transition to object-oriented software development

MOHAMED FAYAD

MAURI LAITINEN

WILEY COMPUTER PUBLISHING

John Wiley & Sons, Inc.

New York ◆ Chichester ◆ Weinheim ◆ Brisbane ◆ Singapore ◆ Toronto

Publisher: Robert Ipsen
Editor: Marjorie Spencer
Assistant Editor: Margaret Hendrey
Managing Editor: Brian Snapp
Text Design & Composition: North Market Street Graphics

Designations used by companies to distinguish their products are often claimed as trademarks. In all instances where John Wiley & Sons, Inc., is aware of a claim, the product names appear in initial capital or ALL CAPITAL LETTERS. Readers, however, should contact the appropriate companies for more complete information regarding trademarks and registration.

This book is printed on acid-free paper. ♾

Library of Congress Cataloging-in-Publication Data:

Fayad, Mohamed, 1950–
     Transition to object-oriented software development / Mohamed Fayad,
Mauri Laitinen.
         p.   cm.
     "Wiley computer publishing."
     Includes bibliographical references and index.
     ISBN 0-471-24529-1
     1. Object-oriented programming.   2. Computer software—
Development.   I. Laitinen, Mauri, 1947– . II. Title.
QA76.64.F39   1998
005.1'17—dc21   98-8274
                                                                     CIP

Printed in the United States of America.
10 9 8 7 6 5 4 3 2 1

contents

PART ONE

A TRANSITION FRAMEWORK

The transition to object-oriented software engineering (OOSE) is a mission with problems. Object-oriented (OO) approaches to software development projects are becoming increasingly prevalent. Even though research concerning the technical aspects of developing object-oriented software is plentiful, many divergent opinions exist. There is little guidance for OO software development project managers on how to transition to OOSE. Transitioning to OOSE addresses several managerial topics critical to the success of OO software development projects. The OO transition process encompasses three stages:

1. Planning and preproject stage
2. Object-oriented technology insertion stage
3. Project management stage

The planning and preproject stage includes activities that condition the development environment for project start-up. The OO technology insertion stage includes activities that identify and plan for the required OO resources. The project management stage includes activities that monitor and provide direction to the project.

This part examines all of these transition stages with respect to three central themes:

"What makes the transition to OOSE a mission with many problems?"

"How can the transition to OOSE be accomplished with minimum impact on the cost and schedule?"

"Why is it important to adopt an object-oriented software development methodology?"

This part has two chapters. Chapter 1 is an introduction chapter and discusses and defines some of the notions associated with the transition framework. Chapter 2 presents a transition framework based upon lessons we have learned from real-world experience. We suggest several effective practices that managers can implement. We provide tips and lessons for completing the transition to OOSE smoothly.

chapter one

Introction

This book focuses on lessons learned and experience gained from transitioning to object-oriented software development (OOSD). It draws on experience from applying software patterns, developing and adapting object-oriented (OO) application frameworks, developing OO distributed systems, and using OO techniques, such as Booch, Coad-Yourdon, Colbert, Fayad, Jacobson, Rumbaugh, Shlaer-Mellor, Unified Modeling Language (UML), and others. The lessons learned are presented from two distinct perspectives: managerial and technical. Based on our experiences, we present a transition framework to OOSD.

1.1 The Promise and Pitfalls of Object-Oriented Technology

The stakes are getting higher every day as more companies bet on object-oriented technology (OOT) for military and commercial application development. Instead of being an academic exercise, making a commitment to the use of OOT is a very serious managerial and technical decision. This is a decision that can impact careers, projects, and entire companies.

On the *positive side* is the promise of a higher quality and more competitive applications. Object-oriented technology promotes a better understanding of requirements and results in modifiable and more maintainable applications. Object technology provides other benefits such as reusability, extensibility, and scalability. Object-oriented technology promotes better teamwork, good communication among team members, and a way to engineer reliable software systems and applications. Object technology helps to build software applications that satisfy human needs and meet the following four objectives:

1. Operational objectives, such as reliability and efficiency
2. Development objectives, such as understandability, reusability, and maintainability
3. Managerial objectives, such as teamwork, productivity, and engineering of right products
4. Business or economical objectives, such as cost efficiency that leads to higher return on investment (ROI)

Object-oriented technology holds the promise of applications that can be quickly extended to satisfy the changing requirements of customers or increase the lifetime of the application. Software products tend to have a much longer usable lifetime than originally planned. The so-called Year 2000 problems are a result of the continued usefulness of programs their developers and users assumed would be long gone by the millennium. Significant applications are more often modified than completely rewritten, and the cost of modification is quite high. Object-oriented technology promotes applications that are shielded from the continual flux present in operating systems and programming language technologies. Because OOT requires a greater explicit emphasis on design with independent modules and clean interfaces, revisions to object-oriented applications do not demand the same level of systemic analysis and testing that a traditional application would. In addition, by taking a conservative approach to legacy systems, OOT can be successfully used to add new functionality to existing systems without incurring the prohibitively high costs of reverse engineering or reengineering and redevelopment. Object-oriented technology should result in applications that sell better. All of this is the promise of OOT: one change in concept that leads to a multitude of benefits that lead to better software products.

On the *negative side* is the significant learning curve involved in bringing teams of system software project organizations, including requirements analysts, system engineers, software engineers, software designers, and software managers, up to a level of competence on OOT. This learning curve implies a longer time to market or a longer development time for initial projects, which is always a bitter pill to swallow. In addition to introducing a new way of developing software, OOT requires new tools, new programming languages, new metrics, and new software development processes.

Transitioning to object-oriented software engineering (OOSE) is a task with a lot of potential hazards. Transitioning to OOSE complicates the software manager's job. It requires the manager to deal with a different set of problems: staffing, training, scheduling, planning, object-oriented processes, tools, cost estimation, standards, documentation, metrics, and a transition process. While managers may already address some of these areas, OOSE requires a modified approach to this management task. The authors have already encountered many of the surprise aspects of OOT and want to introduce our readers to them and help our readers become familiar with these surprises so they are no longer surprises at all.

The future of OOT will bring us a mixture of satisfaction and disappointment. We should expect the disappointment, because developing software is always a painful process when new ground is being broken by the application of new processes. The lessons learned from the satisfying experiences will help sell the technology inside the organization. Readers should seek to understand the benefits of OOT and learn how to capitalize on it for their organization's advantage. Reducing the problems will be the result of higher-quality software products, such as classes that provide cross-platform portability. Tools will evolve that maximize the productivity of software personnel and minimize the process downtime or lost time from problems with the development process that cause developers to be unsure of how to continue. New methods and techniques will emerge that will help software development teams over the OOT hurdle and reduce the learning curve. Software products will help people manage complex projects more efficiently.

1.2 The Reality of Object-Oriented Technology

Although any new software project presents serious issues, a project that includes moving to OOT makes those issues more acute, partly because of the hype surrounding object orientation and partly because object orientation significantly changes the development environment:

> **It is hard to develop a good software architecture—object-oriented or not.** In many non-object-oriented techniques, the success of the proj-

ect may depend on selecting the right architecture during the last part of the analysis or early in the preliminary design. With these techniques, project success may depend on identifying the right set of objects to represent the problem domain during analysis.

It is hard to find/buy/make good reusable software components. Reusability is not a free by-product of the development cycle. Careful consideration of future applications must be undertaken. This extra effort to achieve reusability is often sacrificed because of schedule pressures.

The interconnection technology between software developed with traditional methods and that developed with the various OOTs is poor. Three situations can be identified:

- ◆ The first case is reuse interconnection between software components that were developed using different techniques within OOT, such as Shlaer-Mellor, Colbert, or Rumbaugh. This interconnection is either difficult or impossible, because the interobject communications models for the various OOTs are inconsistent.

- ◆ The second case is reuse interconnection between software components developed using non-object-oriented techniques and new OO components. This interconnection is for all practical purposes impossible, because non-object-oriented models do not provide the logical communications mechanisms that the new OO application needs.

- ◆ The third case is the reuse of object-oriented software components on new non-object-oriented application developments. This practice seems to work very well, because non-object-oriented development uses the communications interconnection required by the OO model.

Key object-oriented standards are missing. This lack of standards is causing much confusion. It is ironic that across the various OO techniques there is not a standard, consistent definition of what an object is. While proposed standard terminology has been published [Snyder93], there are numerous techniques that are based on unique meanings of commonly used object-oriented terminology.

There are many snakes in the grass, and snake oil sales is a major occupation. So, watch out! New techniques are being published nearly every month. Many have not had adequate testing by applying them in multiple-problem domains. Developers are getting hungry for OO information and jump at anything with "object-oriented" in the title. Take care that the bandwagon you jump on has a firm set of wheels (foundation) and has been fully proven.

Object-oriented environments and tools are not completely developed. There has been a strong focus on tools for OO analysis and design for several years. Object-oriented programming tools are starting to mature and show progress. However, OO testing tools are still in their infancy. Tools that apply a consistent technique to object orientation need to be in place for all phases of software development.

Object-oriented professionals (we mean real professionals) are needed. As noted earlier, these people need to have real experience applying OO techniques on real projects. Organizations need to decide if they will develop their own OO professionals or contract for the services they need.

Object-oriented software engineering increases managerial problems. What might have been the development of a single, large, process-oriented application becomes, instead, the development of a collection of objects with a potential for reuse. So OOSE tends to lead to more pieces to manage in getting to the same application, and more interface design attention needed to address future reuse possibilities.

Transition to OOSE is a mission with problems—you need help. All of the above confusion makes it very easy to get off to a false start on early attempts at applying this technology. Find someone that has the kind of experience that has led to the development of a successful OO application to guide your initial efforts.

Despite all of the preceding challenges, OOT is showing up in every major software application area, including operating systems, languages, databases, embedded systems, project management, and more from other domains, such as aerospace, avionics, banking, and insurance. Organizations moving to OOT do not generally move back. After mastering the development discipline, developers do feel that OOT is superior.

Object orientation is more than a fad. It is a significantly different way of developing software. Of course, it uses many of the same constructs that traditional methods use, and the technology itself can be traced to Simula 67 from 30 years ago. But the detailed programming techniques of OOT that get the most publicity—inheritance, encapsulation, and polymorphism—are far less important than the analysis and design methods that they make possible. The ability to model real-world objects and their interactions at multiple levels becomes the basis for OOT real value. If the full value of object orientation were only a few programming constructs, it would be difficult to justify the costs of the transition.

Among the difficulties with OOT is that it doesn't eliminate the need for programming skills, and in many cases it requires software developers to have an even stronger grasp of programming details than before. Why then do we recommend OOT if we guarantee that the transition to it will be demanding in terms of cost, training, management, and initial efficiency? Isn't this a strong recommendation against the adoption of the technology? We think it is not, for the following reasons:

◆ Existing software development has produced essentially mono-lithic applications that are hard to evolve and harder still to evaluate in terms of cost and value. System integration and testing have been such a large part of the development cost that most other cost items have been obscured. Likewise, the value-added functionality of the system is too hard to extract, making it unavailable for derivative and next-generation products. Such applications may be viewed as liabilities as much as assets. One specific value of OOT is that functionality can be found, extracted, and reused.

◆ Object orientation reduces the portion of development devoted to system integration and integration testing and places greater emphasis on the analysis and design of the system and its components. This shifted emphasis gives both the customer and the development team a better understanding of the product being built.

◆ The use of third-party OO components has been growing dramatically to the point where there is a viable source for real pieces of an application. Often these components represent needed functionality but do not provide unique value. Examples are graphical user interfaces (GUIs), printing, and networking capabilities. In-house development of these capabilities does not necessarily contribute to the core competency of the organization [Prahalad90].

◆ Frameworks, software architectures designed to create applications from families of components, appear to offer the highest levels of reuse with all the advantages such reuse implies: lower cost, faster development, and greater reliability. To use framework architecture with third-party components, the core application software must be object oriented.

◆ Object-oriented technology lends itself to iterative and parallel development. Iterative development makes it possible to incorporate feedback from stakeholders more quickly than traditional waterfall methods would, and it allows decomposition into smaller, more understandable units. The earlier fixing of object functionality and interfaces means that object development can be more effectively parallelized and hence more quickly completed. Again, the reduced number of unintended object interactions also reduces the system integration effort.

◆ Finally, we feel that OOT makes itself more accessible to non-programmers. Using the traditional, functional decomposition, only the high-level analysis is accessible to customers and management. They must take on faith the connection between the analysis in terms of application objectives and the more detailed analysis and design in terms of programming constructs. Object-oriented analysis and design allow a deeper view. For business applications, we talk about business objects that model well-understood entities such as credit checking and customers, and we describe the interactions and the data movement between objects as workflows. Similarly, other applications comprise objects that represent meaningful entities in their domain. An automobile control system might have engine and fuel pump objects, and the relationship between them

would be described in a way that reflected the physical association between the real-world entities. At deeper levels of the
analysis and design, more details and interactions appear, and
ever greater skill in software development is required to understand the details, but there is not the abrupt and disconnected
barrier between the top and lower levels that functional decomposition presents.

These reasons, when taken together, imply that a substantial change is
occurring. Object-oriented development is becoming standard. Practitioners find that the adoption of OO programming is beneficial. Systems built
with OOT are inherently more flexible than traditional systems. Components and frameworks allow more reuse; more development choices,
both economically and technically; and more concentration of the organization on its core competencies. Iterative development makes a closer
temporal connection between development decisions and the understanding of their consequences. This technological combination can be
seen as a *disruptive technology,* that is, a technology that advances from a
disadvantageous position with respect to the current technology to one
that surpasses and replaces it [Bower95]. Although the pieces are not radically new, their combination is. Object-oriented technology is not just a
set of new techniques or programming constructs; it is a different way of
development that is finally developing a significant advantage over the
development methods it is replacing. Object-oriented technology is thus
the future of application development over a broad spectrum of problem
domains.

1.3   What Is the Difference between Standard, Methodology, Technique, and Process?

One source of confusion within the OOT community is the variety of
meanings associated with the various terms we use to discuss OO techniques. This section will present the definitions of terms to be used
throughout the remainder of this book to discuss and compare techniques. When discussing each technique, the published terms used to
describe the technique by its developers will be mapped into the terms

defined in this section. Hopefully, this will reduce the confusion attendant with the technique's inconsistent usage of terminology.

A primary source of semantic confusion seems to center around the hierarchical set of terms used to classify the levels of detail of the ways software development is accomplished. Among these terms, we find the following: methodology, method, technique, paradigm, process, and standard.

In this book we hope to avoid contributing to further confusion by defining a small set of common English language terms and using them to discuss all of the techniques. The terms we will be using are: standard, methodology, technique, and process.

Standard

According to *Webster's,* a *standard* is "established for use as a rule or basis of comparison in measuring or judging capacity, quantity, content, extent, value, quality, and so forth [*standards* of weight and measure]." Standards imply regulations, guidelines, rules, laws, and so on. Standards can dictate named methodologies, such as IEEE standards or DOD standards, such as DOD-STD-2167A. Anyone who is working with government standards quickly learns that a standard alone is not sufficient for getting a task completed. The reason for this is that standards focus on the attributes of the results instead of how the results will be achieved.

The concept of standards also includes a type, model, or example commonly or generally accepted or adhered to, such as a criterion set for usage or practices (moral standards). Standard applies to some measure, principle, model, and so on, with which things of the same class are compared to determine their quantity, value, quality, and so forth (standards of purity in drugs).

Methodology

Methodology is used to refer to the very highest levels of the way we do things. It implies a systematic process for handling the ideas that are involved in doing something. In fact, dictionaries such as *Webster's* define methodology as "the science of method, or orderly arrangement." Thus this word refers to the very top-level science of defining order.

Methodology also refers to "a system of methods, as in any particular science." The particular science we are addressing is computer science. This science has a growing set of systems of methods, and the term methodology in computer science can refer to one of these systems of methods.

So, what are the methodologies or systems of methods associated with computer science or software engineering? There are methodologies associated with almost every aspect of computing, from booting the computer software system to operating the system and finally to shutting the computer down. The booting methodology includes methods for loading operating systems on various hardware platforms. The methodologies for operating a system include methods for user interfaces, among other things. Methodologies for shutting down systems, again, include methods for safely getting various combinations of software and hardware to a point where they can be powered off without the risk of losing information or causing damage.

However, our concern is in a much more specific aspect of computing—software engineering. In this area the methodologies group methods for getting from the concept of a software application, through the development of the application and delivery to the customer, to the retirement of the application when it is no longer needed. The methodologies we will consider here cover only the development of the software application.

A methodology might also be called a process model or *macrodevelopment process.* A methodology serves as the controlling framework for the *microprocess* [Booch94]. The macrodevelopment process represents the activities of the entire development team on a scale of weeks or months at a time.

Methodology applies to object-oriented as well as non-object-oriented systems. Throughout this book, we shall use the terms methodology or macroprocess development instead of process model or XYZ model, as shown in Figures 1.1 and 1.2.

Technique (Method)

A *method* implies a regular, orderly, logical procedure for doing something, such as a method of finding software requirements, according to *Webster's.* Other software engineering methods include: waterfall model, spiral model [Boehm84], and fountain model [Henderson-Sellers90]. A search of various references indicates that a method may be thought of in

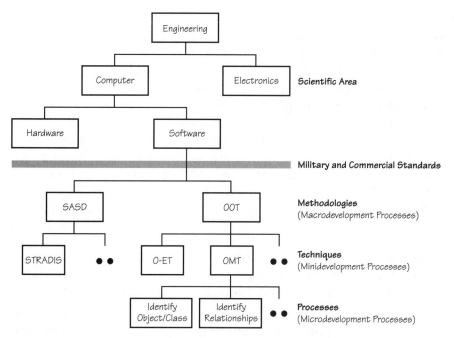

Figure 1.1   Engineering process hierarchy.

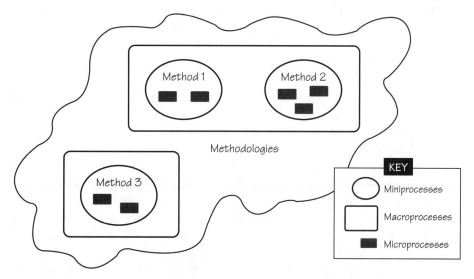

Figure 1.2   Three-level development processes.

a number of ways. A method may be a disciplined process for producing software products or a particular way of applying the concepts of the methodology. In more general terms a method may be a way of doing anything: mode; procedure; process; especially a regular, orderly, definite procedure or way of teaching, investigating, and so forth. A method implies regularity and orderliness in action, thought, or expression; a system of doing things or handling ideas. From this we see that methods define an approach to accomplishing a task in general terms. Jacobson defines a method as a planned procedure by which a specific goal is approached step by step [Jacobson92]. Examples of a software design method are a set of work procedures, a set of notations, or a set of heuristics.

Software engineering methods can be divided into three major categories:

Process-oriented methods. Top-down functional or structured methods that concentrate on representations of software algorithms [DeMarco78; Yourdon89; Yourdon-Constantine79].

Data-oriented methods. Information engineering or data structure design techniques that concentrate on data flow and data representation [Martin90].

Object-oriented methods. Methods that concentrate on objects and the relationships between objects and their operations [Coad-Yourdon91a, 91b; Colbert89; Fayad93, 94a, 94b; Fayad98; Rumbaugh91; Selic94; Shlaer-Mellor88, 92; Rational96; Wirfs-Brock90].

The terms *technique* and *method* are interchangeable throughout this book.

The process-oriented and data-oriented techniques are traditional techniques that imply constant paradigm shifts, because they manipulate different concepts at each phase of the software development life cycle. The OO technique offers a seamless process that helps in viewing the software architecture in terms of problem space elements [Nerson92].

Of these available philosophies, the OO approach is currently receiving the most attention from academia as well as the commercial and DOD software sectors. Once the desire to introduce an OO technique has been established, a particular OOSD technique must be selected. The available techniques provide a multitude of techniques to develop OO software. Some techniques are based on structured analysis—they begin with a functional decomposition of the system into data flow diagrams (DFDs) that are then used to derive low-level objects [Bailin 89]. These low-level objects are then combined somewhat arbitrarily into higher-level objects that define the system. Other OO techniques, such as Colbert's OOSD technique, allow developers to begin with high-level abstract objects that are methodically decomposed during requirements analysis and design phases.

The choice of a particular technique should be made based on the development team's knowledge of the system requirements and the system's operating environment. If the system is data intensive and the individual data elements are mostly understood before requirements analysis (such as a database system), then a data object–driven, bottoms-up technique should be chosen, such as Shlaer-Mellor's Object-Oriented Analysis [Shlaer-Mellor88]. However, if the system details and data requirements are not fully understood at the outset, then a top-down requirements analysis technique should be selected that develops lower-level objects from abstract objects, such as Colbert's OOSD [Colbert89]. Most of the OO techniques concentrate on OO analysis and do little or nothing with OO design, testing, and maintenance.

Process

A *process,* as shown in Figure 1.3, defines specifically who does what, when, and how [Fayad97]. According to *Webster's,* it is "a particular method of doing something, generally involving a number of steps or operations." Now we begin to see why there is confusion. Earlier, we saw that a method is a disciplined process, and now we see that a process is a particular method. We want to emphasize that a process implements one part of a method in sufficient detail, such that the results are repeatable by any number of similarly trained individuals following the steps of the process. However, processes are generally locally documented implementations of methods. Processes tell what tools will be used to implement a method.

Processes generally define *what* needs to be done, but they are only one part of what a method defines. They may define a set of high-level or low-level activities that need to be performed during the software development effort. They are usually partially ordered by time (for example, activity A must precede activities B and C, and activities B and C must be done concurrently). Software processes may define a set of reviews, or

Processes define exactly who, what, when, and how—but remember to see the "big picture."

Figure 1.3 The big picture.

they may define how a review is to be conducted. Any complete set of processes will list the deliverables that result from each process. Processes put OO techniques to work.

Where a method or a technique defines the theory behind an approach, a process addresses the practicalities of using the method in a given development environment. A technique explains the ideas that are to be applied, while a process lays out the concrete actions that have to take place. A technique can only predict results, while a process might define the metrics to be used to verify result. Figure 1.4 illustrates the differences between a method and a process.

We divide the software development processes[1] into three-level processes [Fayad97], as shown in Figures 1.1 and 1.2:

> **Level 1.** The macrodevelopment process represents a span of monthly or yearly activities and is equivalent, for example, to the object modeling technique (OMT) methodology, which consists of analysis, system design, object design, and implementation. The

[1]Booch divides the software development process into two-level processes, which are macro and micro, that map to methodologies and techniques [Booch94].

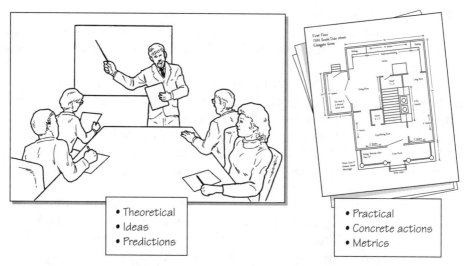

Figure 1.4 The differences between a *method* and a *process*.

macrodevelopment process is considered to be a highest-level process and is shown in Figures 1.1 and 1.2 as equivalent to software development cycle, methodology, or paradigm.

Level 2. The minidevelopment process represents the daily to weekly activities of a small team of developers. The minidevelopment process represents activities dealing with a single phase, such as OMT's analysis or OMT's object design. The minidevelopment process is shown in Figures 1.1 and 1.2 as equivalent to OO technique.

Level 3. The microdevelopment process represents the daily activities of an individual developer, such as identifying object and classes, or inspecting or reviewing a part of a document. The microdevelopment process is considered to be a low-level process and is shown in Figures 1.1 and 1.2.

Modeling

Building a model is a well-established human process. We build models for most every project we undertake. The best way to convey the beauty and functionality of a new building is to first build a model for the users of the building to examine. Designers of electronic products use a schematic model to represent the circuits to be built. Physicists use models to conceptualize and visualize their theories of the physical processes in the universe.

All models are descriptions of something. They allow us to answer questions about a real thing before we build it. Models capture only those features deemed essential by model builders for their goals. A single thing might be represented by a large number of models.

Models can be validated (that is, checked against the original thing) by experimenting with physical things and/or quizzing experts in a field of endeavor about a conceptual entity.

Our focus here is on a model-designing approach to system development allowing an early explicit representation of the system to be built (functionality, data, interfaces) and to reason about the implicit properties of the system (response time, completeness). In particular, our focus will be on the graphical modeling notation, "A picture is worth a thousand words."

Modeling Can Be Tangible or Intangible

Tangible modeling is a modeling technique in which special symbols denote and distinguish those things that must be physically presented. For example, a context diagram of a new system is a way to use tangible modeling. Intangible modeling abstracts away the physical content of things and focuses on their properties and behavior. It is a technique that frees the observer from the consideration of limitations inherent in real-world mechanisms. An intangible model of a system represents:

- What type of system inputs are converted into what type of outputs
- When, in a sequence of processing, a conversion takes place
- What needs to be stored in the system between processing
- Which things are dependent upon each other for information flows

The Major Properties of an Essential Model

The model is an abstraction of reality and lets you see the relationship between the parts and the whole. Modeling is a well-established human activity. All models are descriptions of something (that is, a representation that is not the real thing) that allow us to answer questions about the real thing, that capture only those features deemed essential by the modeler, and that can be validated by experimenting with physical things or by quizzing experts. A single thing can be represented by a large number of models. There are two types of modeling: intangible modeling (such as logical models, behavior models, object models) and tangible modeling (for example, physical models).

The logical model represents the key abstractions and mechanisms that define the system's architecture. The logical model also describes the system behavior and defines the roles and responsibilities of the objects that carry out the system behavior. Logical modeling frees the analysts from the consideration of limitations inherent in real-world mechanisms. Colbert uses object-interaction diagrams and object-class diagrams to illustrate the key abstractions in systems, state transition diagrams (STDs), and state charts to model the behavior of the system [Colbert89]. Object modeling technique and Shlaer-Mellor both use object model and STDs for the same purposes [Rumbaugh91; Shlaer-Mellor92].

The physical model of the system uses symbols to represent things that must be physically present. In the software sense, the physical model is used to describe either the system's context or implementation. Colbert and Object-Engineering Technique use system context diagrams as a physical model of the system [Colbert89, Fayad94c]. There are six properties essential to any good model.

1. **Simple.** This property covers those attributes of the object-oriented model that present modeling aspects of the problem domain in the most understandable manner. This property measures the technique complexity in terms of number of process steps, notational aspects, constraints, and design rules.

2. **Complete (most likely to be correct).** This property ensures that model artifacts are free of conflicting information, and all the required information is present. For example, component names within the model should be uniform, and no incomplete sections of the model should exist. This property determines if the object-oriented model provides internal consistency and completeness of the model's artifacts. The model must be able to convey the essential concepts of its properties.

3. **Stable to technological change.** Unfortunately, object-oriented models are fuzzy due to the absence of quantitative heuristics, and most object-oriented models are built upon false assumptions.

4. **Testable.** To be testable, the model must be specific, unambiguous, and quantitative wherever possible. For our purposes, we define simulation as an imitation of the actual model. This definition leads us to validate the characteristics of the model against the user's requirements.

5. **Easy to understand.** In addition to the familiarity of the modeling notations, the notational aspects, design constraints, and analysis and design rules of the model should be simple and easy to understand by the customers, users, and domain experts.

6. **Visual or graphical.** A picture is worth a thousand words. As a user you can visualize and describe the model. The graphical model is essential for visualization and simulation.

1.4 Summary

We believe that software development is undergoing a dramatic change and that OOT is a key piece of the change. While there are many difficult issues to address in the transition to the new technology, we feel that staying behind is not an option. Object-oriented software is much more than a fad; it is a fundamental reordering of software development processes that will manifest itself in new technological and economic realities. Our aim in this book is to alert you to the larger issues surrounding the move to technology.

The first hurdle in understanding OOT is to understand some of the commonly used terms. In brief, the following points outline the relationships between concepts of standard, methodology, method, and process that we shall use in this book to discuss our experiences with a collection of OO techniques:

Defined processes are the baseline for improvements. You can't improve anything that you can't repeat. It is very difficult to repeat anything without a documented process.

Software process hierarchy.

- ♦ Standard level—Industry/Government.

  IEEE standards.

  ISO 9000 series.

  Military standards.

  DOD standards.

  FAA standards.

  FDA standards.

The macrodevelopment process corresponds to a collection of processes that conform to one or more of the above standards.

The minidevelopment process corresponds to OO techniques that are used by different projects.

The microdevelopment process corresponds to the software development team process within a project.

- ♦ Macro/mini/micro—Processes are especially important for new OO development teams to maximize individual contribution.

- ♦ Macro/mini/micro—Processes interpret the applicable standards in the company or project environment.

- ♦ Macro—Processes must be tuned for specific projects. This process tailoring is required to satisfy unique project requirements within the context of company standards.

- ♦ Mini—Processes must be tuned for specific problem domain. This process tailoring is required to satisfy unique domain requirements within the context of company standards.

- ♦ Micro—Processes are often treated as a methodology or method. This creates confusion.

1.5 Organization of This Book

This book is organized into five major parts based on the transition framework: Part One: A Framework, Part Two: Planning and Preproject

Activities, Part Three: Object-Oriented Insertion Activities, and Part Four: Object-Oriented Project Management Activities. Part One includes two chapters (Chapters 1 and 2) that define several poorly understood object orientation terms and concepts and describe a complete transition framework. Part Two has Chapters 3 and 4, which include activities to condition the development environment for project start-up. Part Three, comprising Chapters 5 through 10, describes actions to identify and plan for the required object-oriented resources. Part Four, consisting of Chapters 11 through 18, describes activities that deal with software quality assurance and software configuration management to monitor and provide direction on the project.

References

[Bailin89] Bailin, S. C. "An Object-Oriented Requirements Specification Method." *Communications of the ACM* 32, no. 5 (May 1989): 608–623.

[Boehm84] Boehm, B. W. "Verifying and Validating Software Requirements and Design Specifications." *IEEE Software* 1, no. 1 (January 1984): 75–88. Reprinted in R. H. Thayer and M. Dorfman (eds.). Tutorial: System and Software Requirements Engineering. Washington, D.C.: IEEE Computer Society Press, 1990.

[Booch94] Booch, G. *Object-Oriented Analysis and Design.* 2nd ed. Menlo Park, CA: Benjamin/Cummings Publishing Company, 1994.

[Bower95] Bower, Joseph L., and Clayton M. Christensen. "Disruptive Technologies: Catching the Wave." *Harvard Business Review* (January–February, 1995).

[Coad-Yourdon91a] Coad, P., and E. Yourdon. *Object-Oriented Analysis,* 2nd ed. Englewood Cliffs, NJ: Prentice-Hall, 1991.

[Coad-Yourdon91b] Coad, P., and E. Yourdon. *Object-Oriented Design.* Englewood Cliffs, NJ: Prentice-Hall, 1991.

[Colbert89] Colbert, E. "The Object-Oriented Software Development Method: A Practical Approach to Object-Oriented Development." *Ada Technology in Context: Application, Development, and Deployment Proceedings, ACM TRI-Ada '89* (October 1989): 400–415.

[DeMarco78] DeMarco, T. *Structured Analysis and System Specifications.* New York: Yourdon, Inc., 1978.

[Fayad93] Fayad, M. E., et al. "Using the Shlaer-Mellor Object-Oriented Method." *IEEE Software* (March 1993): 43–52.

[Fayad94a] Fayad, M. E., et al. "Adapting an Object-Oriented Development Method." *IEEE Software* (May 1994).

[Fayad94b] Fayad, M. E., W. T. Tsai, R. Anthony, and M. L. Fulghum. "Object Modeling Technique (OMT): Experience Report." *Journal of Object-Oriented Programming.* November 1994, pp. 46–58.

[Fayad94c] Fayad, M. E. Object-Oriented Software Engineering: Problems & Perspectives. Ph.D. Thesis, UMI, Ann Arbor, Michigan, June 1994.

[Fayad97] Fayad, Mohamed E. "Software Development Processes: The Necessary Evil." *The Communications of the ACM* (September 1997).

[Fayad98] Fayad, Mohamed E. "Object-Oriented Software Development Process: A Comparative Study." *Elements of Software Process Assessment and Improvement* (eds. Khald El-Emam and Nazim H. Madhavji). Los Alamitos, California. IEEE Computer Society Press, 1998.

[Henderson-Seller90] Henderson-Seller, B., and Edwards, J. M. "The Object-Oriented System Life Cycle." *The Communications of the ACM* 33, no. 9 (September 1990).

[Jacobson92] Jacobson, I., et al. *Object-Oriented Software Engineering: A Use Case Driven Approach.* Reading, MA: Addison-Wesley, 1992.

[Martin90] Martin, J. *Information Engineering* (Books I, II, and III). Englewood Cliffs, NJ: Prentice-Hall, 1990.

[Nerson92] Nerson, J. M. "Applying Object-Oriented Analysis and Design." *Communications of the ACM* 35, no. 9 (September 1992): 63–74.

[Prahalad90] Prahalad, C. K., and Gary Hamel. "The Core Competence of the Corporation." *Harvard Business Review* (May–June 1990).

[Rational96] Booch, G., Rumbaugh, J., and Jacobson, I. *The Unified Modeling Language for Object-Oriented Development Documentation Set,* Version 0.9. Santa Clara, California: Rational Software Corporation, 1996.

[Rumbaugh91] Rumbaugh, J., M. Blaha, W. Premerlani, F. Eddy, and W. Lorensen. *Object-Oriented Modeling and Design.* Englewood Cliffs, NJ: Prentice Hall, 1991.

[Selic94] Selic, B., P. Ward, and G. Gullekson. *Real-Time Object-Oriented Modeling.* New York: John Wiley & Sons, 1994.

[Shlaer-Mellor88] Shlaer, S., and S. J. Mellor. *Object-Oriented System Analysis: Modeling the World in Data.* Englewood Cliffs, NJ: Yourdon Press Computing Series, 1988.

[Shaler-Mellor92] Shlaer, S., and S. J. Mellor. *Object Lifecycles: Modeling the World in States.* Englewood Cliffs, NJ: Yourdon Press Computing Series, 1992.

[Snyder93] Snyder, A. "The Essence of Objects: Concepts and Terms." *IEEE Software* (January 1993): 31–42.

[Wirfs-Brock90] Wirfs-Brock, R., B. Wilkerson, and L. Wiener. *Designing Object-Oriented Software.* Englewood Cliffs, NJ: Prentice-Hall, 1990.

[Yourdon89] Yourdon, E. *Modern Structured Analysis.* Englewood Cliffs, NJ: Yourdon Press, Prentice-Hall, 1989.

[Yourdon-Constantine79] Yourdon, E., and L. Constantine. *Structured Design: Fundamentals of a Discipline of Computer Programming and Design.* 2nd ed. New York: Prentice-Hall, 1979.

chapter two

Transition Planning

Object-oriented software engineering (OOSE) introduces a software development model based upon the way humans think; promises remarkable benefits; and it allows the reuse of software components, potentially saving substantial development costs. Also, OOSE reduces the scope and side effects of software changes, potentially saving substantial maintenance costs.

2.1   The Problem

In spite of these potential benefits, many software development groups still hesitate to use OOSE. Many of these groups are fully occupied by their current software development work and fear being overwhelmed by introducing a new development paradigm.

Other groups interested in OOSE do not know where to begin. "What's the first step?" "How long will it take?" "Is it really worth it?" These are common questions among groups striving to determine whether OOSE is right for them. Eight years ago, members of various software development groups in which one of the authors was working as a consultant asked these questions when they decided to confront the task of developing a large software system using OOSE. They were confident that they understood the benefits of object-oriented (OO) techniques, but they did not understand the theory behind OOSE. They lacked a firm foundation from which to start and practical experience on which to build. Furthermore, many of these teams had never applied any formal or semiformal techniques.

To make matters worse, these groups had additional problems.

1. Their most recent development efforts were in most cases, let's just say, inconsistent.
2. They were usually behind schedule; perpetually 90 percent complete.
3. They were constantly finding problems late in the development, feverishly applying Band-Aids to plug the leaks.

Fixing one problem frequently created others. Also, despite having a highly centralized decision-making organization, individually developed software parts still looked radically different. Each programmer or software engineer developed software by applying his or her own unique process. Occasionally the software integrated smoothly, but frequently major problems suddenly developed. In retrospect, their software development process was chaotic.

On average, the transition of a single software development team to OOSE takes at least a year. Throughout this transition period, they transitioned their organization out of this chaos into an efficient OO development team. Along the way they diligently evaluated several OO development techniques, processes, and practices and integrated the best of these practices into their OO development process. By the end of the first project, they were eager to apply their evolving process to new projects.

During the last eight years, we have been involved in transitioning large software development teams from chaos into OOSE [Fayad 93; Fayad 94a; Fayad 94b]. The transition became quicker and easier on each new project. We have fine-tuned the transition plan in this chapter on several subsequent object orientation efforts. This chapter presents the most significant, evolutionary steps, many of which were not initially apparent.

This chapter presents a road map for getting from an ad hoc development process to a managed, efficient OO approach. This chapter provides recommendations based on our experiences. The chapter also provides a transition plan to OOSE.

2.2   Why Is Moving to Object Orientation Important?

Compare any commonly used program to its equivalent, if one exists, from 1990. The newer programs are far more capable and are usually considerably easier to use. Ignoring the debates about the value of new features, ease of use, and capability are the result of far larger, more

complex programs in equally large and complex operating environments. We rely more on our software now than we did before. We rely
on automated teller machines, airplane controls, and point-of-sale systems completely and unconsciously to the extent that existing without
them is almost unthinkable.

Software in modern product development similarly cannot be untan-
gled. For example, the design of an electronic device includes trade-offs
between hardwired and software components; logic design, circuit simulation, and layout are all software driven; and planning, documenting,
and illustration all depend on software tools.

New View of the Software Crisis

We hear so much about the software crisis that we ignore the changes
that have occurred in software in the last few years. According to Glass,
business software applications are growing in size and complexity by a
factor of 50 every ten years or so [Glass97]. While ad hoc adoption of
tools helps deal with the increasing demands of complexity, size, and
reliability, the fact is that most programs have exceeded the capacity of
casual development approaches. Previously, as shown in Figure 2.1,
programs smaller than 100,000 lines of code were common and could
be adequately managed by a small group without undue organizational
effort. And because the relative cost seemed excessive given the overall
expenditure on the software, requirements, design, and maintenance
documentation was not kept. This was not as foolish as it seems. The
duration of most applications has generally been underestimated.
Pieces of applications get rewritten and translations are made to new
languages and hardware, but the same functionality and overall design
is retained. Given that continuity, combined with a less mobile workforce, a company could expect to have staff on hand who would be
familiar with an application. And for smaller programs, hiring outside
help to analyze and modify programs was not out of the question.

Now, however, 100,000 lines of code may be a small application. At the
upper end, there are Department of Defense projects, such as support for
the Advanced Tactical Fighter (ATF) containing 12 to 15 million lines of
code. This application has hundreds of developers spread across many
teams in different companies. The size of the project requires extensive
coordination, and even if it were not a mission-critical system design and
test, coordination requirements would be great.

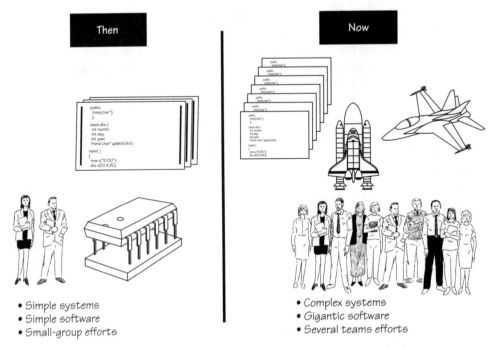

Figure 2.1 In the beginning. . . .

The typical shrink-wrapped software package is also more on the order of one-half to two million lines of code and has a user constituency that expects continuity with previous releases and compatibility with other products. The requirements are thus greater and more complex than earlier efforts. In general, these projects are worked on by multiple groups within an organization and often integrate third-party components. Regression testing becomes increasingly important to assure compatibility with previous releases. As projects grow larger and more people work on them, they become more demanding to maintain. In any sort of organization, intergroup coordination becomes increasingly difficult as the size of the individual groups increase and as their number expands. Separate subcontractors compound the difficulty. Maintenance becomes both harder and more necessary. These factors alone make modern software less tractable than it was even five years ago.

A survey of 500 major projects shows that 43 percent of maintenance costs could be attributed to changes in user requirements [Graham91], as shown in Figure 2.2. Another 17 percent was consumed in adapting to changes in data formats. In other words, a full 60 percent of the cost of maintaining software comes from changes to either keep using it in new environments or to adapt it for new requirements. It also suggests that we still don't look at software as an asset. We tend to think of maintenance as activity required just to keep things going as they have been. But if a large portion of what we call maintenance is actually adaptation, it confirms that valuable software evolves over time. Implicit in this assertion is that changing requirements are an inextricable part of useful software and that we should design software to be able to adapt to new requirements. Unfortunately, the older development methods do not handle changing requirements well.

Additionally, many traditional approaches, such as the waterfall method of development, have never worked well for a large class of development problems. Developing and understanding requirements to the point where they can be translated into designs is most often an iterative process that takes a significant portion of the development time. Traditional development methods do not have straightforward ways to reuse software and, likewise, do not exhibit mechanisms that enforce modularity. They do not provide a useful means of managing complexity. As a

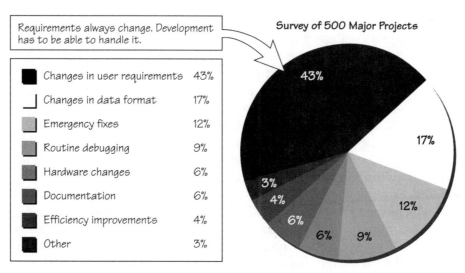

Figure 2.2 Breakdown of maintenance costs.

result, even small changes can have serious side effects, and errors are hard to find.

In short, engineering high-reliability software is not well understood. Even now, larger projects are likely to suffer many kinds of failure. Many projects are paid for but never delivered, abandoned, or subject to extensive rework. A current example of this is California's child support tracking system done by Lockheed-Martin. As of this writing, the majority of California counties are not using the system, now in a pilot testing phase, and those who are find it excessively difficult to master. Lockheed-Martin cannot yet specify the final cost or delivery schedule for the system. We are not attributing blame here; we are merely pointing out that even after 30 years of active efforts in software engineering, large, complex software projects are excessively risky.

And although software professionals for the most part understand that the linear sort of progression of the waterfall method will not work, it still appears to be the way management, customers, and the public think software development should be done. We must all change our view of development.

How Complexity Has Been Handled

Part of the reason for the development shortcoming is the way development handled complexity. They tended to simplify by decomposing things to do. The system would be decomposed into a hierarchical set of functions that performed the necessary functions of the system. Data flow analysis would trace the flow of information in the system. The result of such a design method was a unique system in which the only reusability was at the subroutine level. Because the analysis identified the functions of the system, and the design led to the implementation of those functions, extensibility was limited and maintenance costs were generally high, as shown in Figure 2.3. The costs were especially dear for implementing new functionality that didn't fit well with the original set of processes implemented in the system. The processes then became the least stable part of the system.

The most obvious difficulty in functional methodologies was their limited ability to scale up. The interactions between various processes might be manageable in a smaller system, but in general, there was no discipline in the way interactions could exist. As the system was scaled up,

Structure analysis approach decomposes systems into series of processes…

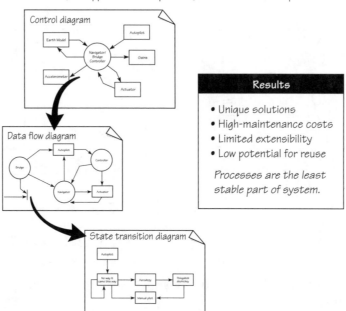

Figure 2.3   Early methods managed complexity by decomposing things to do.

the number of interactions (and their second- and higher-level side effects) would quickly grow to unmanageability, as shown in Figure 2.4.

How Does Object-Oriented Development Help?

Object-oriented development is one of the key technologies to allow larger levels of integration and reuse. Abstraction allows the assembly of simple components to create complex systems, and because the interfaces are laid out first, it allows parallel development. Large teams may be composed of many small groups, each of which is responsible for one or a few objects. Well-defined object interfaces allow the groups to proceed with parallel development, managing the details of their own objects without affecting the work of other groups. With abstraction, encapsulation dramatically reduces the complexity of interactions between objects and, thus, makes both the communication between

The interactions manageable for a small system...   ...often become unmanageable for a large system.

Figure 2.4   Functional methodology successes often do not scale up to larger systems.

objects simpler and more comprehensible to human analysts. Encapsulation reduces the impact of corrections, because changes to objects don't usually have effects on other objects unless their interfaces change. This consequently reduces the cost of maintenance and enhancement, as shown in Figure 2.5.

Objects also provide more reusable pieces for other systems. Because they can be implementations of higher-level abstractions, they provide more generally useful components. Object orientation reduces the knowledge each developer needs to implement a particular piece of functionality. It is possible to generalize an object's capability so that it can work in many environments. Good objects represent only essential features, ones that are most likely to have widespread applicability. Encapsulation hides implementation details while collecting an object's essential properties, both data and associated operations, in one place. Thus, an object is a good way to make a generally usable component, as shown in Figure 2.6.

Encapsulation taken with abstraction enables information hiding, a quality that enhances localization. There is a lingering view that the point of information hiding is to apportion knowledge among developers

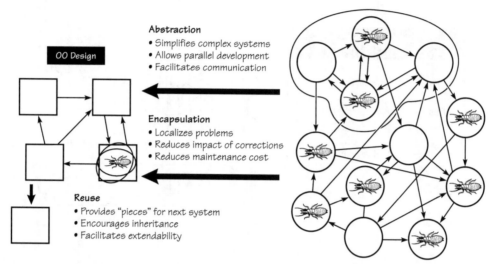

Figure 2.5 Object orientation is the result of software development maturity.

so that no one person has a complete picture. While object orientation can be used in this way, it is a perverse reading of information hiding's value. Rather than keeping information from developers, we want to keep developers from being forced to know more about the environment than is necessary to do a task. Inheritance, if used wisely, makes objects extensible without forcing endless new functionality on components where it is not needed.

The multileveled abstraction in OO analysis and design enhances communication. The highest level of abstraction maps the problem and solution domains in a way that the users and implementers of a system can both understand, and the lowest level provides information that programmers need. A critical point of the mapping is that there is no massive break where abstractions used to describe the system must be translated to a completely foreign design or implementation representations. In a functional approach, the transition from analysis to design is a many-to-many relationship where relatively large design elements have multiple functions that satisfy multiple requirements. Tracing between requirements and design necessitates analyzing all the multiway relationships. Object-oriented analysis and design is different. Starting from the

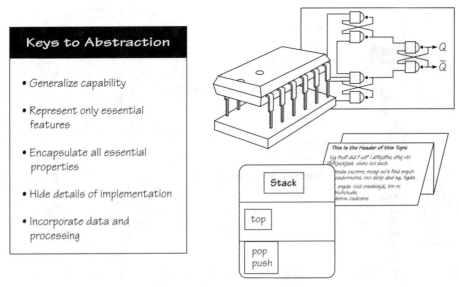

Figure 2.6   Software abstraction promotes reuse.

bottom up, source code can be identified as part of an object specified in design. The design object can be traced back to an analysis object that implicitly or explicitly satisfies some set of requirements.

Object orientation similarly enhances a system's maintainability. Multiple levels of abstraction effectively communicate functions of complex systems in ways that help pinpoint where both corrections and improvements should be placed. By having well-defined interfaces, the number and complexity of connections between system parts is simplified and made more robust. Objects package related information and operations, and make access available only through their interfaces. This encapsulation makes it possible to change specific objects without corrupting details in other parts of the system, as shown in Figure 2.7.

In a sense, software is following the progress of electronic hardware in the way it is integrated, as shown in Figure 2.8. Discrete electronic components were first used to create logic functions. Then logic functions, such as flip-flops, buffers, and counters became encapsulated into integrated circuits. From there, multiple logical functions were integrated to create more complex functional entities on a single chip. Examples would be interrupt and CRT controllers. Finally, standard interfaces

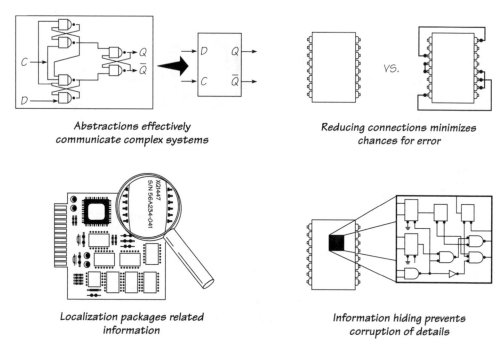

Abstractions effectively
communicate complex systems

Reducing connections minimizes
chances for error

Localization packages related
information

Information hiding prevents
corruption of details

Figure 2.7 Object-oriented principles enhance maintainability.

allowed the combination of many functions into subsystems, and the
market for subsystems was made possible by standards for interconnection. The equivalent development for software matches functions with
discrete components, objects with integrated circuits, object groups with
more complex chips, and frameworks with subsystems.

Object orientation, then, is a more mature level of development and a
necessary prerequisite for even larger-scale software integration.

Challenges in Moving to Object Orientation

Moving to OO development carries with it all the basic software engineering issues that affect other development approaches, as well as
adding new problems. Many of the challenges are merely well-known
management issues; however, with object-oriented development, many
items that once were optional become mandatory. For staff members,
training and adaptation to new ways of working are required. For man-

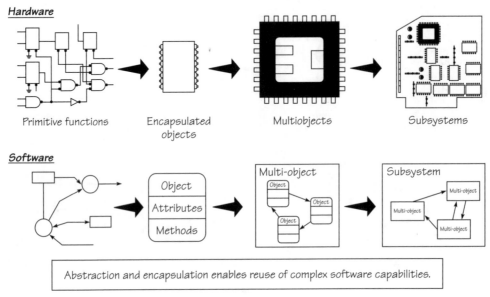

Figure 2.8 Software takes clue from hardware evolution.

agement, training and adaptation come in addition to new administrative and leadership practices.

Challenges for Team Members

It is important to emphasize that moving to object-oriented development entails much more than just adopting a new method or a new language. For team members, it means relearning roles and methods while learning a different way of development. As an example, C++ is one of the most commonly used object-oriented languages, and its syntax is very similar to C. But for staff members familiar with or even expert in C, the effort of becoming proficient in C++ is immense. It is not the few changes to syntax and keywords that cause the difficulty, but rather it is the entirely different way of understanding and ordering programs that causes trouble. Only training and time will ease the transition.

Challenges for Management

Managers must not only train themselves, but they must provide the leadership to overcome the resistance to change that occurs naturally in any organization. Here we mention some of the most common forms of resistance to change. We discuss culture change more in Chapter 4.

Dealing with Vicious Cycles

Making the transition means getting past vicious cycles that enforce stasis. The first cycle revolves around the costs and benefits of the technology, as shown in Figure 2.9. Looking at the total life cycle, object orientation reduces costs making maintenance and enhancements, both minor and major, much easier. To move to object-oriented technology (OOT), however, there is a significant up-front training and transition

Figure 2.9   Object orientation costs and benefits vicious cycle.

cost. But adopting object orientation makes it possible to use components created by others. However, until more people adopt object orientation, the availability of components is very limited. The only way past the first vicious cycle is to decide whether long-term benefits will outweigh short-term costs. In making the decision, it is also worthwhile to look at trends in the industry and to project whether current practices will be adequate and competitive in the future.

The second vicious cycle is a result of the fact that there is never a best time to start an object-oriented project, as shown in Figure 2.10. At the start of a project, there is usually not much time to spend evaluating OO methods and tools. Getting the organization up to speed will certainly add significantly to the schedule. In the middle of a project, changing method-

Figure 2.10   Best time to start object-oriented vicious cycle.

ologies guarantees schedule slippage and confusion, and the end of a project is too hectic to spend significant effort on change. The best way to deal with the second vicious cycle is to sidestep it. Abandoning a working development approach and rushing headlong into a new technology, no matter how potentially valuable, is dangerous. Experience shows that about six months is required to select and refine methodologies and tools. Adding six months to any but the largest of projects is unreasonable, and during that time, false starts can waste resources and frustrate team members. It is better to have a pilot project that makes the transition, from which other parts of the organization can learn and adapt.

Management Must Work Harder

We discuss a series of challenges that face managers in making the transition to object orientation. What we describe here sounds daunting, but most of the issues are ones that management must already be aware of, and the transition will not occur immediately. Moreover, we feel that there is not a significant choice: Current methods already do not satisfy the needs of current development, and future development will require change. In many software environments, that future has been here awhile.

Current employees will probably not have all the technical skills, much less the depth of experience, needed for the new work. Object method experts will be among the new job specialties, as will reuse librarians. New hires must be interviewed to learn how their backgrounds match the organization's new requirements. In particular, the ability of potential employees to work in teams and to document their work must be assessed.

If an organization is not adopting a new technology, or if it is changing slowly, training may not have a major impact on regular operations. It may be done in a more-or-less ad hoc way, allowing individuals to take courses as they desire and as schedules permit. With the insertion of a new technology, however, a more orderly approach to training must be taken. Object-oriented programming is considerably more than just the adoption of a new programming language; it is the adoption of a new approach to analyzing and implementing software. Management must be ready for a sharply higher investment in formal training, along with the disruption in regular operations that will ensue. Moreover, if the training is to be successful, it must be spread out over an extended period and must be tailored to the specific project. The logistics of training will make a significant impact on management's time.

Scheduling and estimating requirements increase as well. Previous tasks such as staffing, organizing, and training as just discussed, will change qualitatively and quantitatively. Historical information about project resources, based on previous technology, will be less accurate as sources for future development estimates. Meanwhile, the existing methods of project estimation will be changing. For many groups this will mean moving from either ad hoc or traditional waterfall methods to an iterative (or at least spiral) approach. A considerably greater emphasis on analysis is inherent in the object approach and will affect the shape of development, pushing coding milestones much farther out. New factors such as reuse-budgeting review cycles, postmortems, and process analysis further complicate the estimation and scheduling activities.

For groups who do government contracting, standards play a major but changing part. Not only are the standards for software development changing, or in some cases appearing, but standards are now being applied to the organizations themselves. Over the last few years, MIL-STD 2167A has given way to DOD-STD 498 as the preferred and generally required standard for development. At the same time, two standards for assessing the ability of organizations to do effective work have become more widely known and used. In Europe and elsewhere around the world, ISO 9000 certification is increasingly becoming required to sell software or contract software services. ISO 9000 is applied at the company level, so it implies a much greater level of effort than might just moving a particular group up. In the United States, the Software Engineering Institute's (SEI's) Capability Maturity Model (CMM) is gaining acceptance. The CMM rating, from 1 to 5, is designed to characterize a group's ability to develop software. It is likely that in the future, organizations will have to have ISO 9000 certification, CMM level 3 certification, or both to be recognized as legitimate. The United States Department of Defense intends to mandate CMM level 3 for all contractors. The software engineering manager will have to be cognizant of these standards and include meeting their requirements in development plans.

As projects get larger, more information is generated about the analysis and design, and about the progress of the projects themselves. The repository of information is the project documentation. Sometimes documentation is kept in one place, but more likely, documentation will be distributed among specific documents and in output from CASE (Computer-Aided Software Engineering) tools and configuration management logs. Not only does OO development place great emphasis on analysis and design, but elements such as reviews, testing, and V and V (Verification and Validation) refer back to analysis and design activities, so documentation for these activities must be readily available and not just sitting on some manager's shelf. Making documentation more accessible while ensuring appropriate security, perhaps using an intranet to distribute the information, means more active documentation management and more work for the manager.

New factors make planning more important than it has traditionally been, therefore, placing greater burdens on software managers. The first and most obvious reason is that larger projects require more careful planning. Second, software improvement initiatives have planning as an explicit part of their prescriptions. The SEI's CMM, for example, mandates full project plans, and the United States Department of Defense expects a DOD-STD 498–compliant plan for all of their projects. The third and most subtle reason for planning's greater importance is that it is useful. In far too many cases, if a project plan is done at all, it is an exercise in wishful thinking in which events are laid out at a level of detail that cannot be known in advance. The project, however, evolves quite differently, with features added and dropped, and schedules expanding and contracting to match the organization's needs. The plan, more often than not, becomes an artifact that bears no relationship to the finished project. If the plan, instead, becomes the central document of the project, and if it references the other important documents of the project, it will be updated and used throughout the development. The appearance and contents of the plan will be quite different between the start of the project and its delivery because it reflects the evolving understanding of the project. The plan, then, is used as a plan and not as a checkoff item on a list of required tasks.

Metrics are not new to OO projects, but they play an increasing role in software development. At the very least, most projects measure time and effort expended. Many also find that keeping track of defects, especially as the project approaches its release date, is important. Other metrics further break down efforts and output by class or object, by team, or by project phase. The manager's role in software development is to make sure metrics are useful without being overwhelming. This implies a more careful appraisal and understanding of the uses of measurement and a strong will to resist calls for expensive or less important metrics.

All of the above-mentioned issues force at least a candid evaluation of the staffing and management of an organization moving to OO development. We now outline the transition plan, and in following chapters discuss its various aspects in detail.

2.3 Transition Framework

The transition framework, as shown in Figure 2.11, is presented in three major parts, 2 through 4. Part 2 deals with the planning and preproject activities and describes effective planning processes and ways to change

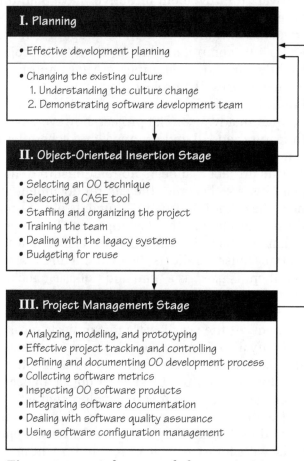

Figure 2.11   A framework for a transition process.

the organizational culture. Part 3 describes how to insert the OOT into a project, such as selecting an object-oriented technique, selecting a CASE tool, staffing and organizing the project, training the team, budgeting for reuse, and dealing with legacy systems. Part 4 describes how to manage a new object-oriented development and how to deal with software quality assurance and software configuration management [Fayad96a, Fayad96b].

Tips and Practical Advice

Lesson 2.1   The transition to OOSE is a mission with problems.

- The adoption of a new paradigm creates fear and uncertainty.
- There is a fear of getting it all wrong.
- There is uncertainty about the process to use.
- Organizations often begin OOSE without any software engineering process to use as a foundation.
- OOSE complicates project manager roles in training, staffing, standards, documentation, scheduling, planning, cost estimation, data collection, and software metrics.

Lesson 2.2   There is little guidance for object-oriented software development (OOSD) project managers on how to transition to OOSE.
Project managers must find their own way through the maze of techniques, tools, and environments with little or no guidance from published sources. Many OOSE training activities only provide often slanted information on their own technique. Object-oriented software engineering complicates the project manager's role and creates several problems related to planning, staffing, training, scheduling, cost estimation, documentation, legacy systems, and software metrics.

Lesson 2.3   Careful selection of the first object-oriented project is very important.
To adapt the OOT well for the first time, the first project must possess three major characteristics:

(continued)

◆ It must be a new project. From our experience, the new project offers the best possibilities. If an existing project is selected, there are a large number of issues that must be dealt with, such as legacy systems, old and established development processes, existing staff, and so on. A new project often has sufficient up-front time to allow for training and experimental prototyping.

◆ It must be large and meaningful enough to influence the other project attitudes toward the OOT.

◆ It must be supported by the customer and/or high-level management. Initiatives die without customer or management support.

Lesson 2.4   On average, the transition of a single software development team to OOSE takes at least a year.

During this year the project team learns to think in terms of objects. For most developers this is an easy transition. A few developers might have difficulty with this transition. However, once a developer has developed one object, future objects become progressively easier. Many organizations find that team-based training is very useful in getting the team through the transition to object thinking. Serious consideration should be given to including the customer/user representative in the transition activities. The customer/user should understand the object-oriented techniques and tools being used on the project.

References

[Fayad93] Fayad, M. E., et al. "Using the Shlaer-Mellor Object-Oriented Method." *IEEE Software* (March 1993): 43–52.

[Fayad94a] Fayad, M. E. et al. "Adapting an Object-Oriented Development Method." *IEEE Software* (May 1994).

[Fayad94b] Fayad, M. E., W. T. Tsai, R. Anthony, and M. L. Fulghum. "Object Modeling Technique (OMT): Experience Report." *Journal of Object-Oriented Programming.* November, 1994, pp. 46–58.

[Fayad96a] Fayad, M. E., W. T. Tsai, and M. L. Fulghum. "Transition to Object-Oriented Software Development." *The Communications of the ACM* 39, no. 2 (February 1996): 108–121.

[Fayad96b] Fayad, M. E., and M. Cline. "Managing Object-Oriented Software Development." *IEEE Computer* (September 1996): 26–31.

[Glass97] Glass, Robert L. "Revisiting The Industry/Academe Communication Chasm." *The Communications of the ACM* (June 1997): 11–13.

[Graham91] Graham, Ian. *Object-Oriented Methods.* Reading, MA: Addison-Wesley, 1991.

PART TWO

PLANNING AND PREPROJECT ACTIVITIES

Planning is the most essential activity in software development. A poorly planned software development is doomed to failure. Software has become a critical part of our daily lives, and planning is required for success. There are five significant points about software in general:

Software is the biggest cost item in any system development. This makes it the highest risk item on the menu and requires careful and continuous planning.

Software has (and will continue to have) the highest impact on the future economy. Currently, the software industry is having a major impact on the U.S. economy with an even greater potential in the future [BSA97]. According to the Business Software Alliance:

- ◆ Revenue: $102.8 billion in 1996 and shrink-wrapped software package sales reached $24.1 billion.
- ◆ Market position: Software is the third largest industry, behind carmakers and electronics, in the U.S. economy in terms of value added.
- ◆ Growth: The software industry grew at a rate of 12.5 percent for the years 1990 through 1996, nearly 2.5 times faster than the overall U.S. economy.
- ◆ Employment and wages: In 1996 alone, the U.S. software industry directly employed 619,400 people. The soft-

ware industry's ripple effect created a total of 2,065,000 jobs and $83.7 billion in wages. By the year 2005, total direct and indirect employment will reach 3,345,000 jobs, paying $139.3 billion in wages.

Software products must be treated as critical assets and essential resources.

Customers will be more involved in the software development process.

Software standards to achieve uniformity, consistency, and completeness are essential.

For all the above reasons, planning is critical for success. The planning and preproject stage includes activities that condition the development environment for project start-up.

A critical component of making the transition is developing an environment conducive to both technical and organizational change. The technical issues are far more extensive than just adopting a new programming language or a set of new techniques (although these must be adopted). Organizations must also adopt a whole different way of looking at analysis, design, and development. On the organizational side, organizations must gird themselves to abandon the function-oriented organization and take on a process-oriented organization. The neat compartmentalization of function, as exemplified by the waterfall method of development, will give way to an iterative development approach in which specifications and design will require a far deeper and longer involvement from customers and the whole organization.

This part has two chapters. Chapter 3 deals with software development planning. Chapter 4 describes how to change the existing culture.

chapter three

Effective Development Planning

"Planning is everything. Plans are nothing."

—Field Marshal Helmuth Graf von Moltke

3.1 Introduction

This chapter covers the software development plan (SDP). It describes the minimum planning activities required and recommends a new planning policy.

Planning is an iterative, multilevel activity. At the highest level, strategic plans set the course for the organization and consider contingencies to handle change. At the development level, the SDP defines the course of the project. For a development group planning to move to a new technology, a transition plan provides both strategy and direction. The current software development processes and personnel must undergo a calculated change. Lack of transition planning assures the change will be difficult and may be disastrous [Fayad96a; Fayad96b].

A high percentage of software projects fail if planning has not been done [Jones96]. When starting a project, it seems obvious that the goal of the project and the expected steps in achieving the goal should be known, but often no such steps have been taken. Although we have more than 25 years of experience in software engineering development and know projects tend to be expensive and frequently disappointing, we tend to avoid some of the basic steps that might make that development more predictable. Nobody would expect an engineering firm to build a skyscraper without first developing plans, but software projects are often done without meaningful plans.

Planning is often viewed negatively, a bureaucratic waste of time that assumes absolute knowledge of the future, or an exercise in wishful thinking that has less bearing on the actual project than a weather forecast has on the weather. There are a number of reasons for this: many plans are created as if every detail of a project can be identified, sized, and scheduled in advance. This is rarely the case with small projects, and it is an obvious absurdity with larger projects. Software projects, even those for relatively well-defined applications such as payroll or process control, vary widely in terms of size and detailed function. In many cases, important features of a project are not understood, much less quantified, until late in the analysis phase. In software especially, small changes in requirements can cause large changes in the scope of design. Planners find it frustrating to deal with such unknowns. Often, if the planners are not familiar with software development, they assume that software estimation is like building construction and do not understand the inability of developers to give reasonable estimates for components such as report writers, databases, and graphical user interfaces (GUIs). The fact is, software does not now (and may never) lend itself to rote estimation methods.

Sometimes planning is equated with the development of program evaluation and review technique (PERT) and Gantt charts, which, while important, are only a small part of planning. Planners in other disciplines rely on implicit assumptions of form and functionality, often embodied in publication of standards and pattern documents, that allow them to focus more on issues of schedules and resource estimation. When building a house, doors are understood to begin at the floor, and windows are understood to be made of transparent material. Software has little in the way of such implicit understanding. Therefore, plans must compensate for the lack of implicit understanding we have about software. But now there is a conflict: How can plans be at once more complete and yet accommodate the lack of information at the beginning of a project?

In fact, planning is a dynamic process in which the first version of the plan will have many unknown areas and generalizations, but as the project progresses the plan will become more complete and more specific. The plan starts by listing those portions that can be determined in advance. Clearly the goal of the project and any firm time, cost, or other resource constraints can be stated at the outset, and any fundamental decisions that dictate the viability of the project should have been made and stated as preconditions of the plan. In addition, the general size and scope of the project should be known. If there is a format for the plan, then adding information can be done in a thorough and orderly way.

3.2 Planning Roles

Two of the major documents of software development, the SDP and the transition plan, are in themselves the result of significant prior planning. The fact that a project is being undertaken implies at least an implicit plan in which the project addresses some need. At the project level, the SDP becomes the controlling document for managing the software development project. We expect that such a plan will describe the project's goal and use.

As the project develops, the SDP will provide a definition of each major task and give ever more detailed estimates of the time and resources required. Detailed task descriptions and schedules are not usually part of the SDP but are referenced from it. The SDP provides an overview of the organization of the project, the resources needed, and the methods that will be used to achieve the goals of the project.

The transition planning, as described in the previous chapter, is a special framework that describes how the organization will change to use a new technology. It addresses some issues, such as culture change and organizational restructuring, which usually would not appear in an SDP. The transition plan describes the way the organization plans to move its people from acceptance of new technologies, to use, and finally to mastery. This will involve at least training and probably some serious organizational changes. At the same time, the plan must show how new methodologies will be selected and integrated into the project along with the tools and other resources necessary to support the move.

3.3 Up-Front Planning

A new business venture doesn't become serious until a business plan is produced. As Bell and McNamara say in their watershed book, *High Tech Ventures* [Bell91], a business plan is:

A set of guidelines for operating the company. The standard of record against which the firm expects its results to be measured. A sales brochure directed at potential investors (although the downside and risks the company faces must also be covered). A place where founders can describe a vision for the firm. [Bell91]

These features apply as well to the SDP. Lest anyone think that a software project doesn't need selling, please think again. Even internal projects need supporters, and given the difficulty of describing complex software projects (the ones that need strong support to justify their cost), an SDP is the best way to get and keep support.

The other essential item for a business plan is a financial model that describes for both employees and investors how the company will make money, given normal assumptions about the business environment. At this point, before too much time and effort has been expended, it can be seen if the business has the first chance of success. For investors, one important business plan area identifies risk factors that threaten the financial model. If the risks seem disproportionate to the potential returns, investors will avoid the company. Software development plans have a similar function, but often the costs are not stated directly. More often, the estimated time and resources are given, especially if the plan represents an in-house project, because dollar costs are subsumed into larger operating budgets.

Obviously, businesses are started without business plans, and some of them become successful, while other businesses with first-rate plans flounder. A plan or lack thereof does not guarantee the outcome, but then going on a wilderness trip without maps and emergency supplies dictates neither success nor failure. Nobody suggests, however, that it is a good idea to embark on a risky journey without preparation. Not only is the risk of failure higher, but failures are more likely to be catastrophic. In business, the lack of a plan isolates the entrepreneur from everyone who might provide support: no banker or experienced investor would waste time on a company that wasn't serious enough to write down what it hoped to do. For software, the same idea holds. A generalized presentation may elicit generalized responses, but it won't give anybody a way to analyze the endeavor at any depth.

For well-financed start-ups, the cost of developing a business plan may vary from 20 percent of the total amount, for an initial funding of 100,000 dollars, down to 5 percent of funding for ventures of a half-million dollars or more. As Bell and McNamara point out, most start-ups will not get funded before a business plan is produced, so the only way to produce a plan is for the founders of a company to work on the plan without compensation. In established organizations, the planning of a new venture may well be funded, but time and resource constraints will be high. Costs can be reduced in these situations by using existing plans as a base and by using plan-writing software programs to help structure and elaborate the document.

In the same way, developing an SDP can be extremely expensive. Costs in large companies range upwards of $500 per page for a meaningful SDP written from scratch. This sort of pricing inhibits writing and modifying a plan, and without evolution, the plan loses its value. By using an SDP template, the documentation cost can be dramatically reduced, the format can be made conformable to the applicable standards, and the chance of omitting important information is diminished.

Software Process Organizations and Planning

In government development, explicit planning is a required part of the project. According to MIL-STD 2167A and its successors, MIL-STD 498 and ISO 12207, the SDP becomes the part of the contract defining the project [Fayad93–98]. For nondefense work, some organizations require the developing group to be assessed at Software Engineering Institute (SEI) Level 3 to be eligible to bid on contracts. Company-wide ISO 9000 certification is becoming a common requirement for companies doing business in Europe. While specific sections and features of these standards may be debated, planning requirements are common to all. These standards convert good method to explicitly required procedure [Fayad93–98].

Software project planning is a key process area starting in Level 2 of the SEI Capability Maturity Model (CMM), as shown in Figure 3.2 (also described in the next section). Each project must document a plan that includes projections of project size, resources, staffing, schedules, and milestones [Humphrey89]. Higher levels make greater planning demands. At CMM Level 3, resource estimation must be done at the activity level, and contingencies must be included in the plan based on historical information. Risk management must be planned, and the staffing plans must be refined. At CMM Level 4, quality improvement plans must be produced, and at Level 5, process and productivity plans are required.

The Capability Maturity Model

The CMM, developed by the SEI, provides software development organizations with guidance on how to gain control of their software development and maintenance processes, and how to evolve toward an excellent culture of software engineering and management. The CMM is designed to guide software development organizations in selecting process improvement strategies by determining current process maturity and identifying issues that are most critical to software quality and process improvement. By focusing on a limited set of activities and working aggressively to achieve them, a software organization can steadily improve its software process to enable continuous and lasting gains in software quality. The CMM is organized into five maturity levels, as shown in Figure 3.1. A maturity level is a well-defined evolutionary plateau toward achieving mature software development and manage-

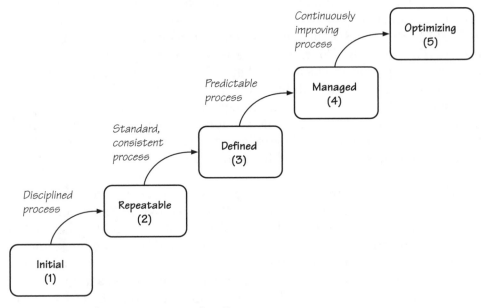

Figure 3.1   CMM's maturity levels.

ment processes. Each maturity level provides a layer of continuous process improvement. Figure 3.2 shows the five levels of the CMM, the characteristics of each level, and the key process improvement areas of each level.

Common Features

The common features are attributes that indicate whether the implementation and institutionalization of a key process area is effective, repeatable, and lasting. These common features are:

Commitment to perform. Describes the actions that must be taken by software organizations to ensure that the process is established and will endure. This includes practices on policy and leadership.

Level	Characteristics	Key Process Improvement Areas
1	Crisis-driven (Ad hoc/chaotic)	None
2	Process still depends on individuals (Intuitive)	Requirements management Software project planning Software project tracking and oversight Software subcontract management Software quality assurance Software configuration management
3	Process defined and institutionalized (Qualitative basis for improvement)	Organization process focus Organization process definition Training program Integrated software management Software product engineering Intergroup coordination Peer reviews
4	Measured process (quantitative basis for improvement)	Quantitative process management Software quality management
5	Continuous improvement	Defect prevention Technology change management Process change management

Figure 3.2   Characteristics and key process improvements (KPIs).

Ability to perform. Describes the preconditions that must exist in the software organization to implement the software process competently. This includes practices on resources, organizational structure, training, and tools.

Activities performed. Describes the roles and procedures necessary to implement a key process area. This includes practices on plans, procedures, work performed, tracking, and corrective action.

Measurement and analysis. Describes the need to measure the process and analyze the measurements. This includes examples of measurements.

Verifying implementation. Describes the steps to ensure that activities comply with established processes. This includes practices on reviews and audits for quality assurance and management.

ISO 9000

ISO 9000 standards require systems to be documented, controlled, auditable, monitored, improved, and effective. To achieve these requirements, plans must be in place describing the necessary work [Fayad96–98]. ISO 9000-1, Section 4.4, requires a project plan, essentially an SDP, that must cover each design and development activity. Included must be plans to set up and execute design reviews. The project plan itself must be under configuration control. In addition, other plans are required for a project:

Planning documents required by ISO 9000

Build plan	Training plan
Quality plan	Test plan
Defect control plan	Service plan
Packaging, storage, preservation, and delivery plan	

3.4 Contents of a Software Development Plan

The next section describes the elements that constitute a fully developed SDP. With appropriate detail, the sections from this contents list, along with the other referenced plans and manuals, can be used to satisfy requirements for ISO 9000, SEI CMM Level 2 and above, and MIL-STD 498.

By itself, an SDP does not guarantee a successful project, but without such a plan, failure is far more likely. Note that even in its complete form, the SDP does not include all documentation required for effective project management. The transition plan, analysis and design documents, process documents, test plans, and so forth, are pointed to by the SDP and contain vital information as well. The SDP is probably the developer's most important document, because it lays out the scope of the project and enumerates the project's milestones.

SDP Contents

The SDP is the guide that controls all of the software development activities. The SDP should include proven methodologies, techniques, and processes from past successful projects. The SDP should address the following areas:

Organization. What are the organizations responsible for developing the system? Who is responsible for each software development task (for example, analysis, design, testing, and so on), and what is the reporting chain for people and organizations?

Management/technical control. What is the management philosophy? How will the software development be managed, and what management controls will be employed?

Schedule and milestones. What are the detailed schedule and specific milestones for the software development effort, and how do they relate to the overall system development schedule?

Status monitoring and activity networks. What is the activity network for the entire software development? How will management know where the project is regarding the schedule, and how will they use an HL activity network to gain this knowledge?

Documentation. What document will be produced and when, according to the contractual agreement and/or SDP policy? What are the techniques and tools that will be used to generate the documents? How will the documents be reviewed and approved?

Methodologies, standards, and guidelines. What specific methodology will be used to develop the software? What specific standards (military, commercial) will be followed in the software development?

Development/test resources. What are the resources needed for analysis, design, coding, and testing activities? What support software and hardware is required, and how will these resources be obtained, maintained, and documented? When will these resources be obtained?

Security. How will classified or proprietary data, documents, technologies, and software products be controlled? How will the development facility be controlled and operated? What provisions will be made for disaster backup and off-site data storage?

Management and Development Processes

Project management process. What management processes will be used for managing the project effectively? What specific processes will be used for staffing, tracking, controlling, directing, staff training, and monitoring the project? What management tools will be used for all the management activities?

Software planning process. What are the contents of the SDP? What other planning documents will be in place, such as transition plan, test plan?

Software development process. What software development processes will be used for developing the software? What influenced the selection of these processes? What tools and environments will be used to support these development processes? What are the deliverables of these processes?

Software testing process. What testing processes will be used for system and software testing and verification and validation activities? What tools and environments will be used to illustrate the software testing process? What are the testing process deliverables?

Software evaluation process. What evaluation processes will be used for evaluating the development artifacts and deliverables? What are the evaluation criteria and checklists for each of the development deliverables? What tools and environments will be used for this purpose?

Configuration management process. What configuration management process will be used for controlling the software development products and deliverables? What software products will go under configuration control? When? How will the software configuration management process interact with other system configuration management activities? What tools and environments will be used to support the configuration management process?

Software quality assurance process (SQA). What techniques will be used for ensuring the integrity and quality of the software products? What tools will be used to support the SQA process?

Corrective action process. What process will be used for the corrective action process? How will errors in software products be reported and documented? What tools and environments will be used to support the corrective action process?

Process improvement. How will processes be defined, measured, and improved? What methods will be used to replace and modify processes? How will process interaction be determined?

Technology transfer process. What process will be used for inserting new technologies into the project? How will effectiveness of new technology be determined?

Delivery process. What processes will be used to deliver and service the final product? How will maintenance effectiveness be determined?

3.5 Minimum Planning Requirements

The plan outlined above provides a full-featured plan for development. A new organization or one that has limited resources may find the list somewhat daunting. With all the effort required to do a new project, it may be prudent to start with a sparse plan and expand it as need and experience allow. The minimum features of any SDP are the following:

Minimum SDP features

Project organization

Management processes

Software engineering processes

Size and cost estimation
Schedule and activity network
Budget

3.6 Planning Policy

The software transition framework may be seen as a necessity to move to object-oriented development, but time pressures and skepticism about its value can tempt development organizations to skip SDPs. For organizations certified under SEI CMM or ISO 9000, such omission can result in a breach of contract and suspension or loss of certification. To avoid this, a planning policy should be put in place [Fayad93–98; Fayad96–98]. The policy itself need not be long, but it must be visibly supported by senior management.

A Sample Policy

This policy ensures that all project managers perform effective planning by developing and maintaining software development plans (SDPs) for the major software development projects within their responsibility. Every SDP will conform to this organization's standards and guidelines for such plans.

3.7 Issues in Planning

As we stated, the plan must evolve to be useful. Attempting to plan everything in advance virtually guarantees a document that remains on the shelf and becomes increasingly irrelevant to the unfolding project. Software development requires an odd collaboration of detailed and general information to be successful. Many architectural details must be evaluated for technical feasibility, prototypes created and analyzed, and analysis and design issues revisited as a project becomes more fully understood. Avoiding some details can lead to serious failures in the system. On the other hand, attempting to nail down every detail in advance seems to be a waste of time: not only are many issues not understood until the project is well underway, but requirements have a way of changing while development proceeds. It may be comforting to attempt a full up-front plan, and it certainly makes official estimating easier, but the comfort comes from a false sense of security. One must be careful, however, not to assume that plans are always wasted effort. Discussion of a few issues may help guide the planning process.

Identifying Wishful Thinking

Beware plans that combine the adoption of new technology with reduced development times. This is highly improbable. If the new project involves even a new language, the time for staff to adapt to and master the changes will add to the time, and while future projects may proceed more quickly, the first one will take longer.

Revised estimates that show reduced duration of later phases (usually called for to offset schedule overruns earlier in the project) are almost always fantasy. It may seem harsh, but every shortened estimate is suspect. Unless there is solid evidence of substantial misestimation beforehand, no estimates should be shortened.

Beware plans that assume all activities will occur without problems. This form of wishful thinking assumes that plans mean problems won't occur. This sort of inflexibility is common and is often driven by the desire to meet a completion date. But a project in which nothing unforeseen happens is so rare that there is little point in contemplating it. A plan that deals with contingencies is more likely to succeed.

Look actively for signs that the plan assumes a static environment. Examples of this are lack of risk analysis, assumptions of no personnel turnover, no contingency planning for subcontractor delays, and no accommodation for changes in the hardware and software development environment.

Consider Scenarios

Planning for every eventuality is clearly impossible. Even if it were somehow practical, the amount of information produced would be so great that it could not be understood by the project team members. This is a common failing of risk analysis. The identification of every risk and its corrective action can result in an impenetrable mountain of data, even if the risks are ranked according to likelihood and impact. One way of dealing with large amounts of planning data is to use scenarios to evaluate possible situations and responses.

A planning scenario takes into account a variety of influences, internal and external, controllable and uncontrollable, and projects possible outcomes based on the different ways these influences can affect a project. For example, significant management changes in a client's organization can affect the project's viability. If new management does not consider the project worthwhile or cost-effective, then its long-term viability is compromised. Another example of risk is a changing technical environment. Advances in hardware, software, and communications may make a project obsolete before it is delivered.

Peter Schwartz, in *The Art of the Long View,* describes techniques in developing and using scenarios to prepare for eventualities. Scenario building requires identification of key issues in the local environment and driving forces in both the local and global environments, which are then assessed in terms of their uncertainty and importance to predict possible outcomes. The end result is usually a small group of possible future scenarios, which can then be used to build contingency plans. The point of doing this sort of planning is that it provides more guidance than merely identifying and ranking possible situations in the planning process. It is probably the best way to deal with risk issues involving non-technical problems, such as organization and management.

The downside of scenarios and of risk evaluation itself is that it can be unsettling. It requires dropping the fiction of total control and requires honest approaches to decision making. By dealing with risks and planning for contingencies, it makes explicit that uncertainty is a large part of any large project. In response to that uncertainty, there are a variety of possible outcomes for a project, not just success or failure. By addressing the uncertainty, multiple decisions will be required during a project that can substantially change its direction. In terms of planning, then, it is a process that does not end with the issuance of the first revision of the SDP, but rather continues throughout the project and is reflected in updates to the plan.

3.8   Summary

Planning for OO projects is different from traditional projects in a number of ways. First, much greater emphasis must be placed on the analysis and design phases of the project. This affects the initial estimates for

Tips and Practical Advice

Lesson 3.1   An SDP must be the first document produced.
A small business must have a business plan before talking to the
bank, the small-business administration, and investors. We see mil-
lions of dollars (sometimes billions) allocated for a software development project with no planning. The software development plan
(SDP) is one of the most critical documents and plays important
roles for any software development project.

   The SDP is the controlling document for managing a software
development project. It provides a definition of each major task, and
an estimate of the time and resources required. It provides a framework for management review and control. In almost every situation
in the Department of Defense (DOD) environment, a draft of an SDP
must be provided by the software development contractor and
included as part of a prospective contractor's proposal.

Lesson 3.2.   An SDP policy should be in place.
The SDP policy will insure that each project manager performs
effective planning by developing and maintaining an SDP for the
major software development projects under their management
responsibilities.

   Because the SDP controls the software development activities, it
must be prepared and approved by upper management in the commercial environment or by the program manager at the beginning of
the development contract in the military environment. In the commercial environment case, the SDP will be the project manager's
contract with his management or his company. In the military and
DOD environment, the SDP will be the vehicle by which the development contractor tells the program manager how the contractor
will do what he promised to do. The SDP is also the contract
between the project manager and all the software development
teams.

(continued)

Lesson 3.3   The existence of a complete and responsive SDP is not a guarantee of project success.

Often, a good SDP is ignored by the software development teams. The SDP may have been written by a consulting firm or by another group who does not participate in the management or development activities, and the majority of the development team members may not even be aware of the existence of the SDP.

> **In commercial settings.** The upper management must enforce the SDP policy and make certain that their product managers do what they promised to do in the SDP.
>
> **In military and DOD settings.** The program manager (PM) must make sure that the contractor delivers the promises in the SDP. The PM must verify that the contractor's activities are in compliance with the SDP.

An update cycle, such as quarterly, for the SDP must be established to make sure that a living or timely plan always exists. The upper management (in the commercial setting) or PM (in the military or DOD setting) must make sure that the vital processes of the original plan are not eliminated from the SDP with each update. This may be controlled by placing the SDP under software configuration management after the initial management approval.

staffing, resource usage, and scheduling. Second, training to make the transition will be higher in the project and exist at the front end of the project. Third, new staff in the form of domain experts, object methodologists, and prototyping experts must be hired. Fourth, an explicit part of the planning must be to choose the appropriate OO methods and tools. Assuming a transition from procedural programming, the transition plan must be done. Expect start-up costs to outweigh other costs. Fifth, object development proceeds at different times and rates through the project. Some objects and program functionality may be complete earlier while other parts are complete later. This means that prototyping, simulations, coding, and testing will occur at different times, some earlier than usual, during the project and must be planned for. Finally, the overall impact of adopting new approaches to software development must be taken into account. The SDP and transition plans will be critical elements of the successful transition.

References

[Bell91] Bell, G. G. and J. McNamara. *High-Tech Ventures: The Guide for Entrepreneurial Success.* Reading, MA: Addison-Wesley, 1991.

[Fayad93–98] Fayad, M. E. "A Complete Guideline Based on DoD-STD-2167A/SDD: Software Development Plan for OO Software Projects." White Document (January 1993 to present): 450 pages.

[Fayad96–98] Fayad, M. E. "Software Development Plan for OO Software Commercial Projects." White Document (January 1993 to present): 250 pages.

[Fayad96a] Fayad, M. E., W. T. Tsai, and M. L. Fulghum. "Transition to Object-Oriented Software Development." *The Communications of the ACM* 39, no. 2 (February 1996): 108–121.

[Fayad96b] Fayad, M. E., and M. Cline. "Managing Object-Oriented Software Development." *IEEE Computer* (September 1996): 26–31.

[Humphrey89] Humphrey, W. S. *Managing the Software Process.* Reading, MA: Addison-Wesley, 1989.

[Jones96] Jones, C. *Patterns of Software System Failure and Success.* Boston, MA: ITP, 1996.

chapter four

Dealing with Culture Change

"The greatest difficulty in the world is not for people to accept new ideas, but to make them forget about old ideas."

—JOHN MAYNARD KEYNES

4.1 Moving to Object-Oriented Software Engineering Is a Major Change

If the change to disciplined, object-oriented software development (OOSD) were just a matter of adopting a new programming language or implementing a few new processes within the software development groups, the behavioral changes and learning curve would challenge the whole department. However, moving to a software engineering approach that includes iterative object-oriented (OO) analysis, design, and development crosses not only departmental boundaries but can involve the customer in the change process as well. This change, extending across the organization, will take longer and will require more effort with greater resources to accomplish than the adoption of some new programming techniques would. It constitutes a change in the organization's culture, which must be taken very seriously. As we indicated in Chapter 2, this transition will take at least a year and requires not only mastery of new technology, but also new roles and modes of interaction within the whole organization.

To make the change, the following conditions must exist.

1. There must be a compelling need to change.
2. There must be people who can and will champion the change.

3. There must be an understanding of the organization's current culture and state.

4. There must be a vision of what the result of change will be.

5. There must be a process to move from the current state, through the transition, and to the goal.

We discuss each of these items in turn.

A Compelling Need to Change

We made the case for the transition in previous chapters, and rather than ascribing miraculous benefits to object-oriented technology (OOT), we stated that it was, along with some more established software engineering practices, a necessary basis for further advancement in software. The difficulty of this argument is that it is not especially glamorous, and to some it is not compelling. Without a firm view that change is essential, attempting cultural change will not be effective. Changes of such magnitude cannot be justified based purely on convenience or on the attractiveness of the idea. Direct or indirect economic advantages must offset the cost and effort of making the transition.

As components and frameworks become commercially viable as sources for software functionality, the economic argument for their use strengthens. Few software products are becoming smaller, less complex, or less functional, and the cost of developing whole applications from scratch therefore increases. This means that software developers have no real choice if they wish to remain competitive but to incorporate third-party components in their products. Components imply object orientation (OO). The nature of the marketplace and the workforce are changing as well. The following items describe areas of change that affect virtually all organizations and that require adaptation.

- ◆ Software products continue to get larger, more complex, and must increasingly interact with other products and components in an increasingly distributed environment. Distributed environments are increasingly built as OO entities.

- ◆ Hardware platforms and software environments rarely last more than a year or two now; as systems become more powerful, expectations of greater utility and performance rise. To meet expectations, faster cycle time and parallel development will be necessary.

- The proportion of contract and temporary workers is rising in software development groups. At the same time, permanent employees can expect assignments to change more often and have a more temporary character. Permanent employees must adapt at a higher rate than before. This adaptation also implies that organizations cannot rely on individuals remaining available to maintain complex systems. Classes and objects are designed to localize code and data, thus reducing complexity. A person who is unfamiliar with a whole system will more readily be able to understand an object than a function with many inputs and outputs throughout a system.

- Competitive pressures will increase. The era of a completely closed software industry has ended. Highly trained and experienced software developers with powerful computers exist around the world, and the nature of software lends itself to almost instantaneous electronic distribution. Even one-off software products will no longer necessarily be done locally.

- Development of the Internet and intranets has changed the character of software development and the distribution of the customer base. *Development in Internet time* is now a serious business concept in which development times are compressed, more frequent revisions and additions are completed, and installation and distribution are immediate with a more diverse customer base.

- Change doesn't last forever. If it did, you wouldn't have to be changing now. This implies that an explicit goal of the transition is to become more adaptive. This, in turn, implies that everyone must learn to accept change in a manner that doesn't cause continuous agony.

Selling Change

If we are selling services or providing contract work, the transition will have to be sold to the customer, and in many cases, we must overcome customer resistance to using object-oriented software engineering (see

Figure 4.1). This is especially true if the customer knows it is our first OOSE project. Customers frequently associate new technology, such as OOSE, with *high risk.* The principal selling job, then, becomes one of explaining the ways risk will be minimized and clearly identifying the risks involved in *not* moving to object-oriented technology.

The way to convince the customer is to provide capability briefings emphasizing minimization of risks. Because the customer is usually negative toward software projects with any element of risk, it is important to identify the greater risks in staying with the old development approach. However, people may consider an OO development high risk because they feel the tools and techniques are immature and the technology has been overhyped. The main purpose of the briefings is to demonstrate that we have thought through our transition plan and provide the least risk for the project. The more we prepare, the less risk will be perceived. Some example topics include the following:

> **Benefits versus cost.** We previously discussed this.
>
> **Training schedule.** The training should include both the customer and the internal development team project. Bringing customers up

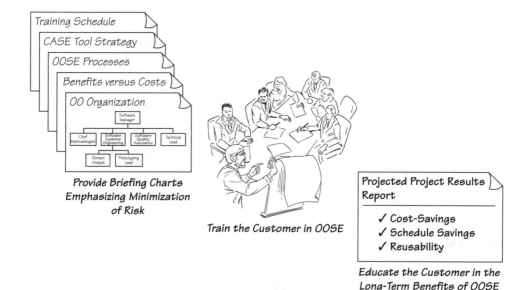

Figure 4.1   Selling OOSE to customers.

to speed on the technology is necessary both to develop confidence in the approach—otherwise, they may feel they have no control of the project—and to be able to participate in the analysis and design phases, which rely heavily on OO.

Computer-aided software engineering (CASE) tool strategy. The CASE tool strategy is covered fully in Chapter 6.

Object-oriented process documentation. Process documentation gives the customer confidence that this is more than just another passing fad that will cost more than it benefits.

Organizational issues. The result of the organization will be to increase efficiency, which will be realized by higher total output per person.

Return on investment (ROI). Note, however, that issues such as ROI must be approached carefully. In larger organizations, technical managers may have limited control over various budget areas that affect returns.

Change Champions

Object-oriented programming has been around long enough and has enjoyed enough success to no longer be considered a fad. As we have already said, most new software is based on object technology, and it is likely that some proportion of the software organization will be familiar with OO concepts. If not, the learning curve will be steeper and resistance to the transition will be higher, but it will still be possible. The essential issue in the development groups will be to find people willing to make OO work. Being a change champion cannot be assigned as a spare-time activity, and it must be performed by someone with experience in the group who is well regarded by peers.

At the same time, it is not enough to change only the software development group. The nature of iterative development requires continuing participation of other groups. No longer can customers or marketing throw requirements over the wall to development and then wait for software. Software estimating must change from a single up-front guess to a series of steps in which estimates are produced with greater accuracy over a longer analysis period. Depending on the type of software produced, sales cycles will change along with maintenance and distribution methods. All of these new approaches mandate the support and active leadership of senior management. In fact, management will have to change as much as subordinates will if the transition is to be successful. Part of the software engineering package is more realistic estimates of time and resources for a project. Estimates and resource support have traditionally been abused, with management mistaking unrealistic expectations for motivation. It is a practice that must stop. But management's greatest challenges will be to stay committed to change, ensuring that resources are available for the transition and not abandoning change when crises arise or setbacks occur.

Understanding Current Culture and State

It is no surprise that many organizations will not immediately be prepared to make the transition. The technical challenges in many ways are the most amenable to change. Experienced software developers have some feeling for the time and effort required to move to new programming languages and development environments. They can identify a series of actions to adapt. However, anyone who has ever been in an organization of any size recognizes that there are as many *political* obstacles as technical ones in making any change. We identify the way an organization views change and reacts to changes as artifacts of corporate culture.

Varieties of Corporate Culture

Any sort of noncontractual interaction in a business is a manifestation of culture. Culture can be viewed in the context of small groups or the whole corporation. At most levels, culture has two types: formal and informal. The formal version of corporate culture is communicated through policy and vision statements. It provides clues about how the company views itself and how it may react to certain aspects of change, such as employment security and willingness to try new approaches. But formal expressions of culture can also be just hype and wishful thinking. Informal corporate culture is passed by word of mouth and often expresses conflicts between the formal expression of culture and the "way things really work around here." An instance of this conflict is a formal statement extolling the company's *can-do* attitude but an informal understanding that failure is always punished. Another example of informal cultural expression is the unwritten rule in many groups that people must work long hours to get ahead. Examining informal culture will yield information about the current state of the organization and conflicts that must be addressed to change.

Sometimes we describe the culture as either chaotic or orderly, a *cowboy* or *engineering* culture. The problem with these descriptions is that orderly engineering cultures are not always efficient, and chaotic cowboy cultures are not always as inefficient or ad hoc as they seem. When we use these terms, we focus on the software development groups rather than the whole organization. These views give us a distorted picture of the way things work and how they might be changed. Let's look at some ways to rethink culture.

Corporate culture is usually described as a monolithic entity: Company A's culture is loose and unceremonious, whereas company B's is structured and formal. But cultures are considerably more varied and complex. Within a company, cultures vary by department, job activity, and function. This variation implies two things: culture is so complex that it can't be changed by working on people's attitudes, and management must be aware of the differing outlooks and agendas of subcultures when planning for change. The interfaces of these subcultures are prime areas where resistance to change will manifest itself. But we do not suggest that companies undertake extensive analysis of culture and cultures before starting a change program. The job is so complex that it will be hard to do effectively, and the results will describe a culture that will soon not exist. Instead, we suggest that management and staff be aware of general culture issues as they map out their change strategy.

Subcultures

Part of understanding the current situation is to assess the current state of various groups in the organization so that they can be enlisted for their support, or in some cases, so that they can be sold on the idea of change. Regardless of company hype about *pulling together,* different groups have differing responsibilities and concerns that must be addressed in an appropriate way.

Schein describes three separate groups of subcultures inside most organizations: the executive culture, the operations culture, and the technical culture [Schein96]. We discuss each of these subcultures in turn and describe their influence on a software development organization.

Executive Subculture The executive culture is made up, naturally, of senior management. Members of this group have limited direct involvement in detailed technical or operational decisions and must, therefore, use the processed information they receive and exercise control at a macrolevel with budgetary and large, organizational initiatives. They are expected to, and tend to, look at issues from an economic viewpoint.

- What are the trade-offs between using the existing technology and a new technology?
- How much will it cost to develop this product or make this transition?
- How will we evaluate the cost of using this new technology as it unfolds?
- How can we verify the cost and value of process improvement?
- What are the risks of not adopting a new technology?

None of these questions is unreasonable, unimportant, or obvious. Senior managers' performance is judged on how well they answer these questions, and far too often the technical groups recommending the technology provide extremely poor information to make the decision. An experienced executive, having been burned before, will also be skeptical of claims of competitive advantage from new technology; dramatic improvements from using a new technology; or widespread demand for some new, highly technical product. Technical management, in contrast, is notorious for dealing poorly with economic arguments when presenting new initiatives to top management. This happens because technical managers are often members of the engineer subculture and think in different terms.

Since top management's active support will be required, they should be given a careful analysis of current costs, transition costs, and benefits expected, all cast in economic terms (including staffing costs and retention, operating costs, and maintenance efforts). The sorts of questions posed above should be answered by the presentation without making unsupportable claims for the transition. We cover some of these issues in greater detail in the following sections.

Operator Subculture   The operator culture is considerably more involved. It consists of the grouped interests and understanding of operational groups, from manufacturing to sales. Each individual group will have its own view of how the organization works and how it should work. From the standpoint of software development, there are quite a few significant interactions. Understanding these interactions will identify current and future areas of conflict.

- ◆ Sales people, to be successful at their jobs, must have a solution-oriented outlook. When discussing a product, they must have a view of its benefits and will find discussions of problems not only tedious, but may well think the people discussing problems are overly negative and nit-picking. In contrast, software engineers must discuss details and potential problems as a necessary step toward finding solutions. This cultural difference suggests that the two groups must be educated about the validity and job appropriateness of the two different outlooks and that meetings between sales and software development groups have experienced moderators.

- ◆ Much of the notorious friction between marketing and software development groups can be traced to differing cultures. Limited understanding in each group of the other group's roles leads to conflict. Each group tends to think the other is trying to control how work should be done. In mass-market software companies, marketing people, rather than contract negotiators, are the voice of the customer. The marketing groups tend to underestimate how much information will be needed to specify development objectives and tend to bridle when developers ask detailed questions about software features and their intended use. Software developers, for their part, bridle when marketing suggests technical approaches and questions development estimates. In an object-oriented development environment, these groups will have continual, detailed interactions. In many cases, domain experts will be part of the marketing groups.

- ◆ In physical product development, concurrent engineering is now an established practice. Concurrent engineering requires collaboration between at least design, manufacturing, and support to assure that what gets created can also be mass-produced and maintained. In software organizations, object-oriented development lends itself to a similar organization. There are traditional conflicts between development and distribution and between development and help desks. Part of the cost reduction in transitioning to object orientation will be found in making the software distribution and support operational groups interact with development starting during the analysis phases and continuing throughout the product life cycle.

◆ The quality assurance (QA) function may be part of the operator subculture or part of the engineering culture. In either case, there is usually a structural conflict between QA and software development that tends to retard progress.

Technical Subculture   The technical culture, ostensibly the target of this chapter, has its own objectives, the first of which in software organizations is the creation and continuation of computer and software products. Regardless of recent progress, there is still substantial uncertainty and ambiguity in software development, and the technical culture must be comfortable and productive in this inherently difficult milieu. The outlook of members of the technical subculture is both safety-oriented and optimistic. They must believe that they can make things work, and, unlike sales and marketing subcultures, they must always keep reliable operation in mind.

The technical culture's greatest shortcoming is that people in it tend to see solutions as overwhelmingly technical. This applies to software products as well as culture change. One of the hardest accommodations members of this culture must make is that technical superiority means little without overall high-level performance, and to achieve such performance, intergroup collaboration is essential. Thus, in the new organization, problems are overwhelmingly personal.

The Organization's Current State

As we said earlier, the formal expressions of corporate culture often bear little resemblance to the actual realities of the organization. This disparity between corporate culture and corporate reality must be understood and the reality used to assess the issues affecting change. The first task is to ask a few questions that identify what you do know about the change and what you don't know. Understanding the current state is a necessary starting point [LaMarsh95].

1. Have compelling reasons for the change been explicitly defined? Goals have financial, strategic, and cultural components. Have clear goals for the change in all these areas been established [Kaufman92]? Is management support confirmed, and are continuing resources guaranteed?

2. What information are you using to explain the need for change and the predicted change? How are you using this information? Answering these questions requires honesty about the limits to prediction. Even if the goal is accomplished, many of the routes to the goal will be different than expected.

3. What does the organization think of its current technical capabilities? Is there in-house object-oriented expertise, or must everyone learn object technology from scratch? What general software engineering skills, such as configuration management, formal reviews, and development planning, does the department already have?

4. What does the organization think about its general state of operation? Does it feel competent to deliver the current product? Compare this answer with the answers to question 1. If the organization feels competent, how does it feel about change? Have any of the groups had experience with change?

5. What areas have the largest likelihood of generating resistance to change? Are these areas local to the department, or will long-standing processes in multiple processes require change? If the latter is true, an assessment of the effort and cost of change should be done.

6. How realistic are the goals of change? Do they look too much like a *silver bullet* that will cure all the department's ills and provide many multiples of current productivity? If so, the goals must be revisited and made more realistic. Is there a model company of equivalent size and product that has made a similar change, or will your group be the first.

7. What resources exist to aid the transition, such as training, team building, conflict resolution, and so forth?

A Vision of the Future

Answers to some of the above questions will help identify the next factor in the change, a vision of the results. Without this vision, the change efforts will be meaningless. There will be no way to evaluate progress, assess costs, or calculate returns. The vision of the future must be more than a glossy advertisement with marvelous predictions. The vision we need will go through many iterations and generate, for a time, constant revisions. To do this will require seemingly endless meetings, conducted at many levels of the organization. The meetings, evaluations, and resultant vision will disrupt current work, cost money, and fray nerves. At the end, however, should come a general view of what the organization should look like after the transition. While fixating on exact outcomes is not productive, because not everything can be predicted, the general outlines can and should be identified. Too much formalization at first can be wasteful. It may have to be redone often, and trying to firm up situations in flux just slows things down. The results of this plan for the future are really the first part of the transition process. We identify a few areas below.

1. What do you know about the change already, and what don't you know? For example, if staff increases or reductions are part of the future, how and when do they happen?
2. How are trade-offs to be decided? It is reasonable to assume that some goals will conflict. So which goals have we decided in advance will take precedence?
3. Can individuals see how they fit into the new organization? Will their responsibilities change or remain essentially the same? Are the expected changes in reporting identified? For example, if the department is to be reorganized as teams, are people aware of who they will report to and what departments they will work with?
4. What changes in resources are planned? Does the new way require new software development tools, programming lan-

guages, or development hardware? What happens when the cost estimate exceeds our change budget (as it almost certainly will)? What will happen when an unforeseen or overlooked issue comes up that has a significant cost impact. Will the transition be canceled, delayed, stretched out? What are the acceptable parameters for delay?

5. What is the time frame for change? What information are you using to explain the change, and how are you using it? Be sure to emphasize the limits of prediction. No matter how well prepared, subtle interactions and unforeseen problems will affect plans. Developing too rigid a plan or too rosy a change scenario will guarantee trouble.

A Process for Moving to the Future

Having identified the current state and the desired state, the next step is to develop a process for moving to the future and implementing that process. Up to now there have been many changes, but now the change will be continual and sometimes jarring. For some parts, a gradual change will be possible, but for some parts of the effort, the change will be intense and abrupt. If an organization has a history of collaboration, then learning new ways will be easier. If it doesn't have this history, more radical change that tends to break down existing structures will be necessary to achieve the equivalent effect. The first steps in the process have already started, and next is a more detailed planning for immediate steps, doing those steps, and dealing with the inevitable obstacles.

We believe that the organization can best be prepared for the change by identifying certain tangible goals that must be reached quickly. Corporate cultures are so complex as to defy any but the most rigorous analysis, and superficial analyses are worse than useless. Trying to prepare people for change without having a reason is, we feel, wasted effort [Beer90]. If it is possible to start the transition to object orientation with a noncritical project, it will make people feel freer to try new approaches without the severe consequences for failure.

A first goal could be identifying and ordering new CASE tools within two months. This is an aggressive but reachable goal. Our recommendation in Chapter 8 calls for a ten-week schedule of training. Using this guideline, another goal of completing the first analysis iteration of at least one class per team in 90 days can be set. This implies analysis and documentation using the new CASE tools. This approach of moving toward tangible goals is in direct contrast to spending time trying to analyze the culture or prepare the organization before going for tangible results.

Trying to make everyone comfortable during the transition is impossible, so we recommend that the discomfort be used to advantage. If the current environment is made unstable, it makes the difference between the current state and the desired state less problematic. For example, prohibiting the use of structured analysis or function-based analysis for any new work would cause instability and tension that could only be resolved by adopting the new OO approach. While we suggest making some substantial changes at one time, we don't think trying to change absolutely everything at once will be effective. The transition to OO development has a steep learning curve, and adopting all the other software engineering and organizational changes at the same time may well be too stressful.

Adoption of object-oriented analysis and design will necessarily be a relatively abrupt change. It is essential that the team starts thinking in terms of objects and does not try to mix function-based design and analysis with object approaches. In our experience, mixing of this sort is just not successful. As we state later, a concerted training program for the whole team will be essential and should be an integral part of the transition process. The training must be tailored to the particular team, project, and object-oriented methods used. To assure this, the teams must have a strong say in designing the training. They must learn what they need to know, not what someone else thinks they should learn.

Once started, management must strictly enforce the new OO process. There will almost certainly come a time when a member of a software team wants to bypass all the rigorous OOSE activities and develop the source code directly. These individuals will undoubtedly provide numerous reasons why going directly to coding will save time and money. Managers should not back down from the process change under any circumstances. Backing down, even in the most trivial of cases, sets a bad trend, but also demonstrates a lack of commitment to the newly defined process.

To do this, the proper tools must exist. Although CASE tools are often expensive, we believe they are essential to the new object-oriented process. Without proper tools, software engineers waste effort and creativity on trivial tasks instead of the analysis and design of the software system. By not committing any capital to the purchase of tools, management sends a wrong message of being unsure about the paradigm shift and the success of the new OO process. Software engineers will justifiably interpret this as a lack of management commitment to the new OO process.

Management must continually reinforce the idea that software development is no longer being done the way it had been and must reiterate the reason change is being made [Strebel96]. Continuing reinforcement is absolutely necessary. Changes take time, and people can become tired of the uncertainty and strain of transition. People in the midst of change must feel free to express their feelings, which at times will include confusion, weariness, dislike of the new way, and even fear of failure. Management's job is to foster open communication and reassurance that such feelings are normal. As we said, the change will be stressful, so management may develop destressors to let people decompress from time to time. This can include days off, movie breaks, or other nonwork approaches.

One of the dilemmas of modern organizations is the need and desire on the part of management for high-level commitment to projects, which is especially needed when making major changes, and the desire to keep the *employment-at-will* view of employee dispensability. The change in itself makes roles unclear, makes employees feel less competent and valuable than usual, and makes the future less clear. The result is even greater fear of job loss than usual.

A way to offset the fear is to involve the staff fully in the transition planning process (see Figure 4.2). This is a necessary step, anyway, to get people to buy into the change. If orders for change are handed down from management, there is little motivation to make sure the process is successful. Another facet of team-based development is giving teams the larger share of responsibility in managing schedules and work assignments. As shown in Figure 4.3 this can be termed participative management. It becomes the team's responsibility to define milestones and meet them. Because they cease to be passive recipients of management edicts, they have to buy into the OO processes, and they have to make them successful. This provides another motivator to master OO and software engineering techniques. The idea of participative management is essential for the whole organization to embrace; otherwise, the effectiveness of the teams will always be limited.

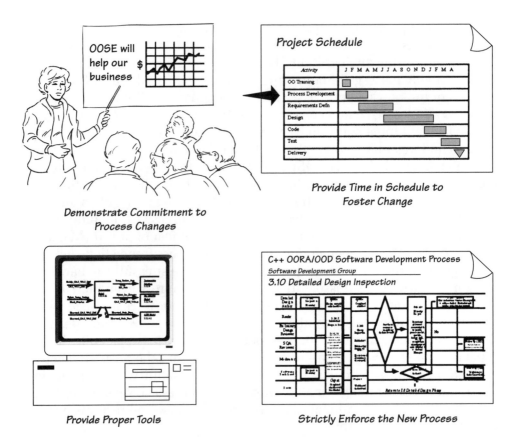

Figure 4.2   Everyone must be involved in the transition.

If the organization has a software engineering process group (SEPG), it can play a large part in documenting the project software processes. The purpose of the SEPG is to start the procedure but not to control it. Ultimately the team must take responsibility for the processes and be in charge of documenting the new processes. This approach forces the software engineers and other members of our team to understand the development processes so they can claim ownership of them. Both the understanding and the ownership of the process are important parts of a successful OO transition.

Open communication means that communication is direct and consistent from all levels of management. While information about major cor-

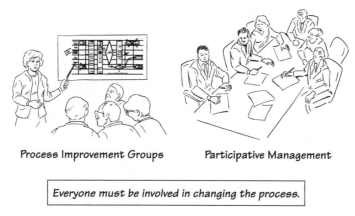

Process Improvement Groups   Participative Management

> Everyone must be involved in changing the process.

Figure 4.3 Features of change.

porate restructuring may be delivered by senior management, most of the changes in departments during the transition, including staffing changes, should be communicated directly by line management rather than Human Resources or executive memos.

Frustration and uncertainty during the transition come in part from the fact that people will have to try new procedures they think won't work. Part of the difficulty of software engineering is the unacknowledged discrepancy between idealized software engineering and its actual application. The problems that plague real-world projects tend to be dealt with in an ad hoc fashion. Developers, then, start distrusting all manifestations of software engineering as impractical, and when faced with an edict to use them, they think they won't work. This is an area where management will have to do some pushing (or if the change comes from the technical staff, it's where they will have to push management). While people must be pushed and encouraged to try approaches that they suspect, they have to feel they are not being set up to be punished. Open communication, reiteration of why the transition is important, and truthful assertions that honest efforts won't be punished are all needed here.

In our experience, software engineers who were proficient at procedural programming tended to spend more time on implementation issues than on object design. These engineers moved quickly from the early stages of designing the objects, to the implementation of the behaviors of the objects. Instead, they should have been more concerned with the relationships of the objects to one another and the role played by inheritance.

For designers, the tendency to focus on the specification of the behaviors of the objects was due to the designers' experience with procedural approaches and their lack of experience with OO approaches. On the other hand, designers who were familiar with data modeling, as used in database design, tended to develop more elaborate models of the objects and their aggregations and associations than they did on inheritance or the behaviors of the objects. While these designers had a good grasp of the objects and their relationships, they often had difficulty identifying inheritance and polymorphism in their models.

Experts and consultants must help the organization work on specifics, not on changing attitudes. Changing attitudes directly is counterproductive.

4.2   Tough Issues in Transition Management

In the best and smoothest transition, there will be difficulties that must be addressed. We start with a few general issues and then cover one of the biggest difficulties that any transition faces: resistance to change. Being aware of the problems will help prevent the disillusionment and demoralization that cause so many change programs to fail.

Problem Issues

1. To move to OO, the whole organization has to change. It is not optional. Even more importantly, some groups that seem to be running just fine the way they are will have to change as well to accommodate the new processes. For example, the technical documentation group may work perfectly well for the current development environment, but the very nature of iterative development will force it to change how it must deal with information and how group members will have to work with designers.

2. Change is expensive, and resources will be less than needed. People will be taking on more tasks than before, and many of those tasks will be unfamiliar. They will need training, and they

will need adaptation time. Training will be far more expensive than expected. It will take a couple of months for OO concepts to jell, 9 to 15 months for habits to change, a year for mastery of object-oriented concepts, and months at a time for each new piece of the change. There will be serious conflicts in some cases between existing project needs and new initiatives in time, personnel, and software resources. It is absolutely essential to understand that current tasks cannot be continued at the same level of effort during the transition.

3. Just because the system is improving (we hope), that doesn't mean that complaints will disappear. This is very demoralizing to some managers who only notice that complaints continue and miss the fact that the subject of the complaints has changed. In the past, working conditions, stupid management, and repressive conditions were the norm. Now, complaints discuss the failure to do even better. This means that people are buying into the change.

4. Both managers and workers may have trouble with the transition from a command structure to one of contribution and coordination. Control structures in an organization are very ingrained. People just want to isolate themselves in their own area of interest. For example, programmers don't want to discuss marketing issues, they just want to deal with software and hardware issues. Marketers may not want input from naïve software developers or may not want to discuss software developers' ideas with customers. If left alone during the transition, people will fall back into the same sort of management routines, reporting responsibilities, and intergroup interactions as before. Management must watch for and redirect these lapses.

5. People will be insensitive to the way things were done in the past. They will put down the people and processes currently in place as examples of stupidity or pathology. Management may do this as well. It is important to understand that the old ways were not bad or stupid, nor were the people doing them. The state of the organization is just the way things evolved. To avoid resentment, it is essential that we identify the need for a change without labeling the old way bad and the new way good.

6. Tensions will increase between people in groups with structurally conflicting missions. Management and the people within these groups may ascribe the tensions to personality conflicts and will ignore the fact that the positions force conflicts and the bad feelings that are attendant to these conflicts. The first action is to study the situation carefully and identify the structural causes of conflict. For example, if a test group is judged on errors found and the programming group is evaluated on how few errors are generated, a structural conflict exists. Changing the evaluation structure so that both groups are in alignment is not too hard and reduces bad blood between the groups.

7. Management will usually assume that it does not have to change. Iterative development cycles, team orientation, and new estimation processes affect more than just the development group. These changes also affect the way software is planned and sold. If managers assume they can just come up with a new formal structure for the organization and then return to business as usual, chances for success are limited. Constant rededication to the new organization is mandatory. Failure to keep the level of dedication up is a major cause of failed transitions. If management balks when it discovers how much the transition will cost and how long it will take, the process is doomed.

Resistance to Change

One of the most difficult issues in making a transition is the unavoidable resistance to change from developers, managers, and customers. Unfortunately, during a change that requires significant expenditures of resources, effort, and dedication, the existence of resistance will be taken by many managers as a sign of laziness, stupidity, or just plain perversity on the part of employees. But resistance to change generally has a real basis that must be understood to be dealt with [Senge90]. Resistance to change often is a result of structural conflicts in the organization. Among these are the following:

◆ Cynicism due to previous improvement initiatives that had no lasting impact is one such structural conflict. Employees have had to put up with fads that were applied on top of what they were doing, for which they didn't have adequate support, and that often jeopardize their security and productivity. After a few cycles that were either explicitly or more often tacitly dropped in a few months, employees have become cynical. Management, similarly, may develop a cynical view of the efficacy of change programs. In many cases, the change programs are canned solutions that have limited results and significant costs. Canned solutions for organizational change just don't work. The only antidote for cynicism is a dogged determination to make a successful transition. The determination is most important in top management, and it must be backed up by resources and a refusal to back off when problems arise.

♦ Incentives and rewards that don't correlate with the changes is another structural conflict. For example, if the new team-oriented assignments still provide individual merit pay and individual bonuses, then a tension exists that will generate resentment and resistance. An illustration of an antiteam incentive is providing monetary rewards only to programming staff while ignoring testing and administrative staff. In addition, structuring rewards as zero-sum prizes is another problem. That is, for one person to get a bonus (or stock options or a promotion), somebody else on the team has to get nothing for his or her effort on the project. Of course, using lines of code (LOC) as a productivity measure is misleading, and it conflicts with more reasonable productivity incentives—a perception (or realization) of punishment of failure. In a major change, there will be a good number of failures. If people are punished, it will be difficult indeed to effect change.

♦ If one group changes its mission, but the groups it must interact with do not, then conflicts will develop and retard changes.

♦ Lack of a clear view: current state, change goal, and process will cause justified resistance. One of the major lapses in a transition is to attempt to keep current projects going at the same rate while making the transition. This will not work. Adequate time must be allocated to the transition—not spare time, not overtime. If the current projects must be continued by the same staff, then both the transition schedule and the current project schedule must be adjusted accordingly. During initial training and change planning, however, the staff must give their full concentration to the new tasks, and no other project work should be scheduled.

♦ If management's actions are inconsistent with the new goals, then people assume a lack of commitment and hypocrisy. Even if management inadvertently contradicts itself, people will assume a lack of candor and will resist. The most common example is asking for participation from all the staff, but then ignoring recommendations. Even if the recommendations cannot be implemented, they must be discussed and dealt with openly. Change can also be threatening to managers. Some changes can reduce authority, number of reports, and other symbols of status. Rather than accept such changes, managers may retreat from it. When this happens, the retreat appears to be just another management fad and people become highly discouraged.

♦ If reporting relationships are inconsistent with the goals or processes of change, opposition will ensue. The major example of inconsistency in relationships is to implement a halfway team organization, where people report for their assignments to multiple groups. If the conflicts in prioritization between the reporting structures aren't handled, people resist being put in no-win positions. Another example is to have people work in a team but to have a manager who expects individual performance that might hurt the team, then resistance is likely.

♦ Inertia can be a factor. When people become comfortable with existing operations, they may not be eager to confront the discomfort of change. This is at least as big a problem in management as it is in workers. Management has the difficulty of trying to identify what practices do and do not work in organizing teams to achieve company goals. When they find a method that seems to work without generating too much conflict, they tend to keep with it.

♦ Change of status can be the biggest factor. This has three aspects: formal, psychological, and social [Strebel96]. The formal aspect is change of duties, pay, and authority. Psychological issues include employees' and management's expectations about the employment agreement—relationship between loyalty and commitment and the security and rewards offered by the company. Social issues include personal interactions with people and the congruence between stated company goals and values and actual performance.

- ◆ High-level commitment versus diminished job security is another resistance generator. In return for meaningful contributions, people expect tangible rewards in addition to pay, including bonuses and formal training. Intangible rewards include honest appraisals of the business situation, a clear expression of how the company's goals and strategy compare with workers' concerns, and recognition of accomplishments.

- ◆ There are even more subtle problems that can cause resistance. For example, in a small company, capitalization of hardware and software can skew the costs of development and reduce its ability to spend money on transition necessities such as hardware, software, and training. Another example is a sales cycle that requires new and updated products on a different schedule from the development schedule. Incentive problems can be difficult to identify and often cause unexpected resistance to change. Employees will always choose to work systems in a way that's best for them, even if it is damaging to the organization.

4.3 Summary

Culture change will be one of the hardest and longest-lasting parts of the transition to OOT. Once the initial transition is complete, the change will be a continuing part of the organization. The company will become more adaptable and will have the confidence to attack new technology as it comes. Although there are many obstacles to overcome in the transition to OO, the largest obstacle comes from management. Line managers are concerned about losing control; they must continue to deal with ingrained processes that subtly work against the change; they may be cynical about the likelihood of success and regard OO as a fad; and they

Tips and Practical Advice

Lesson 4.1   Transition planning is critical.
The software management team must carefully plan the transition and must fully engage the whole team. The transition is going to have an impact on other groups and virtually all activities. The transition process will impact each team member. The team members must take part in developing the plan.

Lesson 4.2   Thinking in terms of objects is essential.
Identifying and designing objects require the requirements engineer's and the designer's focus be placed on the object as the unit of design.
   Rumbaugh points out that in object modeling, the emphasis is on object structure, not procedure structure [Rumbaugh91]. This paradigm shift can be difficult for programmers who have only developed software using procedural approaches.

Lesson 4.3   Upper management must fully support the transition and provide the support and resources needed to change.
Managers must continue to push the change and resist returning to the previous way of doing things. At the same time, they must not denigrate the old ways or they will generate resentment and resistance. They must provide the time, training, and equipment that support the change if there is to be any chance for success.

Lesson 4.4   Management must change as much as the team.
Managers must be ready and willing to change. They must look for new ways of control and give substantial autonomy to development teams. They must avoid all-knowing paternalistic attitudes, because they can't know how everything will change. They must give up the unrealistic views they've had about project estimation and costs.

Lesson 4.5   Resistance must be actively managed.
Any change will encounter real and often justifiable resistance. Rather than ignoring or punishing resistance, the causes of the resistance should be identified and dealt with.

(continued)

Lesson 4.6   The customer must understand the transition of project processes and tools.
It is important that the customer fully understands the object-oriented techniques and the tools used to develop and represent the software system. The customer must be fully aware of the impact of OOA and OOD on the entire software development life cycle. Compared with SA/SD, a typical Object Modeling Technique (OMT) produces software documents (e.g., Software Requirements Specifications (SRS), Software Design Document (SDD), etc.) that describe requirements in terms of graphical representations rather than text and may require unique tailoring of standards. The customer must understand the underlying object-oriented concepts to adequately review the software documents and support the software reviews.

Lesson 4.7   The culture must be prepared.
Changing culture is likely to be the most difficult task of the transition. Culture includes the people, the organization, and the internal systems of the company (policies and politics). Regardless of the project, each of these cultural issues will be affected to some extent, and without culture preparation, these issues will slow the progress of the project.

Lesson 4.8   The change must be sold to the team, to the customer, and to management.
In addition to the right education and good training, professional salesmanship is a critical element to help the project to implement the desired changes.

Lesson 4.9   Personality conflicts usually aren't.
Clearly there are situations in which two people just don't get along with each other because of personal differences, but more often, conflicts are the result of structural differences that give two people goals that conflict. The manager must be extremely sensitive to such conflicts because they are not only destructive, but they are also indicators of organizational problems. Structural causes of individual conflict should be identified and eliminated.

often find it difficult to deal with the significant costs of training and equipment. Finally, they have the major responsibility to keep the change going once the excitement of newness wears off, and they must continue to enforce OO techniques and reinforce the reason for the move.

References

[Beer90] Beer, M., R. Eisenstat, and B. Spector. "Why Change Programs Don't Produce Change." *Harvard Business Review* (November–December 1990).

[Kaufman92] Kaufman, R. S. "Why Operations Improvement Programs Fail: Four Managerial Contradictions." *Sloan Management Review* (Fall 1992).

[LaMarsh95] LaMarsh, J. *Changing the Way We Change: Gaining Control of Major Operational Change.* Reading, MA: Addison-Wesley, 1995.

[Rumbaugh91] Rumbaugh, J. et al. *Object-Oriented Modeling and Design,* Englewood Cliffs, NJ: Prentice Hall, 1991.

[Schein96] Schein, E. "Three Cultures of Management: The Key to Organizational Learning." *Sloan Management Review* (Fall 1996).

[Senge90] Senge, P. M. *The Fifth Discipline: The Art & Practice of the Learning Organization.* New York: Doubleday/Currency, 1990.

[Strebel96] Strebel, P. "Why Do Employees Resist Change?" *Harvard Business Review* (May–June 1996).

PART THREE

Object-Oriented Insertion Activities

Object-oriented insertion is the rather awkward term used to describe activities surrounding the preparation for implementing an object-oriented development environment. This constitutes the second phase of the transition framework. Laying a firm foundation helps to maximize the benefits of an object-oriented development.

In our experience, the following six activities are essential in moving to an object-oriented paradigm.

1. Chapter 5 covers selecting the right object-oriented technique: The first and possibly most important task is to select one of many available object-oriented techniques. This activity develops the criteria for selecting the right object-oriented technique for your project.

2. Chapter 6 deals with selecting the right CASE tool: This activity develops the criteria and guides the selection process for choosing an appropriate CASE tool for your project.

3. Chapter 7 covers staffing the project: Staffing an object-oriented software development requires special considerations. This activity deals with these special considerations, such as specialized positions and organizational structures.

4. Chapter 8 discusses training the team: Training is essential for new object-oriented development teams. This activity deals with providing good training for the team.

5. Chapter 9 deals with legacy systems: This activity examines how to deal with legacy systems and explains how to reuse legacy systems in object-oriented settings.

6. Chapter 10 covers planning and budgeting for reuse: Designing for reuse is harder than it seems. Reuse requires a large investment up front. This activity concentrates on software reuse artifacts, such as components, classes, patterns, and application frameworks. We also discuss how to budget for reuse.

chapter five

Selecting the Right Object-Oriented Technique

5.1 Introduction

A great variety of object-oriented (OO) techniques exist and are promoted through advertisements, books, and magazine articles. While OO approaches have some similar elements, they all have specific strengths that make them more suited to particular types of development. In this chapter, we examine the features provided by OO techniques. By doing this, we will see why different object-oriented techniques exist and develop selection criteria to match the needs of the project to the proper technique. We will also examine how follow-up projects allow for more flexibility in OO technique selection.

The first insertion activity, and possibly the most important task, is to select one of the many available object-oriented software development (OOSD) techniques. There are many widely known to choose from, such as object-oriented analysis/design [Shlaer-Mellor88, 89; Fayad93], object modeling technique (OMT) [Rumbaugh91; Fayad94], and unified modeling language (UML) [Rational97]. An object-oriented technique provides the step-by-step activities that lead from analysis to implementation. An OO technique provides a set of graphic notations for use in reviews, inspections, and documentation. In addition, an object-oriented technique provides communication media between developers and customers, a framework for modeling the domain problem, and standards for transitioning the problem from analysis to final deliverable products, as shown in Figure 5.1. Therefore, the OO technique selection will have an impact on almost every step in the software development.

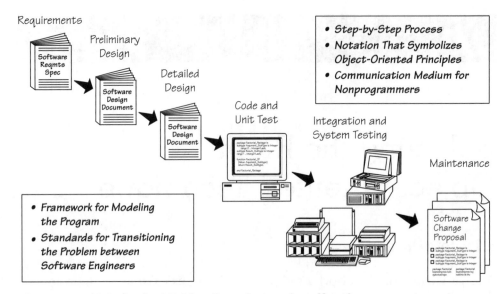

Figure 5.1   Method provides foundation for all software engineering.

As object-oriented software engineering (OOSE) has matured, the number of projects applying OO techniques has multiplied. Choosing some of the more popular methods and trying to determine which one is the best fit for the target application is a difficult area to master. We summarize our experience in Tips 5.1 through 5.7.

Effective software engineering (like other engineering disciplines) guarantees neither success nor perfection, but for all significant projects, the lack of software engineering virtually guarantees failure. While consultants continue to thrive on projects that have no organization or documentation, such projects become increasingly intractable as they age. Major upgrades benefit little from previous work or scheduling. The implication, of course, is that most projects have a life span that will see maintenance and enhancement, and these phases will cost as much as or more than the original development. Without documentation of the design, development plans, and maintenance history, a system must be analyzed anew each time. Predictability, repeatability, and documentability, then, are the cornerstones on which software engineering is based, and all three depend on methods.

Remember that a project is more than a technical operation and that people outside the development group have a valid interest in its progress and outcome. The use of defined methods provides a way for all groups to gauge the progress of a project. It is not completely necessary for people in other groups to understand all details of methods, but it should be possible for these people, if necessary, to examine the methods and understand the process.

5.2 Myths of Object-Oriented Techniques and Tools

There are no meaningful one-size-fits-all software development methods. The approach one takes to a very large project must include explicit forms of planning, coordination, and control that would be out of place or even harmful in a small project. A system that affects human life or safety would require extensive and rigorous specification and review that, in terms of time and effort, could not be justified in a mass-market system. A well-defined extension to an existing system calls for different processes from a whole new system in an ill-defined environment. And a program having a very specific function with a short life span, such as a one-shot data converter, would have very different requirements from a system intended to be in place for years.

Methods used, then, depend on such conditions as system size, reliability and safety requirements, cost constraints, implementation schedule, maintainability, and expected system life span. Each different requirement affects the methods used, the tools required, the quality assurance functions, the personnel needed, and the documentation required (see Figure 5.2).

This brings up the issue of software development tools. Sometimes vendors suggest that their computer-aided software engineering (CASE) or other software development tools are appropriate for all products and environments and make you believe that, "This CASE tool will solve all of your problems," as shown in Figure 5.3. A little bit of thought will reveal the falsity of that idea. Any tool requires effort to master, and the time required for mastery of some CASE tools may be measured in months. With such a large expenditure of effort, multiplied by the number of people using the tool, the methods that will be used should be

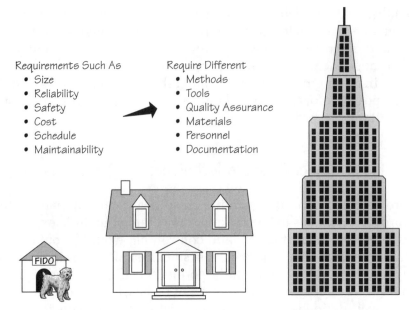

Figure 5.2   The myth of the single software development method.

Figure 5.3   The myth of an ultimate software development tool.

• Look first for methods, not tools.
• Select tools only after you select the appropriate method.

Figure 5.4   The reality.

chosen first. Then, with the method in hand, a tool to implement the methods can be identified. This is shown in Figure 5.4.

For example, if you plan to use OMT as your design method, choosing a tool that cannot handle OMT, regardless of its other worthwhile features, would be a poor decision. Faulting the tool when it is inappropriately used also makes little sense. To repeat, the best object-oriented method is the one that most closely meets your particular needs, as shown in Figure 5.5.

5.3   The Impact of Software Methods

During the past several years, many software methods have been developed to overcome some shortcomings of ad hoc software development approaches. Software methods simplify the decomposition of a software

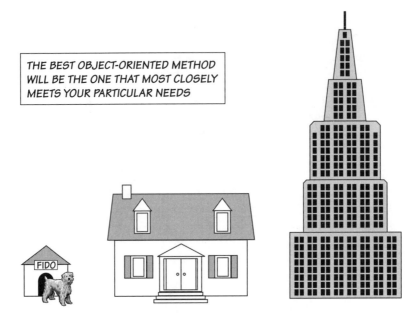

THE BEST OBJECT-ORIENTED METHOD
WILL BE THE ONE THAT MOST CLOSELY
MEETS YOUR PARTICULAR NEEDS

Figure 5.5   The best object-oriented method.

system into manageable pieces and, by implementing paradigms that
govern development processes, support a software development life
cycle. The evolution of software methods has progressed from structured
analysis/structured design approaches to the current object-oriented
approaches. But each method must exist within a methodology that provides an overall software development process. It is this process that
allows the software system to be defined in a manner understood by all
software development participants.

Use of a specific software development method provides many benefits
for the developers, customers, and particularly the ultimate maintainers
of the software system. A primary benefit of using a software method is
that it provides a consistent way of proceeding through the software
development process. Methods additionally focus on a thorough requirements analysis phase to ensure that the problem is well understood and
that the generated solution meets the system requirements. This is in
stark contrast with the ad hoc method where requirements analysis is
rarely performed. Most methods also provide a means of viewing the
software system from multiple perspectives. This feature allows people

with varying software or system backgrounds—system engineers, management, customers, software designers, coders, and testers—to understand those portions of the problem and its solution that interest them.

A frequently asked question is, "If using a software development methodology brings so many advantages to a software project, why don't all developments immediately begin using one?" There are two answers to this question. One answer relates to the nature of software projects and the other to the nature of software engineers. The majority of software projects are not completely new developments. They are either upgrades to an existing system or projects that must be integrated into an existing system. Management, in an effort to reduce cost and schedule risks, avoids a complete redesign of the system, and thus avoids implementing a new development methodology. Additionally, the time and training required to adopt a more orderly method costs enough that management often shies away.

And software engineers, for their part, may be comfortable with the way they have always developed software and don't want to make radical method changes to perform their duties. Besides, most software engineers in today's workforce have not had training in organized software development. In fact, in typical college programming courses, they were graded on getting the correct output turned in on or before the due date, but not on the methods that they employed to complete the project. Thus, formal software training, time and resource development constraints, and lack of opportunity all retard the progress from ad hoc to method-driven software development.

5.4   Object-Oriented Techniques Survey

A software methodology provides a uniform approach to developing software through the application of a system of software engineering methods. The methodology provides the abstract software development concepts and a transition to more detailed and specific techniques. Methods provide necessary processes for producing each software product required during the software development life cycle. Software methodologies can be divided into three major categories that are defined by their approaches to software development: functional oriented methodologies that concentrate on representations of software algorithms, data structure design methodologies that concentrate on data flow and data representation, and object-oriented methodologies that concentrate on objects and the relationships between objects and their operations.

The majority of popular OO methodologies have existed in some form for several years, so there is adequate literature available that describes their basic concepts and how they can be used for developing software systems. Of these available approaches, the object-oriented way is currently receiving the most attention from academia, commercial, and DOD software sectors. Once the desire to introduce an OO methodology has been established, a particular method must be selected.

The available methods provide a multitude of approaches to developing object-oriented software. Some methods are based on structured analysis techniques. They begin with a functional decomposition of the system into data flow diagrams (DFDs) that are then used to derive low-level objects. These low-level objects are then combined into higher-level objects that define the system. Other OO methods, such as Colbert's OOSD, allow developers to begin with high-level abstract objects that are methodically decomposed during requirements analysis and design phases. The choice of a particular method should be made based on the development team's knowledge of the system requirements and the system's operating environment.

If the system is data intensive and the individual data elements are mostly understood before requirements analysis (such as a database system), then a data object–driven, bottom-up method should be chosen. However, if the system details and data requirements are not fully understood at the outset, then a method should be selected that uses a top-down requirements analysis approach that develops lower-level objects from abstract objects.

A particular class of OO techniques usually supports the application domain. Partitioning the available techniques into unambiguous classes is impossible. However, one simple guideline that we use is to distinguish between a top-down abstract object approach and an information-modeling approach.

The top-down abstract object approach uses a successive breakdown of objects. The analyst successively decomposes high-level objects into lower-level objects until the lowest-level objects are all easily understood. Systems that are computation intensive, where the data is not initially well understood (e.g., digital signal processing, pattern recognition), map better to a top-down abstract approach. Examples of OO techniques using a top-down approach are Colbert's OOSD [Colbert89; Fayad92b, 93d], Fayad's object engineering technique (OET) [Fayad94], Firesmith's object-oriented requirements analysis and logical design [Firesmith93; Fayad-Fulghum94], Berard's object modeling method, and Selic's real-time object-oriented modeling (ROOM) [Selic94; Fayad93d].

An information modeling approach uses data objects as the starting point and builds up from there. Information management systems, such as payroll systems, scheduling systems, and insurance applications, map better to an information modeling–type approach. Because the analyst fully understands much of the data early in the project, building objects from the data is reasonably clear-cut. Examples of information modeling OO techniques that use a bottom-up or middle-in/out approach include Coad-Yourdon's object-oriented analysis (OOA) and object-oriented design (OOD) [Coad-Yourdon91a, 91b], object modeling technique (OMT) [Rumbaugh91], Shlaer-Mellor's OOA [Shlaer-Mellor88, 92; Fayad93a], and document-driven analysis [Drake92]. Figure 5.6 shows this breakdown.

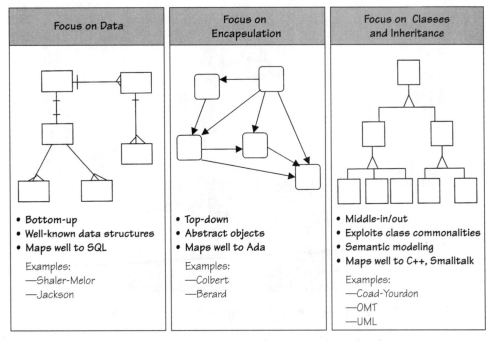

Figure 5.6   General categories of object-oriented methods.

Some object-oriented techniques conform to the features of a particular target language. For a first OO project, it is best to use a technique that easily maps to the target language. For example, if the target language is Smalltalk or C++, choose a technique that fully uses the features of these languages. Object-oriented techniques, like Fayad's OET [Fayad94], use inheritance as a major feature of the technique. Other techniques may not use inheritance at all. Because Smalltalk and C++ feature inheritance as an integral part of the language, with these languages we want a technique that has inheritance. Figure 5.7 illustrates the recommendation.

Any object-oriented technique has a good side, a bad side, and an ugly side. These sides vary from one OO technique to another. The ugly side represents high risks, and it increases the cost of software development. Many of the risks that cannot be identified from descriptions of the technique will not become obvious even during training with experienced instructors. Unfortunately, each object-oriented technique's risks will be discovered only during and after the application. Some of the risks of this type include voluminous documentation produced by the method (or the CASE tool), many different artifacts of analysis and design, and

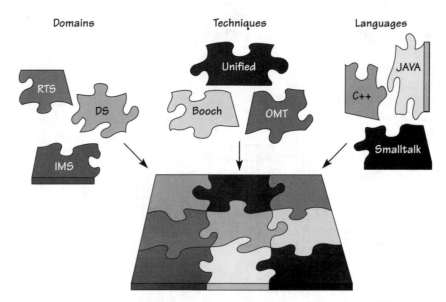

Figure 5.7 Appropriate method must map domain and language.

inability to handle complexity. Other problems include difficulties in integration, inability to model certain functionality or class interactions, and problems with testing. Although detecting these problems early cannot always be done, it is useful to find other organizations who have used the selected OO method on a real problem and talk to them about problems they encountered with it.

Extensive testing and verification and validation (V&V) during the development of software is essential for building reliable software [Fayad92]. Unfortunately, most OO techniques do not adequately address testing and V&V activities. Currently, V&V activities are most widely performed in defense-related applications, where because of their ad hoc nature, they are costly to perform. Verifying and validating OO specifications and programs still need much research before effective practical approaches can be developed. Recent attempts include multilevel specification checking [Fayad93a] and test case generation from methods and message specifications [Fayad93b]. Kirani points out that if successful testing and V&V activities for OO paradigms are not developed, there is a great risk of failure of OO paradigms as a next-generation software development technique [Kirani94]. Extensive review of the object model and other artifacts, along with inspections covering the whole development life cycle, are still the most V&V tools.

Software engineers often experience frustration in the first application of object-oriented methodology to software development. First, they must be trained in the method to be applied. This requires integrating a new way of thinking about development, including the changing relative importance of initial development phases. Second, since software standards currently in use do not always apply to OOSD efforts, the team will be compelled to define their own standards. The success of these efforts will not be immediate. As the team gains proficiency in the methods and tools, the needs will change, and the standards used will be found inadequate and need improvement.

5.5 Object-Oriented Technique Selection Criteria

In the previous section, we listed some considerations about matching object-oriented techniques to the environment. Here we consider some additional areas that are important in selecting a particular OO technique. Some of these are intrinsic to the method, and some relate more to the domain and the commercial viability of the method. These areas, as shown in Figure 5.8, are life cycle coverage, CASE tool support, availability of training, availability of expert advice, domain compatibility, and language compatibility.

Life Cycle Support

It is important to choose an object-oriented method that covers as much of the software life cycle as possible. As we show in Figure 5.9, this means the method should not only include analysis and design, but development testing as well, and if possible, enhancement and maintenance. While none of the current methods covers the whole life cycle, it is still important to think about how the cycle phases will be covered. Using different methods at different phases will invite model shifts that tend to dissipate the OO focus and inhibit reusability. A customized solu-

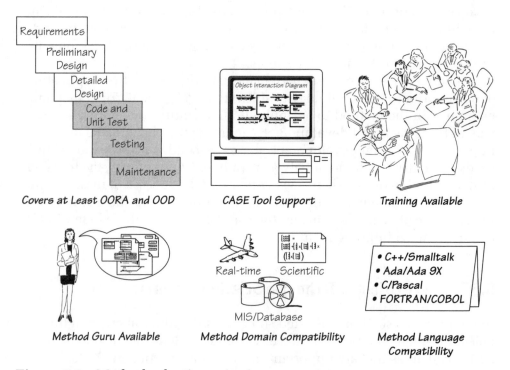

Figure 5.8 Method selection criteria.

METHOD SHOULD COVER AT LEAST OORA AND OOD.

Why use OO to cover as much of the software life cycle as possible?

- Prevent paradigm shifts.
- Avoid interoperability.

What to know before selecting a method:

- All existing methods lack full life cycle coverage.
- Most important activity is object-oriented requirements analysis (OORA).
- Beware of methods that cover only object-oriented design.

Figure 5.9 Life cycle coverage.

tion addressing only the current problem should be avoided, because it will be hard to adapt to the next problem or group in the organization. A better solution is to find an OO method that works in your environment and adapt it to your particular problem domain. The analysis and requirements phase is the most important phase of the life cycle. It is where the problem domain is captured and forms the basis for all subsequent work. A failure of requirements analysis in any significant system virtually guarantees failure of the project.

Other phases in which model shifts can be especially harmful are between analysis and design, and again during maintenance. In the first case, using a non–OO analysis technique with an OO design invites the problems of both missing important requirements and substantial rework between the phases. Therefore, methods that cover only object-oriented design without analysis should be avoided.

The second case is more insidious. An organization that has not fully made the transition to object-oriented development means that the maintainers, often a separate group, will not understand the methods used to develop the system. It is then likely that the maintenance group will introduce changes that violate the OO paradigm. Over time, this will result in inconsistencies between the design and implementation and, thus, will result in reduced system maintainability. Unfortunately, there are no current methods addressing the maintenance phase of the life cycle. The only available solutions to this problem are to take maintenance very seriously, to train staff members who maintain OO systems in OO methods, to make sure the original analysis and design data is available to the maintainers, and to carefully review modifications.

Computer-Aided Software Engineering Tool Support

Given the complexity of moving to an object-oriented project, certain criteria are extremely important when selecting the OO method. As mentioned above, the method must include both object-oriented requirements analysis (OORA) and design. Too much will be lost trying to translate to design if OORA is not included. Computer-aided software engineering tool support should be considered essential for the first project, and the CASE tool must adequately implement the chosen technique. A good CASE tool provides direct support of the graphics and rules of the technique, and it is a learning aid for the development team. The CASE tool lets the developers concentrate on the analysis and design of the system and not on the mechanics and diagramming of the OO technique (see Figure 5.10).

This brings up a serious difficulty in object-oriented method selection. Although we recommend that the object-oriented method be selected before selecting the CASE tool, we also believe that a good CASE tool is essential for effective development, and especially so for the first OO project. If there is no CASE support for the selected method, then it may be worthwhile to find a method that has support. As we state in Chapter 6, an awkward mapping of the CASE tool's output to an object-oriented method is counterproductive. So, at the outset, object-oriented selection must include adequate CASE support, and CASE tool selection must include adequate OO method support. In our experience, we were dissatisfied with the results on projects where we tried to adapt a CASE tool without direct support for the object-oriented method we were using. The difficulties encountered in trying to make the CASE tool do something it wasn't designed to completely offset the supposed benefits of the CASE tool.

Training Availability

Formal training should be considered essential for the whole team. As shown in Figure 5.11 and described more fully in Chapter 8, formal training must be available for the selected technique. Without intensive, team-

---

USEFUL TOOLS WILL SUPPORT AT LEAST THE NOTATION, CONSISTENCY CHECKING, AND A DATA DICTIONARY.

Why have CASE tool support?

- Enhances productivity and rigorous adherence to the method.
- Supports adherence to the method.

What to look for in a CASE tool.

- Accurately supports notation.
  - A simple drawing package is often sufficient for small projects.
- Consistency checking (especially for large projects).
- Data dictionaries.
  - Multiple dictionaries support the OO principle of information hiding.
- Automated documentation generators (a misnomer) often produce documents with poor visual quality.

Figure 5.10 CASE tool availability.

wide training, start-up times will be increased, and uniformity of analysis and design approaches will be lost. These problems increase the risk of the transition. Typically, each software development team member will learn each step of the technique and then apply it to a small example. Each member obviously will not be an expert immediately after formal training. However, at least each member will get to see how an experienced user creates objects using the specific technique. This type of knowledge is often impossible to derive from a textbook describing the technique. As a consequence, an important criterion for training is that instructors have experience in using the technique on a real project.

The training course should introduce the methodology itself, experience with applying the method to a real-world problem, and the use of a CASE tool that implements the method. To obtain complete buy in, class attendees should include software managers and system requirements engineers, as well as the software development staff. Allocating resources

---

TRAINING HELPS GET YOUR FIRST OO DEVELOPMENT OFF TO A QUICK START.

- ◆ Why train?
  - ◆ Reinforces the culture change.
  - ◆ All methods require practical experience to develop expertise.
  - ◆ Learn and ask questions from an expert.
  - ◆ Get off to a fast start (remember—requirements activity is most critical).
- ◆ What to look for when selecting training?
  - ◆ Train the specific method you have selected (not just OO training).

Figure 5.11   Training availability.

for full training is an excellent way to reinforce the cultural changes needed to make the transition.

The close relationship between training and technique selection is illustrated by a large simulation in which one of the authors was involved. Colbert's OOSD method was selected from a short list of several similar object-oriented methods, due primarily to the timely availability of training. Colbert's training material required a full week to complete (eight hours per day for five days), and the entire software development team was required to attend. Training sessions were held off-site so developers could get away from daily activities and concentrate on understanding the training material. The course included training on the OOSD method and the use of a CASE tool that supported the method. The CASE tool, Mark V System's Adagen, was used to develop software solutions for classroom examples, as well as some initial requirements analysis of the simulation project. A few hours spent discussing the system in class helped develop an initial approach to analyzing the simulation system's requirements. One important lesson learned from this training was that the systems used as examples in class were never as difficult as real-world problems. That is why it is helpful to discuss initial ideas for your system with an experienced practitioner.

Guru Availability

A method *guru,* someone experienced in specific OO method and programming techniques, should be available to keep the team from flailing. Figure 5.12 identifies the reasons why a method guru is important. A method guru can assure that whatever method is used gets uniformly applied and implemented. Thus the guru would make sure the method is adapted to the particular project and problem domain, and effectively implemented in the CASE tools. A guru works with both engineers and nonengineers to bridge between the user domain and the system. In addition, an expert in the particular technique can resolve problems in the chosen object-oriented method and develop method extensions that don't breach OO principles.

If no guru is available for the first project, consider using an experienced consultant to both act as a guru and to train an in-house person. A good consultant can save a great deal of time in helping the development team with OO technique evaluation and selection processes. Two items are worth mentioning: first, the consultant must be an expert in the particular OO method chosen, not just in general object-oriented methods. Second, the consultant should be up to date in the techniques. The industry is changing rapidly and the area can be quite complex. A quali-

---

METHOD GURUS SAVE SCHEDULE AND BUDGET BY PROVIDING EXPERT ASSISTANCE DURING THE TRANSITION PERIOD.

- ◆ Why have a guru?
  - ◆ Focal point for method.
  - ◆ Works with both engineers and nonengineers.
  - ◆ Drives method uniformity and resolves issues.
  - ◆ Adapts methods to CASE tools.
- ◆ What to look for in a guru.
  - ◆ Communication skills.
  - ◆ Software and method experience.
  - ◆ If a guru is not available, then develop one.

Figure 5.12   Guru availability.

fied consultant can be worth the cost. Whoever is chosen should have excellent communication skills, method experience, and understanding of the software environment. If possible, find a guru with a strong understanding of the problem domain.

Domain Considerations

The software development method must match the problem domain and the general category of the system. For example, a real-time system must have a way to model performance constraints, and an information management system (IMS) must have rich data modeling capabilities. Selecting a method that fits the problem domain makes the development task easier (or conversely, using the wrong method may make the task exceptionally difficult). In assessing the domain, you should consider the size of the project, how intensive the requirements analysis will be (new systems with ill-defined goals are far more requirements intensive than are well-defined enhancements to existing systems), whether there are significant database or real-time components, and whether the system is highly procedural or computational. Figure 5.13 reiterates these ideas.

In Chapter 7, we discuss staffing and describe people with a position of *domain expert* who are familiar with both the problem domain and the

---

METHOD DIFFERENCES DRIVE SUITABILITY FOR A PARTICULAR SOFTWARE DEVELOPMENT DOMAIN.

- Why consider the domain?
  - Selecting a method that fits your domain will make your software development easier.
- What to consider.
  - Requirements analysis intensive.
  - Database intensive.
  - Real-time requirements.
  - Highly procedural or computational.
  - Size of project.

Figure 5.13 Domain considerations.

development method. Domain experts, like method gurus, bridge between people expert in the problem domain and people expert in the development domain. They must be able to explain development issues to customers and interpret requirements and constraints of the problem domain to developers. For example, in real-time systems, customers will have a strong understanding of the way time-based constraints must be handled, while developers may have little functional understanding of these constraints. The domain expert must be able to explain the constraints to developers and to help frame them as meaningful requirements. Thus, the domain expert must also be not only familiar with OO concepts but well trained in the particular technique selected.

Language Considerations

Method differences and problem domains affect the choice of programming languages. The chosen language must suit the development method so that design constructs can be translated easily into code. In choosing a language for object-oriented projects, some specific features must be considered. If the OO model includes single or multiple inheritance, then the target language must support these constructs as well. Likewise, the encapsulation constructs of the language should map well into the modeling method. Figure 5.14 shows these items.

METHOD DIFFERENCES DRIVE SUITABILITY FOR A PARTICULAR SOFTWARE DEVELOPMENT LANGUAGE.

- ◆ Why consider the language?
  - ◆ Selecting a method that translates easily to your software development language will prevent the need for language workarounds.
- ◆ What to consider.
  - ◆ Inheritance.
  - ◆ Multiple inheritance.
  - ◆ Encapsulation.

Figure 5.14   Language considerations.

There are other ways the language must map to the problem domain. For example, a usual requirement of real-time systems is specifiable performance and repeatability. This tends to eliminate languages that have on-the-fly garbage collection. If the domain includes interaction with legacy systems at the programming interface level, the language must somehow support the legacy language's calling structure. Similarly, database-intensive systems might require the interfacing with a commercial database engine and the ability to generate reports.

5.6   Selecting Object-Oriented Techniques—First versus Later Projects

Figure 5.15 lists some of the differences that exist between the first OO project and later projects that affect the selection of techniques and related tools and services. There are some areas that remain essential to the success of any project, such as keeping a method that covers at least analysis and design and matching the method to the domain and problem type. Other areas that are essential for first projects change their urgency in later projects, such as the need for training the whole group simultaneously and the use of CASE tools. Obviously, any members new to OO or the specific method in use must be trained, but the mass training so necessary to make the first project successful is not necessary later. Likewise, CASE remains necessary, but the level of support and training required to make it useful is not as necessary in later projects.

As the team becomes more adept at a particular method, the need for a specific guru may decrease. Whether or not this position can be dispensed with depends on the difficulty of the modeling, the turnover of personnel in the team, and the evolution of the particular method in use. If the team changes methods, of course, a guru expert in the new methods must be available.

If a team is expert in OO projects using a particular method, it may even become more effective to adapt the known method to the problem domain than to change methods to an unfamiliar one that appears more suited to the domain. Likewise, developers expert in a particular language may find it more effective to put up with certain language deficiencies than to learn a new language. Such decisions are dependent on the

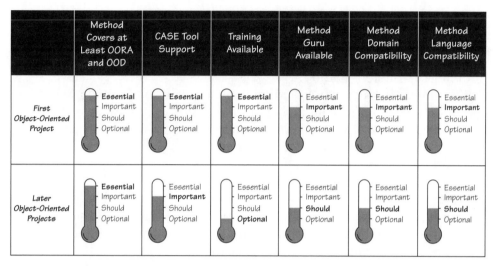

	Method Covers at Least OORA and OOD	CASE Tool Support	Training Available	Method Guru Available	Method Domain Compatibility	Method Language Compatibility
First Object-Oriented Project	**Essential** Important Should Optional	**Essential** Important Should Optional	**Essential** Important Should Optional	Essential **Important** Should Optional	Essential **Important** Should Optional	Essential **Important** Should Optional
Later Object-Oriented Projects	**Essential** Important Should Optional	Essential **Important** Should Optional	Essential Important Should **Optional**	Essential Important **Should** Optional	Essential Important **Should** Optional	Essential Important **Should** Optional

Figure 5.15   First versus later projects.

lack of fundamental incompatibilities in either method or language to the problem.

5.7 Summary

Selection of an object-oriented method is as much an issue of utility as it is of expressive power or theoretical rigor. Unless your resources are virtually unlimited, restrict your selection of OO techniques to those that have some share of use. This means that there are books and articles available that cover their use, and that training suitable to your organization is available. The training must be tailored to include issues in your problem domain. There must be CASE tools available that directly create and manipulate the object diagrams and other graphical artifacts of the method. Moreover, expert advice, either in-house or from consultants, must be available to get the project up to speed.

The method must map to the problem domain and to the nature of the problem. For a project where the problem is well understood, use a bottom-up or middle-in/out method, such as Coad-Yourdon, Shlaer-Mellor, OMT, or UML. For a project where the problem needs significant analysis, use a top-down techniques, such as Colbert and Berard.

Tips and Practical Advice

Lesson 5.1 Avoid use of the functional decomposition front-end to an object-oriented method.

We believe that a purely functional decomposition approach, when used as a front end for an object-oriented approach, may lead to a significant number of problems, such as interface weaknesses and duplication of code [Fayad92, Fayad93b].

Lesson 5.2 Stick to the method.

Once a method is chosen, stick to it. Analysis and modeling take proportionally greater effort in OO projects and form the basis of the rest of the development. Changing methods or mixing methods will generate disagreement and many revisions.

Lesson 5.3 Selecting the appropriate technique is critical to project success.

There are many techniques from which to select. The team should select a technique that will work for them, not one that makes the team work for it. The selected technique should provide organization on the project without requiring various products of questionable value. The team should avoid techniques that require a high level of detailed diagram editing.

Lesson 5.4 Technique selection will impact virtually every activity in the new software development process.

In addition to analysis and design, the technique affects the choice of implementation language and testing. After deployment, the maintainers must understand the OO technique to preserve the integrity of the method. Training and tool selection also depend on the method.

Lesson 5.5 Most V&V activities remain ad hoc.

Rigorous V&V methods for OO techniques have yet to be developed. This means that current techniques do not cover V&V and that traditional methods must still be used. Research in this area is still needed.

(continued)

Lesson 5.6   Software engineers must adapt.
Software engineers must change their understanding of software development to adapt to object orientation. This will require training, practice, and the endurance of frustration during the transition. In addition, every technique has its own idiosyncrasies that must be mastered. No OO technique or software development method will cover every aspect of the process, so engineers will have to develop their own standards and processes in addition to what the OO method provides.

Lesson 5.7   There are some hidden risks that are associated with each object-oriented technique.
Every object-oriented technique has a good side, a bad side, and an ugly side, and each technique's problems are different from those of other techniques. Some problems surface only with application of the technique. If possible, talk to other companies that have used the candidate technique on real problems to find out what risks you will face.

References

[Berard85] Berard, E. V. *An Object-Oriented Design Handbook for Ada Software.* Frederick, Maryland: EVB Software Engineering, Inc., 1985.

[Booch91] Booch, G. *Object-Oriented Design with Applications.* Menlo Park, California: Benjamin/Cummings, 1991.

[Coad-Yourdon90] Coad, P., and E. Yourdon, *Object-Oriented Analysis.* 2nd Edition. Englewood Cliffs, New Jersey: Prentice Hall, 1990.

[Coad-Yourdon91] Coad, P., and E. Yourdon, *Object-Oriented Design.* Englewood Cliffs, New Jersey: Prentice Hall, 1991.

[Colbert89] Colbert, E., "The Object-Oriented Software Development Method: A Practical Approach to Object-Oriented Development." ACM TRI-Ada Proceedings, October 1989, pp. 400–415.

[Fayad92] Fayad, M. E., "OO Software Engineering: Techniques and Tools for Better Software Development." *IEEE/AIAA 11th Digital Avionics Systems Conference,* a full-day tutorial, Seattle, Washington, October 1992.

[Fayad93a] Fayad, M. E., "Managing Object-Oriented Software Development Projects," *7th European Conference on Object-Oriented Programming* (ECOOP '93), a full-day tutorial, Kaiserslautern, Germany, July 26–30, 1993.

[Fayad93b] Fayad, M. E., "Managing Object-Oriented Software Development Projects," TRI-Ada '93, a full-day Tutorial, Seattle, Washington, September 1993.

[Fayad94] Fayad, M. E., Object-Oriented Software Engineering: Problems & Perspectives, Ph.D. Thesis, UMI, Ann Arbor, Michigan, June 1994.

[Fayad96a] Fayad, M. E., "Transition to Object-Oriented Software Development," *First Hong Kong Conference on Quality Software Development,* a full-day tutorial, Hong Kong, April 1996.

[Fayad96b] Fayad, M. E., "Transition to Object-Oriented Software Development," Laval University, a half-day tutorial, Quebec City, Canada, May 1996.

[Fayad96c] Fayad, M. E., "Transition to Object-Oriented Software Development," Canadian Research Institute of Montreal (CRIM), a half-day tutorial, Montreal, Canada, May 1996.

[Fayad96d] Fayad, M. E., "Transition to Object-Oriented Software Development," King Fahd University, a full-day tutorial, Dhahran, Saudi Arabia, June 1996.

[Fayad96e] Fayad, M. E., "Transition to Object-Oriented Software Development," Portugal's Object-Oriented Programming (OOP '96), a half-day tutorial, Lisbon, Portugal, October 1996.

[Fayad96f] Fayad, M. E., "Object-Oriented Experiences and Future Trends," a half-day tutorial, OOPSLA '96, San Jose, California, October 1996.

[Fayad97a] Fayad, M. E., "Transition to Object-Oriented Software Development," ECOOP '97, a half-day tutorial, JYVASKYLA, Finland, July 1997.

[Fayad97b] Fayad, M. E., "Object-Oriented Experience & Future Trends," ECOOP '97, a half-day tutorial, JYVASKYLA, Finland, July 1997.

[Kirani94] Kirani, S., Specification and Verification of Object-Oriented Programs, Ph.D. dissertation, Computer Science Dept., University of Minnesota, Minneapolis, Minnesota, November 1994.

[Rumbaugh91] Rumbaugh, J. et al., *Object-Oriented Modeling and Design.* Englewood Cliffs, New Jersey: Prentice Hall, 1991.

[Shlaer-Mellor88] Shlaer, S. and S. Mellor, *Object-Oriented Systems Analysis: Modeling the World In Data.* Englewood Cliffs, New Jersey: Yourdon Press, Prentice Hall, 1988.

[Shlaer-Mellor89] Shlaer, S. and S. Mellor, "Object-Oriented Approach to Domain Analysis," *Software Engineering Notes,* vol. 14, no. 5 (July 1989): pp. 66–77.

chapter six

Selecting the Right Computer-Aided Software Engineering Tool

6.1 The Role of Computer-Aided Software Engineering Tools

Modern computer-aided software engineering (CASE) tools are the subject of controversy, having been both cited for substantial increases and blamed for decreases in productivity. Few would argue that the right tools in the right hands can effectively increase software quality and reduce costs. The key is identifying these right tools. Section 3 describes an effective selection process for CASE tools.

We found the use of CASE tools essential to successfully transitioning to object-oriented software engineering (OOSE). A good CASE tool can significantly aid the learning process. However, a CASE tool will not eliminate all the obstacles associated with first-time object-oriented (OO) development. There is still no substitute for qualified software engineers who are open to change.

Computer-aided software engineering tools may be either an integrated suite of compatible tools, as shown in Figure 6.1, or they may be sets of compatible tools from various vendors. In all cases, each tool supports a specific task. Those tasks include editors, programming tools, analysis and verification and validation (V&V) tools, configuration and project management tools, modeling tools, and method generators. Editors can be either graphical or text-based and will probably be integrated with databases and modeling and method generation tools. Programming tools include compilers, debuggers, code generators, and programs to aid reverse engineering.

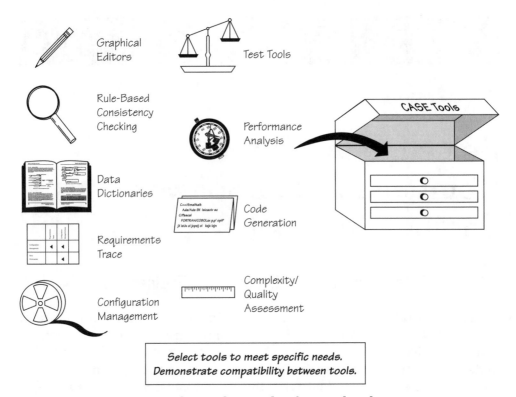

Figure 6.1 CASE provides tools to aid software development.

Analysis and V&V tools comprise test case generators, performance analyzers, and requirements tracers. Configuration management (CM) tools have at least change and version control functions. Measurement tools can have a broad range of metrics and will exchange data with project management systems. Modeling tools exist for process modeling systems and object modeling. Examples of CASE tools include ObjectMaker, Paradigm Plus, Objectory, Statemate, Rational's Rose, and TeamWork.

Computer-aided software engineering tools run the gamut from simple and inexpensive visual editors to complex, fully integrated systems that tightly control every aspect of development. When selecting a tool, or set of tools, the most important criterion is that it meets your specific organizational, technical, and economic needs. Based on this measure, there are four types of CASE tools (refer to Figure 6.2).

WARNING:
All Tools Are Not Equal!

Correct Tool for the Job

- Maximum benefit from realistic expectations
- Simple tools can often be invaluable

Wrong Type of Tool for the Job

- Frustrates users
- Seldom ends in success

Underpowered Tool

- Reduces confidence in CASE technology
- Often arise from unrealistic expectations

Overpowered Tool

- Wastes money and time
- May be inflexible

Figure 6.2 Choosing the right tool for your specific need.

Correct tool for the job. This type of CASE tool provides maximum benefits from realistic expectations. It accurately models the analysis, design, and programming methods chosen for the project. The costs associated with it—product, training, and integration—are consistent with the expected return. Simple tools can often be invaluable: they tend to be inexpensive, easy to learn, and flexible.

Wrong type of tool for the job. The most common mismatches are incompatible analysis and modeling approaches, lack of specific language support, incompatibility with other development tools, and insistence on too much control and too little flexibility. Such CASE tools frustrate users and seldom lead to success.

Underpowered tools. Tools that offer only a visual editor without consistency checking, or that cannot be integrated with other tools, or that scale poorly to larger systems cause users to wonder if CASE technology has any real value. Some tools, of course, are merely victims of unrealistic expectations on the part of customers or of grandiose but unsupportable claims by vendors. Such tools diminish confidence in CASE technology.

Overpowered tools. Some solutions have functions to cover every aspect of software development. The learning curve for such tools is excessive, the purchase cost is high, and adaptation requires a complete change in the organization. The costs associated with such tools make it impractical to change once they are adopted, even though the per-seat cost can be extremely high. Because they are large, complex systems in their own right, they tend to be inflexible. Changes and updates will be slow in coming from the vendor, and compatibility with other development tools will be limited. All of these factors suggest that only a few organizations with special needs will find such tools worth the cost.

6.2   Select the Method before the Computer-Aided Software Engineering Tool

The selection of a method that implements the desired software development methodology is one of the most significant decisions to be made when planning a software project. The selected software development technique provides the process by which all the software life cycle products are developed. The method decision should be made before CASE tool selection and should be reviewed again after the selection of a CASE tool. In any significant project, CASE support for analysis and design is essential, so the first requirement for CASE is that it supports the selected method. If the selected method has no CASE tool support or if the tool that supports the selected method is not compatible with your development environment, then it may be necessary to choose a different method that has CASE support.

One of the hard lessons software development teams have learned is that the transition to object-oriented technology (OOT) may make existing modeling tools unusable because they don't support OO modeling or don't have graphic notation editors. If there is no direct support for object orientation (OO), the CASE tool must be replaced. Attempting to adapt existing tools that use function-oriented design to OO, in our experience, just doesn't work and wastes both time and money. Similarly, if the team attempts to choose a CASE tool before adopting an OO development method (and programming language), it will have insufficient information to make the CASE tool choice. Obviously, the selection of a method and a CASE tool must be made in concert with each other, but the choice of method should always come first.

6.3   Criteria for Evaluating Computer-Aided Software Engineering Tools

Figure 6.3 provides a list of general CASE tool evaluation criteria. It can be used as a starting point for determining the needs of an organization in choosing the right tool. There are five major evaluation categories: utility, extensibility, flexibility, usability, and completeness.

> **Utility.** This section lists a number of desired and specific features that are the basis for evaluation. It includes consistency checking between diagrams, integration of data/object repositories, leveled abstractions of diagrams, templates according to specific documentation standards, and reverse engineering of diagrams from code. It also includes the following areas.
>
> ◆ Method support. This is the ability of a CASE tool to support the chosen method's notation and output the method's artifacts. There are several forms of object-oriented models that can be supported using CASE tools, including class diagrams, context diagrams, object interaction diagrams (OIDs), software architecture diagrams, and state transition diagrams (STDs).
>
> ◆ Model analysis. This is the CASE tool's ability to perform such analysis techniques as consistency checking, completeness checking, behavior analysis, and interface analysis.
>
> ◆ Requirements trace. This is the CASE tool's ability to trace the requirements between software life cycle phases, such as tracing of requirements to software design, tracing the requirements to implementation, and tracing the requirements to software tests. Requirements tracing is an important form of consistency checking.
>
> ◆ Data repository. This is the CASE tool's ability to store, interface, access, and extend different object artifacts,

such as objects, object models, diagrams, code, and documentation. It also covers the tool's capabilities in performing queries, doing CM, and recording project information. It should also include the ability to contain multiple versions and design and analysis history information. The history information provides a way of reviewing analysis and design decisions for later postmortem review and for maintenance.

- ◆ Documentation. This is the CASE tool's ability to support documentation, including the integration of graphics and text, document generation from analysis and design artifacts, and use of user-defined document templates for standardization. It also covers capabilities such as interfacing to other documentation produced with word processors and other programs and support for different text and graphics file conversions.

- ◆ Correctness. This is the CASE tool's ability to generate correct products and to conform to the specifications and standards.

Extensibility. This is the tool's ability to extend any of the object-oriented artifacts, including new modeling functionality, and provide interfaces to different data/object repositories. It should be possible to integrate preexisting class libraries and frameworks into the system.

Flexibility. This is the CASE tool's ability to provide access simultaneously across a network and between multiple development platforms. It covers such aspects as versioning and access granularity. On large systems with many developers, there must be a way to work on the same parts of the system that doesn't force developers to wait excessively for access to objects and prevents artifact corruption. The system should interface with desktop publishing. It also includes the ability to work with other development tools, such as integrated development environments, CM systems, and project management programs.

Usability. This criterion examines several abilities related to the CASE tool's documentation, user interface design, help line for user support, and tool performance.

- **Utility**
  - — Consistency checks between diagrams
  - — Integrated data repository
  - — Leveled abstractions of diagrams
  - — Integration between diagrams and code (2-way)
  - — Method-specific rules enforced
  - — Bidirectional diagram dependency automation
  - — Decomposition of objects (nodes)
  - — Decomposition of arcs
  - — Automated documentation generation (templates)
  - — Automated code generation
  - — Reverse engineering of diagrams from code
  - — Read-only version available for customers

- **Extensibility**
  - — Interface to rules (individual enable, insert new)
  - — Interface to repository

- **Flexibility**
  - — Simultaneous network access
  - — Interface with desktop publishing

- **Usability**
  - — User interface design
  - — Documentation
  - — User support (help line)
  - — Tool performance (speed)

- *Completeness*
  - — Requirements analysis support
  - — Preliminary design support
  - — Detailed design support
  - — Coding support
  - — Testing support

Figure 6.3   Criteria for evaluating and applying CASE tools for OO software projects.

Completeness. This section is concerned with completeness, where object-oriented artifacts (software products) that are created by the CASE tool possess the characteristics of completeness to the extent that all of its parts are present and each of its parts is fully developed. This criterion examines the CASE tool's support of completeness in all the life cycle phases.

6.4 The Computer-Aided Software Engineering Tool Selection Process

When selecting a CASE tool or set of tools, we go through a multistep process. First, we determine the project's needs, including the identification of the smallest list of essential attributes of the CASE tools. Second, we establish the project's resources. Finally, when we have narrowed the list, we use a weighted evaluation method to help with the final selection.

The following, as shown in Figure 6.4, is the CASE tool selection process.

1. Establish specific needs. The project needs for a CASE tool must be justified in many ways, such as life cycle and OO tech-

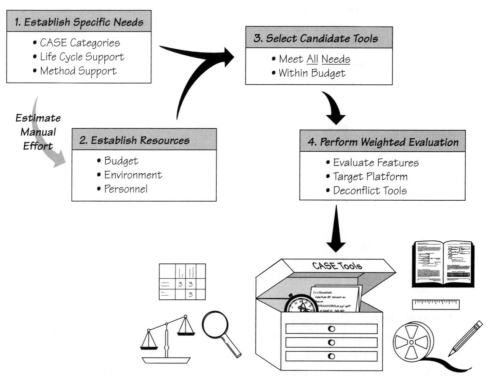

Figure 6.4 CASE tool selection process.

nique support, productivity, reusability, testing, and V&V support. We identify certain items that must be present to even consider a particular tool. Of the essential items, support for a particular method, support for the target programming language, support for development platforms, and consistency checking are universal. In addition, an extensible graphical notation and database/repository support are attributes that disqualify nonconforming tools.

2. Once the needs of the system are identified and the list of absolutely essential tool attributes is made, we establish resources such as budget, environment, and personnel. Full-featured CASE tools can be extremely expensive, so the per-seat cost can quickly eliminate many systems from consideration. If the established needs from the first step don't correspond to the budget and personnel constraints, then the analysis and selection process must start over. It's essential to determine compatibility early. Determining compatibility with the development environment also must be done early in the process.

3. Select candidate CASE tools that meet all project needs and that are within budget. Once we have the CASE tools that have passed the first three checks, we are ready to begin detailed evaluation.

4. Perform a weighted evaluation based on carefully selected criteria. Figure 6.5 shows an example of a weighted evaluation matrix of two CASE tools. In this example, Tool No. 1 is weighted 270 points versus Tool No. 2, which is weighted 247 points. Tool No. 1 should be the project CASE tool, because it has scored better on those criteria that are important to the project than Tool No. 2 has. In practice, the number of items in the weighted evaluation will be greater than our example.

When applying the evaluation, it is important to avoid the checklist mentality. Doing so makes it more likely that features, as specified by CASE tool vendors, will assume a greater role in the selection process than the project's actual needs will have. We provide hereafter some guidelines.

Benefit	Feature	Tool Performance		Project Weight	Adjusted Score	
		Tool #1	Tool #2		Tool #1	Tool #2
		(0–5, where 5 is highest)				
Utility	Consistency checks between diagrams	1	3	5	5	15
	Integrated repository (dictionary)	4	3	5	20	15
	Leveled abstractions of diagrams	4	4	4	16	16
	Integration between diagrams and code (2-way)	0	0	3	0	0
	Method-specific rules enforced	5	5	4	20	20
	Bidirectional diagram dependency automation	1	3	4	4	12
	Decomposition of objects (nodes)	4	3	4	16	12
	Decomposition of arcs	0	0	2	0	0
	Automated documentation generation (templates)	2	2	2	4	4
	Automated code generation	4	0	1	4	0
	Reverse engineering of diagrams from code	4	0	1	4	0
	Read-only versions available for customers	5	0	2	10	0
Extensibility	Interface to rules (individual enable, insert new)	4	4	2	8	8
	Interface to repository (dictionary)	4	2	5	20	10
Flexibility	Simultaneous network access	0	4	3	0	12
	Interface with desktop publishing	4	4	4	16	16
Usability	User interface design	4	4	4	16	16
	Documentation	4	4	3	12	12
	User support (help line)	4	5	3	12	5
	Available training	5	5	1	5	5
	Tool performance (speed)	4	2	4	16	8
Completeness	Requirements analysis support	5	5	5	25	25
	Preliminary design support	5	5	5	25	25
	Detailed design support	5	2	2	10	4
	Coding support	2	0	1	2	0
	Testing support	0	0	4	0	0
				TOTALS:	270	247

Tool Performance Legend

5 Complete, automated implementation

4 Partially addressed, useful implementation

3 Partially addressed, clumsy implementation

2 Addressed only through workarounds

1 Manual effort required

0 Unaddressed

Project Weight Legend

5 Critical, customer/method requirement

4 Consistently saves manual effort

3 Sometimes saves manual effort

2 May save effort someday

1 Nice to have, but not important

0 Not helpful

Figure 6.5 Examples of a weighted evaluation of two CASE tools.

A displayable graphical notation for OO is a must. Customers as well as developers need multiple levels of viewing to understand both large and detailed aspects of a system. Visualizing models without graphical aids is difficult and prone to error. An automated diagram generator is the only way to deal with the complexity and data volume involved.

- Model diagrams rapidly become so complex as to be incomprehensible without some simplifying automated process. Rumbaugh briefly discusses breaking up the model into sheets with each association or aggregation on each sheet and classes divided across multiple sheets [Rumbaugh91]. Exactly what criterion should be used for the decomposition is not stated. Some engineers found that a good approach was to put the detail of the class attributes and methods on one sheet, and to represent the class as simply a name in a box on all other diagrams. This would also make the diagrams easier to maintain when attributes and methods change. In a CASE tool, these levels of detail could be handled as viewing options.

Implement the technique correctly. Numerous CASE tool vendors (and even the authors of OO techniques) have provided a *mapping* of a particular object-oriented technique to CASE tools that implement structured analysis and design. In our experience, attempting to use the graphics developed for structured analysis to implement our OO analysis technique worked poorly. Although it is undoubtedly possible with careful engineering, we found it intuitively difficult. Additionally, people familiar with the functional graphics often had trouble making a complete switch to object-oriented thinking. Avoid using a CASE tool that requires a mapping of the graphical representations to a particular technique.

The CASE tool should enforce the rules of the OO technique as much as possible. The best time to find mistakes is while the developers are first making them. If the CASE tool can catch these faults before reviews or inspections, then a great deal of time will be saved. This is especially important when the technique is new. The continual enforcement of the technique by the CASE tool serves as a good training mechanism for the developers.

Watch out for low payoff features. Computer-aided software engineering tool vendors are constantly trying to add more features to outdo the competition. Features such as *reverse engineering* or *automated code generation* are generally not the most important reasons to buy a CASE tool. We found these items to be marginally useful. The most important parts of the CASE tools were the graphical editors that enforce consistent application of the rules. Consistency checking between diagrams and a data dictionary is also useful.

Evaluate vendors' claims carefully. A CASE tool may not work exactly as the vendor promised in your environment. For example, after several tries, we eventually gave up on a feature called *automated documentation generation* of a CASE tool. The poor quality and high overhead of this feature of this particular tool convinced us we were better off using a commercial word processor. In general, evaluate the actual tool to verify that it has the required features and that they work as claimed. For full-functioned CASE tools, trial use is absolutely necessary due to their cost and impact on the organization.

♦ Our experience with CASE tools indicates that the CASE industry, as a whole, lags behind developments in the OOA/OOD world. Analysis and design techniques are changing rapidly as the methodologists frequently improve their techniques, and the tool vendors are hard-pressed to keep pace with the latest developments. The CASE tool representatives are always promising to provide additional or expanded capabilities in their next release. Such claims should not be used as the basis for choosing a tool.

A CASE tool should support several OO techniques, their development processes, and must be flexible for generating and updating these development processes. In many cases, projects will be moving between different OO methods, and transition support is useful. For example, many projects will be moving from *Booch* [Booch94] and Object Modeling Technique (OMT) to Unified Modeling Language (UML) [Rational95]. Having a tool that can accommodate both notations will ease the transition.

6.5   Summary

In our experience, CASE tools for modeling and design are essential for object-oriented development, and their proper selection helps to make the transition to OO successful. Given the wide range of tools, their dramatically varying cost, and the impact (either positive or negative) they may have on a team, a careful evaluation process is essential.

The keys to effective selection are to first adopt the OO method the project will be using. Then the project's needs should be assessed in the areas of essential features, resources, and environment. This gives a basis for tool evaluation. Tools that don't meet the essential requirements of the project can be eliminated right away. The remaining tools can then be subjected to a weighted evaluation process that reflects the needs of the team. Remember that a blind checklist approach to evaluation is poor, which makes the process especially vulnerable to feature comparisons. In this case, the vendors rather than the team have the most control in the selection process.

There are a few essential features that any CASE tool must have. It must directly and correctly implement the chosen object-oriented notation. It should not be a mapping from the OO notation to a structured analysis and design format. This doesn't work. It should provide a graphical notation and manipulation for the OO technique. It should ensure consistency between diagrams and object-oriented rules, and enforce consistency with a data dictionary as well. It should provide for CM, either itself or in conjunction with a separate CM product. And, it must support the languages and platforms used in development. Finally, don't equate large sets of features, high per-seat costs, and fancy sales approaches with usefulness. Some of the most effective tools are very inexpensive. Even if the inexpensive tools must be replaced later, they often provide a more effective introduction to OO analysis and design than their more expensive counterparts.

Tips and Practical Advice

Lesson 6.1   Computer-aided software engineering tool (CASE) support is important for object-oriented development projects.
The availability of CASE tool support is one of the most important areas that must be addressed before introducing an OO technique to a project. An effective CASE tool can be used throughout the software development life cycle.

A tool should allow system engineers to quickly develop requirements descriptions and easily maintain them, allow software designers to express their designs in a format compatible with the chosen technique, and provide traceability from requirements through design and code. The CASE tool should also allow the engineers to produce requirements and design documents that can serve as working papers during the development, in addition to meeting contractual requirements.

Lesson 6.2   The selected tool must be true to the technique.
The selected tool must fully support the selected development technique. Trying to use a poorly suited tool can be very frustrating. In general, avoid tools that must map the OO technique you've selected to a structured analysis and design format.

Lesson 6.3   Object diagram complexity dictates the need for CASE tools.
Complex object models are usually too large to represent on a single sheet of paper. This complexity can be compounded if the designer wishes to include objects in the diagram to show information such as the number of instances a class will have.

Lesson 6.4   Selecting a CASE tool follows technique selection.
The team must identify tools that support the selected technique and run on the available platform(s). The team will find that many tool developers support only a very limited number of platforms. Attempting to use tools left over from some other methodology or technique can mean disaster for the project. Choosing a CASE tool that supports the selected technique and runs on the required platform is a decision that must be made in an organized manner. We

(continued)

recommend, as a first step, the selection of an object-oriented development technique for one's project. Then, find a CASE tool that supports the OO technique and runs on his or her equipment. If a CASE tool is selected before an OO technique, the ability to tailor the technique to meet your needs will be severely restricted. The CASE tool and OO technique selection must be made, however, hand-in-hand. The chosen OO approach may lack adequate CASE tool support, or the available CASE tools that support the OO technique may not meet other project requirements. If this situation arises, the evaluation process must be continued until an optimal technique/CASE tool combination can be found.

Lesson 6.5   CASE tools can have negative impact if improperly applied.
Any tool takes time to master, and the more complex the tool, the longer the learning curve. Part of any CASE tool evaluation must be understanding the trade-offs between adaptation to the tool, its cost, and the expected performance gain. There will be many cases where the time and cost do not justify the expenditure. Vainly hoping for dramatic productivity improvements guarantees disappointing results.

   Computer-aided software engineering tools produce a large number of diagrams that represent the different aspects of the requirements specifications and the design. These diagrams help the project team to communicate effectively among themselves but not necessarily with the users. A multilevel viewing capability is useful so that users can identify high-level functionality without being bogged down in technical and notational details.

Lesson 6.6   CASE selection must be based on a need-driven process.
Computer-aided software engineering tools don't solve problems by themselves; they are just tools. If they don't fit the needs of the team, then they will not be effective. Relying on vendors' claims about CASE tool benefits is the wrong way to go. Identify the project's needs and resources first. Then, identify tools that meet those needs within the resource constraints. The selection process must include the people who will be using the tools.

References

[Booch94] Booch, G., *Object-Oriented Analysis and Design with Applications.* Redwood City, California: Benjamin/Cummings, 1994.

[Rational95] Booch, G., and J. Rumbaugh. "Unified Method for Object-Oriented Development." Rational Corp., Santa Clara, California, Documentation Set, Version 8, 1995.

[Rumbaugh91] Rumbaugh, J. et al., *Object-Oriented Modeling and Design.* Englewood Cliffs, New Jersey: Prentice Hall, 1991.

chapter seven

Staffing and Organizing the Project

"An idea can turn to dust or magic depending on the talent that rubs against it."

—WILLIAM BERNACH, AS QUOTED IN THE *NEW YORK TIMES*, OCTOBER 6, 1992.

7.1 The Special Needs of Object-Oriented Development

Staffing the first object-oriented software development (OOSD) requires special consideration. From our experience, the standard software engineering organization does not exactly support the needs of OOSD. As development teams continue through the development, they make several improvements to their software organization. Important new positions are shown in Figure 7.1. These key jobs include object orientation (OO) guru, prototyping lead, and domain analyst, and they are essential to successful object-oriented software development. There are two additional and more specialized positions for specific applications: framework developer and distributed object application expert. The new positions have direct responsibility for eliminating several problems that development teams encounter early in the development.

There is no way currently to staff an organization with experienced OO developers. For the foreseeable future, the demand for software development skills will substantially exceed the supply of qualified people. Most existing organizations do not have staffs trained in object-oriented development, even though the technology has existed for decades, and gaining

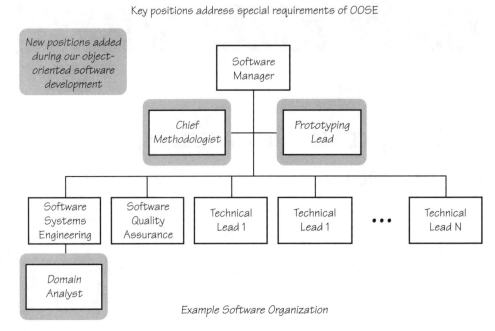

Figure 7.1 Key OO positions.

experience through training takes months to years. Even if it were possible from an organizational standpoint to replace the existing staff with software engineers experienced in OO development, it would be impossible to find that many qualified people. The question then becomes, "How do we acquire the help of a few specialists while we organize and assign our staff to make the introduction of OO successful?" The strategy is to hire or contract a few key positions, train existing staff (as we discuss in Chapter 8), and fill other gaps from the limited pool of new hires and consulting services.

The following sections contain the justification, responsibilities, and qualifications for the new positions. Additionally, we discuss some qualifications that are important for all personnel on the project.

7.2   Object Orientation Guru/Chief Methodologist

An OO guru (also known as a chief methodologist) is required in the organization to refine the use of the selected object-oriented analysis and design technique. Although each team member should receive formal training in applying the chosen technique, many technique-related questions will inevitably remain. Numerous clarifications and extensions of the technique are necessary to accommodate the unique elements of each project. The first issue will be to map object orientation constructs to the selected programming language. In addition, the OO guru must map the technique to reviews, documentation, and adaptation to a particular computer-aided software engineering (CASE) tool. Many of these questions are significant to completing the development within the required schedule.

There are many reasons that the object orientation guru is needed. The most important of these reasons include:

◆ Large software projects expose limitations in the chosen object-oriented technique not encountered during training.

◆ The technique often needs to be adapted to the selected CASE tool. It is rare that a CASE tool would completely implement a specific technique.

◆ Training on an OO technique will normally be completed before the project requirements analysis even begins. New questions must be answered as the development team proceeds through the development cycle.

◆ The technique will need to be expanded to integrate with tools or standards already in use by the project's organization.

◆ Extensions to the technique may be necessary for a particular problem domain (such as real-time or algorithm intensive).

◆ New people will need to be trained when adding staff.

Poor decisions in the application of OO techniques areas can lead to extensive rework. To reduce the likelihood of rework, the object orientation guru must be directly involved with every phase of the project and every person in the development. The OO guru has the following responsibilities, as shown in Figure 7.2.

He or she must tailor the chosen OO technique to fit the needs of the organization's application domain and integrate the CASE tools with both the technique and domain. The guru must also identify how object orientation methods are implemented in the target programming language and must develop necessary extensions to the object-oriented tech-

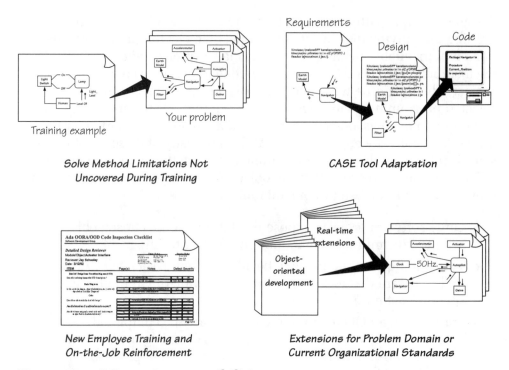

Figure 7.2 OO guru's responsibilities.

nique that fit the development environment. The guru must also develop standards for graphic representation of analysis and design. This is a challenging task, because there must be compatible levels of graphic documentation that run from high-level representations suitable for nontechnical reviewers to low-level representations suitable for detailed design, programming, and test development. In addition, the OO technique must be integrated with other documentation, test, and review procedures, and it must be consistent with any applicable standards (for example, DOD-STD-2167A, IEEE standards, and NASA standards). Directing these tasks also falls to the object orientation guru. Finally, this person must be responsible for coordinating the training of the project staff so that they learn techniques consistent with the chosen OO method.

This object orientation guru position requires a person with a broad range of experience. Formal experience with each activity of the software life cycle, from analysis to acceptance testing and maintenance, is needed. The person must not only have excellent communications skills, but must also understand the necessary organization of technical documentation. The guru should also have experience with other formal techniques (such as structured analysis and design) to bridge between the old approach and the new one. This is a critical position, and it would be best to have this position be a permanent hire, but if necessary, a consultant may fill in with the extra job requirement of helping to find and train a permanent replacement.

7.3   Domain Analyst

A primary goal of object-oriented software engineering (OOSE) is to lay a firm foundation for software reuse. The project needs a domain analyst to specifically address the reuse problem. The domain analyst is also responsible for understanding multiple software projects within the domain, extracting the common elements, and designing practical, reusable software parts and components. The specific responsibilities, as shown in Figure 7.3, for the domain analyst include deciding when

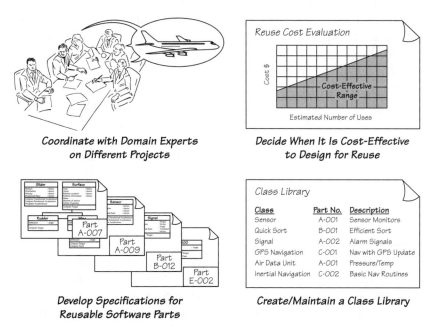

Coordinate with Domain Experts
on Different Projects

Decide When It Is Cost-Effective
to Design for Reuse

Develop Specifications for
Reusable Software Parts

Create/Maintain a Class Library

Figure 7.3   Domain analyst's responsibilities.

design for reuse is cost effective, and when it is, to develop specifications for reusable parts and components. The domain analyst must also create and maintain class libraries, which will involve working with domain experts on the organization's projects.

The domain analyst must be an expert in the application domain and have a firm understanding of classes and objects. Without a thorough knowledge of the application area, it will be difficult to create common parts successfully. The analyst must work to ensure encapsulation of the details within a class or object. If too many internal details are visible, designers will be less likely to use the part.

A domain analyst coordinates with domain experts and developers to translate the needs of each group to the other. In this sense, the domain analyst forms a bridge between the software development environment and the application domain environment. Developers are not necessarily experts in the application domain, nor need they be. Likewise, domain experts are not necessarily expert in software development. To implement reuse, the domain analyst must be able to straddle both environments and explain needs between them.

The job requirements for this person include a strong understanding of both the application domain and object-oriented software methods. Because domain understanding is hard to acquire outside the organization, it is usually better to develop the domain analyst from within. This implies finding someone with domain and programming experience, and training that person in both general object-oriented methods as well as the specific techniques of the selected OO method. During the training period, the domain analyst may place extra mentoring burdens on the OO guru. A consultant may also be hired to augment the domain analyst's object-oriented understanding during the transition.

7.4 Prototyping Expert

Even in the middle of a formal OO development, there is still a need for a pure programmer—someone who can develop a software product rapidly and correctly without necessarily following formal techniques. It is generally the case that certain aspects of a project cannot easily be deduced from requirements or formal analysis. This is especially the case in the area of user interaction, where prototyping can uncover serious problems that would not otherwise surface until product deployment. Therefore, prototyping is always a useful and efficient addition to the development organization.

The activities of the prototypers must be carefully separated from the rest of the software developers. This is especially true when software development teams are using formal techniques. The software product will not be consistent if software designers incorporate prototypes directly into the formal development. Figure 7.4 shows the prototyping expert's responsibilities.

Once the prototypes are complete, the prototyping staff must communicate the requirements to the formal development personnel, who are then responsible for the formal object-oriented development. The first requirement is the ability to program quickly in the development environment of the project. Second, an important qualification for the proto-

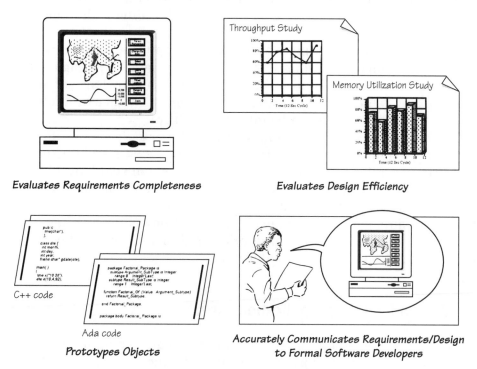

Evaluates Requirements Completeness   Evaluates Design Efficiency

C++ code

Ada code

Prototypes Objects

Accurately Communicates Requirements/Design
to Formal Software Developers

Figure 7.4   Prototyping expert's responsibilities.

typing position is to be able to explicitly communicate the prototypes to the formal development staff. It is also worthwhile if the prototyper has at least a basic understanding of OO principles to communicate with the formal development staff. Prototyping experts may be found inside the organization, or they may be hired or contracted.

7.5   Framework Developer

This is a special position in object-oriented application framework (OOAF) development projects. The application framework project needs a framework developer to specifically address the framework development and framework adaptation. The framework developer is also responsible for designing, evolving, and maintaining the framework architecture. The position also involves using design patterns in developing and documenting object-oriented application frameworks, providing hooks for extending and customizing OOAFs, and dealing with framework integration.

The framework developer must be an expert in application framework development and have a firm understanding of components, design patterns, and software architectures. Without a thorough knowledge of how to develop and to integrate application frameworks, it will be difficult to create reusable framework architecture successfully.

A framework developer coordinates with application developers to explain how to build applications on top of the framework architecture and how to integrate frameworks. In this sense, the framework developer forms a bridge between the framework development environment and the application domain environment.

The job requirements for this person include strong understanding of both software architecture and object-oriented design methods. It is difficult to find a qualified framework developer.

7.6   Distributed Object Application Expert

This is a special position in distributed object-oriented computing application projects. Common Object Request Broker Architecture (CORBA)-based, COM-based, or other distributed object-oriented computing application projects need an application expert to address distributed object infrastructure issues and to be able to deal specifically with addressing the next generation of client–server applications. The distributed object application expert is also responsible for designing and maintaining that part of the framework architecture that deals with distributed OO computing, integrating preexisting components, and building applications that comply with CORBA or other standards.

The distributed object application expert must be an expert in CORBA or whatever distributed object schemes are used. This person must also have a firm understanding of client–server and advanced distributed OO computing applications, distributed software architectures, and system integration. Without a thorough knowledge of how to develop and integrate distributed OO computing applications, it will be difficult to create reusable framework architecture successfully. Again, such people will be hard to find, and consulting services may have to be used until an existing staff member can be trained.

7.7   Other Staffing Issues

It is important that all software personnel understand the object orientation concepts quickly. The authors have had the best success with people experienced in an OO programming language. Although these people had not used an OO technique, they could relate the concepts back to the object-oriented language constructs. Relating object-oriented principles to language constructs is a good way to understand and explain the more abstract concepts of OO development.

Moving to object-oriented development can be a wrenching change, and there will always be some staff members who resist the move. In a large organization, there will be a continuing need for people who are familiar with existing software developed under previous methods. Those who consistently resist may be suited for maintenance on these projects. As shown in Figure 7.5, for the rest of the project, the staff should have an openness to change. Those who can back away from the details of software development and examine the concepts of object-oriented development will find the change easiest. To reinforce the new way of development, training and the use of OO analysis, design, and programming—especially with automated OO tools—must be mandated.

Best Substitutes for Lack of Object-Oriented Experience
- Open to change in culture
- Familiar with at least one object-oriented language
- Persistence with automated tools
- Conceptual thinkers

Figure 7.5   Staffing the rest of the project.

There are two issues in making the transition: the short-term needs of the organization for object-oriented expertise and the long-term requirements of maintaining and growing an OO culture (see Figure 7.6). For the short term, hiring the key positions we have described is essential. For some of the positions, consultants may fill in while the search for qualified candidates goes on. Once hired, there is still the transition of familiarizing the essential hires with the company's environment. Outside consultants may help during the adaptation period. Sharing expertise with other groups is especially necessary during the transition as well. For the long term, essential skills must be developed inside the organization. Continued training is mandatory. Domain analysts and object orientation gurus will remain important players in the organization, and efforts must be made to retain them and replicate their skills in others. This implies a management approach that recognizes the strategic value of these people and works to provide appropriate career opportunities for them.

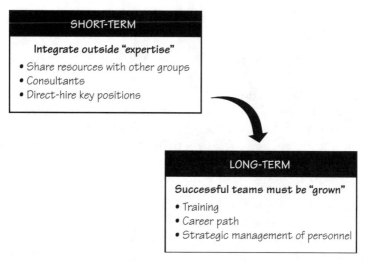

Figure 7.6   Short-term versus long-term staffing.

7.8 Summary

A few key people can make a significant difference in a new OO project. Because expertise in object-oriented development is hard to come by, finding a few people who can help the project along is the best way to make progress. Those people include an object-oriented methodologist (or OO guru), a domain analyst, and one or more prototyping experts. In some cases, one or more distributed object application experts and application framework experts will also be important staff additions.

Even finding a few people with these special skills can be difficult, and their salaries will be high. In many cases, people will have to be trained into the job; however, training is better than waiting until the supply of OO gurus, domain analysts, and prototyping experts increases. Current employment projections indicate the shortage of software experts will continue for another decade at least. The best advice we can offer is to look for people with formal training in object-oriented analysis, design, and programming, and plan to hire consultants to guide them while they learn specialized skills.

Tips and Practical Advice

Lesson 7.1   Staffing the first object-oriented project requires special consideration.
First-time OO project managers will find that their previous organization may not be well suited to object-oriented activities. There may be a need to define or change the definition of some team roles. The people selected for this team should be eager to learn new concepts.

Lesson 7.2   Development teams' or developers' attitudes and attributes are one of the major keys to success or failure of adapting the object-oriented technology on the project.
The team's individuals must be selected carefully to have two personality traits: aggressiveness to push forward new ideas and receptiveness to gain knowledge in new and unfamiliar areas.

Lesson 7.3   Development of a large system may require an object orientation guru to ensure that the methods and tools are rigorously followed, as well as to provide follow-up training to the development team when needed.

Lesson 7.4   Specialized software disciplines (e.g., OORA, OOD, Ada, C++, Java, and testing) help the development process.
We found that it was difficult for one person to work an object through all phases of the development process. The software development proceeded smoothly when the software disciplines were specialized. For example, let a group of engineers be responsible for the OORA throughout the system development cycle, then hand off the requirements product (for example, OIDs and STDs) to a group of designers and programmers.

chapter eight

Training

8.1 Directed Training

Training budgets in software development organizations are usually based on the vague notion that continuing education is an employee benefit and that it is a good idea. We don't usually find a focused plan to provide training that moves a team to a new level of skill. There are a few reasons for this. First, departments are set up to have only a few people at a time absent for training. Second, it is hard to find training that will directly and immediately affect job skills. Therefore, the year's training budget is often underused. In making a serious change to object orientation (OO), the rules change. Our goal is to use a combination of formal and on-the-job training to move the staff as quickly as possible to a new way of working. And this goal finds the first of its obstacles in the up-front training costs. Everyone on the project must get some form of training: managers, developers, subcontractors, administrators, quality assurance staff, and even customers. While some of these groups require relatively limited training, the software engineering staff will need intensive repeated training sessions. Without the training, the success of the project is jeopardized.

In some organizations, there is a penalty for not spending all budgeted money. In others, approved budget expenses must still go through approvals, making the likelihood of actually spending all of the budget small. The key here will be to get the budget and the spending approvals—before the project begins—so that training can start quickly. In a sense, getting the approval will be a sign of management's commitment to the transition, because the training costs will be a real and significant expense. To make an effective transition, teams must be trained together, in multiple sessions, for a total of 10 to 20 days of on-site instruction. The other serious budget consideration is that, unlike the usual training expenses, whole groups will be in training simultaneously and will be unavailable for other work.

Training is essential for new object-oriented development teams. Even experienced software developers benefit from a formal introduction to OO tenets, and existing teams require periodic training to keep their edge. As with most education, early investment pays large dividends in increased quality and productivity throughout the development. Additionally, just as with reusing object-oriented software systems, the benefits of reusing an experienced, highly trained workforce increase dramatically as we can apply their knowledge to the *next* project.

Any new team requires a training period. This is the same concept as spring training in major-league baseball. The teams all go off to neutral settings and concentrate on the fundamentals of the game. Not only does training develop new skills, it helps the team abandon the older, incompatible skills. This alone may be worth any training cost. Software teams also require periodic refocusing. When a team is on the threshold of using a new technique, they must plan for some training to get focused on the new aspects of developing software.

Use Formal Classroom Training

After selecting an appropriate object-oriented technique, we contract for three to five days of in-house training. For a first-time OO development, we recommend contracting with an experienced training organization. Such an organization can provide experience and valuable insight into application of OO techniques and tools. Several vendors currently provide high-quality training and will tailor class examples to the actual project under construction. This approach is helpful for the development team in that it forces the software developers to clearly explain the project to the trainer, who has little knowledge about your application domain. Figure 8.1 shows recommended training approaches.

The training method options include selecting the media for use in training. Effective training may include videotape, computer-based training (CBT), on-line and distance learning, seminars, or combinations of these. We feel, however, that face-to-face training for the basic skills is far

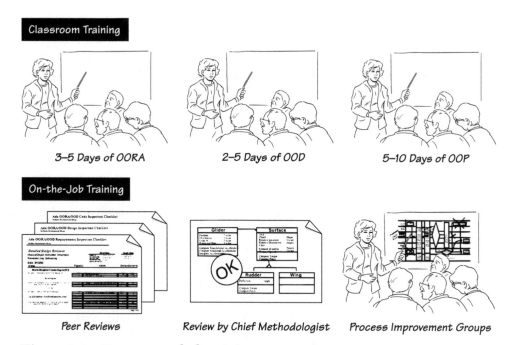

Figure 8.1 Recommended training approach.

superior to the other methods. We will be giving the team a whole new approach to design and development. A change of this magnitude just doesn't work well with self-paced training. Face-to-face training allows customization that the other methods do not. In addition, putting the whole team in simultaneous training forces a commitment that cannot be put off by other tasks and interruptions. Nonclassroom training may be useful for review and for concentration of specialized skills.

Object-oriented techniques have to be practiced. The selected training must include laboratory time, and participation in this activity must be enforced. Similarly, the participants must be polled to assure that the training is fulfilling its objective and is modified if necessary.

Another important decision may be how the training will be scheduled. A requirement for 40 hours of training may be filled in one week if that week is totally dedicated to the training activity. The same training may be spread across two weeks if training is only half-time. The training may also be spread across ten weeks with the addition of a part-time consultant.

The authors favor the latter approach for several reasons. Compressing the training tends to overwhelm the students. They are exposed to too much, too fast. Spreading the training across a longer period allows the student time to reflect on and practice each significant detail. Adding a consultant provides the opportunity for much more one-on-one learning. As Figure 8.1 shows, we suggest a series of formal classes spread out over a number of weeks. The first subject should be object-oriented requirements analysis and general OO concepts. The next subject should be devoted to moving from analysis to OO design. This class should refer back to the analysis course and should be geared to the problem domain the team is working on.

The last formal class will involve object-oriented programming and should emphasize the language already chosen for the project. For a transition to an object-oriented programming language (such as C++, Smalltalk, or Java), you must ensure an extensive training program that includes object-oriented software engineering (OOSE) principles and object-oriented analysis and design methods.

Training examples are much easier than real problems. This makes sense while teaching the basic concepts, but real problems may appear to be intractable when the basic concepts are first applied. To overcome this problem, illustrated examples in the training materials should be taken from the project requirements. Exercises and outside assignments must be taken from the project requirements as well. Note that this implies training tailored to your organization. The difference in cost between standardized and tailored training is not that great, and the benefits of applying OO methods in a familiar domain far outweigh any cost differential.

In many environments, people feel a need to continue work on their other projects, and will slip out of the classes to do other work. In other cases, people are called out for meetings or consultations. The steep learning curve for OO concepts makes such distractions especially destructive. If necessary, conduct the training off-site, or else make it clear to all that the training is serious and that self-generated or external distractions will not be tolerated.

Train for the Whole Life Cycle

Training and education play a major role in improving the object-oriented development process. However, the curriculum should not focus on object-oriented analysis (OOA) or object-oriented design (OOD) alone. A view of the entire life cycle development should be presented, demonstrating how both OOA and OOD support the subsequent development stages.

Requirements traceability through the development life cycle should be emphasized. A requirements analysis and design case study, using an example of similar size and complexity as the target system, would give early indications of the problems that might be encountered during the requirements analysis and design phases. This training should also be made available to customers if they will be evaluating software products, such as requirements specifications and design documents, or if they will be assisting in requirements analysis and reviews.

Augment with On-the-Job Training

On-the-job training is an effective way to augment and reinforce formal training. As Figure 8.1 shows, the main forms of this sort of training are peer and expert reviews and active process improvement efforts. Since the training activities are also integral work components, they are not as disruptive as formal training, and they can be carried on continuously. One of the most important types of peer review is the inspection. We discuss this subject more completely in Chapter 16, but we mention here that inspections can be applied to all areas of the development process. Design reviews and postmortems also can be counted as peer reviews.

During the analysis and development phase, review by the person designated as the object orientation method guru is another important form of on-the-job training. The task of the OO guru is to review objects with respect to the team's object-oriented method and against established design guidelines to make sure developers understand the method. If done properly, this is not a bureaucratic function but a teaching one.

Process improvement groups likewise force developers to look at their own ways of working to improve themselves. To be effective as training, the improvement process should not be used to find fault with individual employees, nor should the data collected be used in performance reviews.

Among the most important forms of on-the-job training are coaching and mentoring. Coaching is an explicit training technique in which a person with special skills and experience actively works with a less-experienced person to develop a particular area of expertise. Coaching is not limited to technical mastery. It can also be used to help people work as members of a team or to interact effectively with people in other departments. Mentoring, in contrast, is a less formal training arrangement in which a senior person assists someone more junior in adapting to the environment of the organization. Mentoring commonly involves advice on both technical issues and those involving company culture.

The drawbacks of both coaching and mentoring are that suitable senior people tend to be in short supply, and their time is already over-booked. Because it is an explicit activity, coaching at least can be sched-uled into a senior person's set of responsibilities, and care can be taken to avoid having it consume all of the coach's time. Mentoring is a dicier proposition. Except in the unlikely situation where there are enough mentors to go around, attempts to formalize mentoring may lead to com-plaints of favoritism. In addition, mentors may find much of their time taken by this activity without any way to account for it. In short, while mentoring can be extremely beneficial for training, it must be handled with care by management.

8.2 Training the Whole Team

Software engineers are not the only people who benefit from training. Each member of the development team, including managers, contract engineers, cost estimators, and system engineers, needs to understand their role in an OO development. A training program should be tailored to complement the entire development team. Figure 8.2 shows the five *W*s for training the project team. Note especially that the training, to be effective, must be done just-in-time and must be taken seriously enough to assure that participants are not distracted by conflicting work assign-ments or daily interruptions.

> **Training software managers.** The software manager must under-stand the basic principles of object-oriented techniques, iterative development, and domain analysis. Senior management and cus-tomers often perceive additional schedule and budget risks in OO developments, especially first-time efforts. In fact, the risks change but are not necessarily greater than with any other development, and object orientation is undertaken to address existing risks that threaten future development. It falls to the software manager to

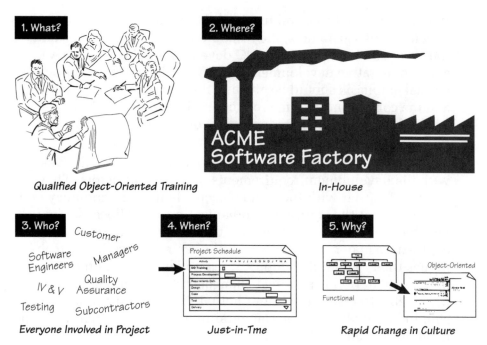

Figure 8.2 The five *W*s for training the project team.

communicate the changed risks to senior management and to assure everyone that the development changes aren't a sign of chaos. Iterative development adds both risk and uncertainty at first. Management training must include an approach to iteration that avoids the risk of endlessly iterating without making progress. Training should also include expectation management to counter the persistent problems of underestimating project duration and overselling the benefits of OO.

Training customers. Customers base their expectations on experience of previous software development projects. The more experience they have, the greater their cynicism about new methods will be. They may expect a waterfall model approach because it seems more orderly, and they may expect the almost adversarial approach to requirements analysis and specification that the waterfall method engenders. They won't expect the higher interaction, domain analysis, and fuzziness in estimation of iterative development. Customers, then, should be trained to understand the procedural differences in OO development. Because early stages of iterative development may seem like wheel spinning, special emphasis should be given to the increased role of analysis and the corresponding time reduction of later stages. Customer training should be hype-reduced to avoid cynicism and to foster reasonable expectations.

Training subcontractors. Subcontractors must align themselves with the development requirements of their contractors. They must be familiar with the same object-oriented methodology and notations that the contracting organization uses. Because they may have less direct contact with the development teams, subcontractors may need a higher level of competence in the techniques than regular development team members. But moving to object orientation is a radical change, and subcontractors may not be able to respond without help. If possible, subcontractors should be involved in the same training that the regular development group gets.

Training administrative personnel. Without good administrative help, a project will disintegrate. While it may seem superfluous at first, administrative personnel should be trained in the fundamentals of object technology. Leaving them behind while the rest of the organization moves forward is destructive. In addition, administrators must develop skills in a variety of new areas, and the fastest and ultimately least expensive way to build these skills is through training. The first is aligning project management procedures with work packages as the fundamental units of progress. Without this alignment, the substantial clerical and administrative effort of tracking a project will become unwieldy. Second is training in configuration management. Third is dealing with reuse and third-party components.

Training testing and QA people. Testing object-oriented software is not the same as traditional testing. Obviously, training in the same OO methodology as the rest of the development organization is necessary. At the lower levels of development, the traditional test areas must be expanded to include such areas as related groups of classes, associations, object flows, and error flows. Third-party components will probably play a significant part in the project and will require new test approaches. In addition, testing responsibilities will change. Developers may be expected to test their own objects. Quality assurance must be involved at the analysis and design stage, so test development will start earlier and will be based on object models rather than specification documents. Formal training for OO testing is more available now, but on-the-job training for organizational changes may be the only option.

Training writers. Writers as well require formal training in object-oriented technology and in the specific OO methodology adopted by the organization. As we describe in the chapter on documentation, the organization of object-oriented documentation is different from function-oriented documentation, and on-the-job training will be necessary to impart the skills for the new approach.

Training software developers. Object-oriented software development requires developers to adopt a different perspective. We found that the approach challenged even experienced developers (experienced software engineers and programmers often stubbornly resisted the change). Successful training must concentrate on the details of the specific technique's theory and application. Plenty of real-world examples, preferably dealing with the project under consideration, are helpful. A one-week training session is sufficient for most of the developers; others required more practice. Therefore, we recommend creating a program in which the trainees train others in the organization.

Training systems engineers. Training systems engineers in object-oriented principles eases project development. Systems engineers are primary contributors to the software requirements. If the requirements reflect an alternate decomposition paradigm, such as a functional decomposition, OO developments are significantly restricted, if not doomed. Alternatively, trained systems engineers cannot only specify, but optimize system requirements to exploit OO benefits. This results in systems that are more robust and easier to maintain.

Tips and Practical Advice

Lesson 8.1 Involve the entire team at early requirements analysis sessions.
It is a good way for members of the team to understand the method and the system.

Lesson 8.2 Training is essential for new object-oriented development teams.
Any new team requires a training period. Even existing teams require periodic training to keep their edge.

Lesson 8.3 Train for the whole life cycle.
The curriculum should not focus on OOA or OOD alone. A view of the entire life cycle development should be presented, demonstrating how both OOA and OOD support the subsequent development stages. Requirements traceability through the development life cycle should be emphasized.

Lesson 8.4 The method of training must be carefully selected.
Effective training may include videotape, computer-based training (CBT), seminars, or combinations of these. However, for the major topics, classroom training is a must.

Lesson 8.5 Training should be spread over a number of weeks.
We recommend a series of classroom sessions in OORA, OOD, and OO programming spread over a ten-week period.

Lesson 8.6 Training examples are much easier than real problems.
To overcome this problem, illustrated examples in the training materials must be taken from the project requirements. Exercises and outside assignments must be taken from the project requirements as well.

Lesson 8.7 Laboratory participation is mandatory.
Object-oriented techniques have to be practiced. The selected training must include laboratory time, and participation in this activity must be enforced.

(continued)

Lesson 8.8   Object orientation learning curve is relatively steep. Once developers begin to understand OO concepts, they will grasp the other facets quickly. The learning curve is a factor. If your team has no experience with object-oriented techniques, you can expect a learning curve of between two and four months. We also found, on the average, that 15 percent of the people trained would not move smoothly to the OO mind-set.

Lesson 8.9   Organize the training so that participants are not distracted.
Conduct the training off-site, or else make it clear to all that the training is serious and that self-generated or external distractions will not be tolerated.

Lesson 8.10   Do not substitute on-line or self-directed training for the major pieces.
While multimedia- and Internet-based training are valuable in many circumstances, they work poorly for active team training. Many concepts require face-to-face discussion to understand fully. Such training will not be tailored to your needs, and discussions cannot include examples meaningful to your group. Self-directed training is only as comprehensive as the person taking it desires. The tendency to skip various topics or allow distractions to interfere will be too great.

8.3   Summary

Blanket training, which provides an overall understanding of object-oriented development process, is essential for all the team members on OO projects. Specialized training is vital for creating a core of expertise in object-oriented analysis, design, and languages, such as C++ or Java. In addition, special training may be needed for framework development, object request broker technology, reusable component technology, and other specialized requirements.

The transition to OOSD requires a concerted approach to training. Providing occasional classes, encouraging employees to train themselves through outside courses, multimedia, on-line instruction, or other canned programs not designed for your environment won't result in an adequately trained team. The costs of providing uniform training will be substantial, but the alternatives cost even more. There is virtually no chance that a whole team with appropriate skills could be hired to replace the current team, and taking a haphazard approach to training jeopardizes the whole project. The very least that inadequate training will do is to slow the whole process down. In today's economy, such a slowdown is unacceptably risky. The impact of training on the development schedule is not trivial, so training must be incorporated into the development schedule. By explicitly scheduling and budgeting training both the time and cost, which are significant, will be understood ahead of time. The cost impact of training is one of the aspects of the transition most visible to management, and approval of the costs is one of management's most visible and necessary signs of commitment to the transition.

Once formal training has been done, it must be reinforced with on-the-job training, practice, and mentoring. Taking a conscious view of the training potential in various tasks like inspections, test development, and design meetings will enhance the quality of the activities and will drive home the lessons of formal instruction.

chapter nine

Dealing with Legacy Systems

9.1 Introduction

The intent of this chapter is to discuss the most effective ways of interfacing with legacy systems in an object-oriented environment. A somewhat humorous definition of a legacy system is a system that is old
enough to be doing useful work. Legacy systems are at once indispensable and troublesome. This definition highlights the cause of the
problems of legacy systems. They represent the results of long effort,
substantial investment, and hard-won adaptation to meet essential
needs of the organization. At the same time, their age, complexity,
and the technology used in their creation make them increasingly hard
to adapt to the new demands placed on them. Thus, legacy systems
cause problems for their users, developers, redevelopers, and the
management charged with their continued use.

   Changing software systems is inevitable. The general term for system
change is *maintenance;* however, it has a negative connotation. A better
name for maintenance, which we will use for the rest of this chapter, is
software redevelopment. Maintenance implies repairing broken or worn-
out parts. Software does not break in that sense, nor does it wear out
[AirForce95]. When a software system suddenly fails, the offending module cannot just be repaired with an identical replacement; the module
must be redesigned. And in order for the redesigned module to avoid
producing side effects throughout the rest of the system, its place in the
system must be analyzed. This effort, from problem analysis to tentative
fix to contextual analysis to specification change, contains most of the
elements of development. This is why we call it software redevelopment.
We categorize in the following list some of the reasons why change,

maintenance, or redevelopment—whatever name we choose to call it—will surely happen.

1. *Preventative redevelopment* attempts to find problems before they cause damage. Testing and inspection are examples of this activity.

2. *Corrective redevelopment* is the repair of defects. Current technology does not give us the ability to make software without defects. Even if it were possible to make software absolutely error-free, it is almost certain that specification errors or oversights would force corrective action.

3. *Perfective redevelopment* adds new capabilities and satisfies new requirements. Software evolution naturally builds on earlier products.

4. *Adaptive redevelopment* accommodates a system to new hardware and operating environments.

Regardless of the reason for change, the cost of changing is dependent on the extent of the changes and the adaptability of the software to change. According to a U.S. Air Force study [AirForce95], the typical cost of redeveloping a software product is from 49 to 80 percent of the total life-cycle cost, as shown in Figure 9.1. This brings us to the question of why we would want to redevelop existing systems. The simple answer is that they have continuing value for the organization, and to preserve their value they must sometimes be redeveloped. Particular reasons to redevelop legacy systems include the following.

♦ **To reduce redevelopment cost.**   Legacy systems are usually built on one (or more) earlier technologies, and making even simple changes can require extensive analysis and testing. Major changes may be all but impossible.

♦ **To reduce defect rate.**   Given the difficulty of changes, every update may introduce new defects. In addition, if the original system was poorly designed, it may be impossible to reduce that rate.

♦ **To use a better language.**   Newer languages have features that make them more desirable. For example, previous language

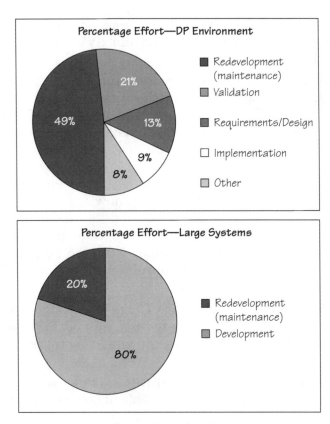

Figure 9.1 Life-cycle redevelopment cost.

implementations might have limitations in memory or I/O access that are no longer necessary in current hardware and operating systems. For longer-lived systems, the shortcomings may include lack of adequate data structure or communication support.

- **To migrate to a new platform.** Hardware evolves rapidly, and keeping a system compatible with the rest of an organization's hardware may require rehosting. Of course, operating system changes and networking capabilities may also require platform changes.

- **To increase the life span of the system.** Legacy systems would not continue in use if they did not provide useful services.

Extending a system's operational life span can be necessary because replacement cannot be immediately considered or because the cost is too great.

♦ **To utilize and use the most current technology.** As software and hardware technology evolve, they offer new functionality and performance. If a legacy system is stuck in an old environment, it cannot make use of features in current technology. It becomes more isolated and less useful.

The preceding reasons for redeveloping legacy systems also hint at the problems such systems cause. We list these now.

♦ **Lack of reuse.** Older systems generally were not designed with modern reuse concepts in mind. The largest unit of reuse in a legacy system is the low-level subroutine or a related group of subroutines.

♦ **Lack of provision for extension.** The previous model for large systems made limited provision for extension. Adding new functionality meant a major system upgrade, a process taking multiple years.

♦ **Lack of adaptability.** This inability to extend a system makes legacy systems inflexible and incapable of being adapted to new, similar uses.

♦ **Low performance and efficiency.** Either basic design limitations or designs intended for less powerful systems and hardware retain those limitations when moved to new systems.

♦ **Difficult for users and developers to understand.** The function-based approach to software development causes a serious dislocation between the way requirements are represented and the way functions are designed. This inherent difficulty with tracing between requirements and code is augmented in many systems with inadequate change documentation and design entropy.

So the reality is that we want to keep the functionality of legacy systems, but we want to make them more tractable and we want to be able to use them with newer systems. In order to have both features, we must reengineer the legacy systems in such a way as to use their functionality without completely reimplementing them.

9.2 Reengineering Approaches

Reengineering, as shown in Figure 9.2, is the process of evaluation and changing a legacy system to produce an implemented new form. The reengineering process combines subprocesses, such as reverse engineering and forward engineering. Reengineering means recovering design from a legacy system and using the recovered design to reimplement some part of the legacy system. Our interest is to use reengineering to interface a legacy system with an object-oriented (OO) system in a fashion which doesn't require full reimplementation of the legacy system and which doesn't break the object-oriented-ness of the OO system. We define the two major reengineering approaches.

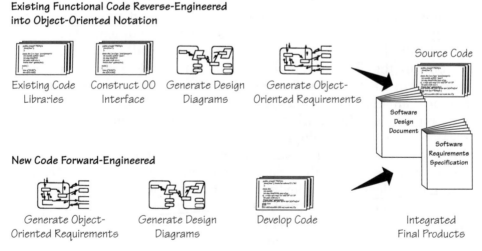

HOW TO INCORPORATE HERITAGE FUNCTIONAL CODE

Existing Functional Code Reverse-Engineered into Object-Oriented Notation

Existing Code Libraries   Construct OO Interface   Generate Design Diagrams   Generate Object-Oriented Requirements   Source Code

Software Design Document

Software Requirements Specification

New Code Forward-Engineered

Generate Object-Oriented Requirements   Generate Design Diagrams   Develop Code   Integrated Final Products

Figure 9.2 Reengineering.

Reverse engineering.　Reverse engineering is the process of examining an existing legacy system to abstract design artifacts and fundamental requirements. It is also used to understand the legacy systems. It is the opposite of forward engineering [Glass92]. These are the steps to reverse-engineer a system to integrate with an OO system.

1. Start with existing code libraries.
2. Construct an OO interface.
3. Generate design diagrams.
4. Generate OO requirements.

Forward engineering.　Forward engineering is the process of using the existing software product derived from legacy software and any new requirements to produce a new software system. See Figure 9.2. Here are the steps required to forward-engineer a legacy system to interface with an OO system.

5. Generate OO requirements.
6. Generate design diagrams and design.
7. Develop code.

To reengineer any legacy system, a feasibility analysis of the cost and risks must be performed. The feasibility analysis must compare reengineering costs against developing a new system that implements the same functionality. The feasibility analysis must identify all development risks and compare the likelihood and cost of each risk associated with reengineering to the likelihood and cost of doing a whole new development. Another evaluation must be done against the cost of doing nothing with the current system. In addition, other factors must be considered. First, the value added in redevelopment must be weighed against the future value of a brand-new and presumably more adaptable system. Second, the expected life span of the legacy system must be compared to the time it will take to develop and the time a new system would take. Finally, other factors, such as the availability of hardware and experienced personnel over time, must be considered for both systems.

Experience and published studies agree that reengineering costs substantially more than starting from scratch. Perry [Perry93] calls this the "rat hole" syndrome, in which money is spent on the legacy system with no hope of recovery. The reality is that legacy systems in most cases have higher continuing costs, and adding redevelopment merely makes the long-term costs much higher than starting over. A rule of thumb is, reengineering is a viable alternative only when the cost of reengineering is not more than 50 percent of the cost to develop from scratch [AirForce95].

One of the issues with reverse engineering is that it is extremely difficult and costly. Consider a large, 15-year-old COBOL program in a typical corporation. Being a typic⁻l program, the specification, if it ever existed, is so out of date and incomplete as to be unusable. Thus, the code is the principal artifact for figuring out what the program is supposed to do. Because the software is regularly used, it has been modified, updated, and possibly adapted to run on a different operating system and target hardware than that for which it was originally designed. This would be bad enough, but not all the software modifications were made to fix software errors or add new features. Over the years, there were data sets that contained errors, so, scattered in various areas of the code are tests for certain values in records that take some special action if the value is found. These changes were implemented in response to emergencies, and completed late at night. Consequently, there are no comments in the code to guide the person trying to understand it.

Being judgmental about the state of the system does no good. It got this way because it evolved over time and it was useful to the company. Trying to reverse-engineer this program will be very hard, and when the project is done, a detailed specification will exist for a program that must be substantially modified. Moreover, just maintaining it in its current form will be expensive. This is a typical, or possibly simpler-than-average, legacy system. Unlike the enthusiastic recommendations for legacy systems, the reality of the situation is considerably more grim. This is why we do not recommend full reverse engineering as an effective method for redevelopment.

9.3 Object-Oriented Shell or Wrapper Techniques

There are three principal ways of dealing with legacy systems: use as is, reverse-engineer them, or modify them to fit with object-oriented systems. All of these approaches have their problems, but the one that offers the most promise is the third way, where a shell or wrapper is put around the legacy system to make it look like it is object-oriented. Some experiences using this approach are described in [Fayad96]. As Figure 9.3 shows, the shell approach provides cleaner interface because the target object-oriented system will interact with the shell modules as if they were objects or classes. The benefits of developing object-oriented shells or wrappers of preexisting modules are the following.

1. They make the preexisting legacy components look and feel like objects, classes, or object-oriented components.

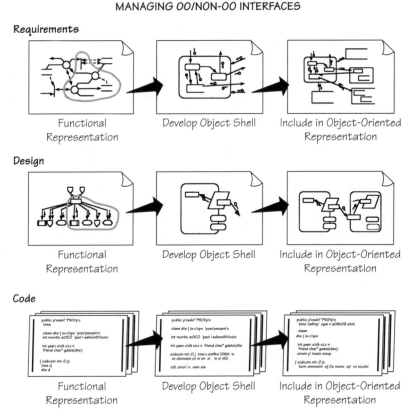

Figure 9.3   Object-oriented shell.

2. They allow easy integration of non-object-oriented legacy components with object-oriented components.

3. They provide substantial cost benefits comparing to other forms of reengineering or developing new software.

Object-oriented wrappers can be used with requirements, design, and code. As Figure 9.3 shows, the requirements and design methods for creating wrappers take existing functional designs and requirements from which object shells are created. The principal difficulty with this part is as previously described; it depends on the accuracy and completeness of the functional specification and design. If these are lacking (or if they don't exist), then the source code must serve as the requirements and design spec. In this case, the analysis costs become very high indeed. On the coding level, there are three properties that must be provided in the language interface when building a shell:

1. No data coupling. Data information inside the wrapper should be handled as private data. No direct links should exist between the legacy data and outside objects. If necessary, create messages that pass the data in and out of the wrapper.

2. Well-defined interfaces. The wrapper looks like other objects to the object-oriented part of the system. The interfaces should have the same stability and properties as other objects.

3. Information hiding. Each wrapper should make the underlying legacy functionality inaccessible through the object.

9.4   Summary

The apparent paradox of legacy systems is that the more valuable and used they are, the more complex, ugly, and hard to manage they become. As other systems using object-oriented technology grow, there will be a need to either reimplement the legacy systems in an object-oriented form to integrate with the new systems or to reengineer the legacy systems so they can be used with the new systems. The costs of keeping legacy systems in their current form are high as are the costs of reimplementing them or reengineering them. The most cost-effective method we have

Tips and Practical Advice

Lesson 9.1   Legacy systems must be recognized and dealt with effectively.
The presence of legacy software is one of the major obstacles to advances in software development methods. Developers do not know what to do about all of those applications that are implemented in some other language using some other development technique. Object-oriented developers have at least three options for integrating legacy software into new applications: (1) use it as it is; (2) reengineer it into an object-oriented implementation; (3) create an object-oriented shell or a wrapper around it. Option 3 seems to offer the best solution.

found so far that strikes a balance between cost and utility is the use of object-oriented shells or wrappers to make legacy systems appear to be object-oriented.

References

[AirForce95] *Guidelines for Successful Acquisition and Management of Software Intensive Systems.* Software Technology Support Center, Air Force (February 1995).

[Fayad96] Fayad, M. E., W. T. Tsai, and M. L. Fulghum. "Transition to Object-Oriented Software Development." *Communications of the ACM,* 39, no. 2 (February 1996), pp. 108–121.

[Glass92] Glass, Robert L. *Building Quality Software.* Englewood Cliffs, New Jersey: Prentice-Hall, 1992.

[Perry93] Perry, William E. "Don't Pour Money Down Rat Holes That Infest Your Budget." *Government Computing News,* December 6, 1993.

chapter ten

Budget for Reuse

10.1   Introduction

The object of reuse is to save time and money. The rise of interest in software reuse mirrors the realization that the time and cost of software development is not a fluke or a result of carelessness. Software development remains a complex, demanding activity that shows little sign of becoming quick and easy. Thus, other methods of reducing the time and cost of software development have arisen.

Effective reuse of software artifacts, such as processes, diagrams, requirements, designs, code, test cases, and test procedures from previous software developments, has been one of the primary ways of increasing productivity, software quality, and performance. Reuse itself is not a new idea. The earlier forms of reuse include function libraries (now class libraries), documentation templates, and utilities. Newer reuse forms include components and parameterized classes. But these methods of reuse have real limitations. They exist at relatively low levels and their use requires the construction of a program which includes them. They do little for the reusability of the larger system. Barnes [Barnes91] suggests that human problem solving rather than software artifacts is the value in software reuse. Current reuse methods look at higher-level forms such as design patterns and application frameworks, which have just that characteristic. These reuse approaches include not only low-level functionality but also higher-level design and domain knowledge that is embodied in an application. Most of this chapter is devoted to the reuse capabilities of frameworks.

When looking at reuse, it is important to understand that it is not just a simple by-product of software development. It must be planned, budgeted, and maintained. The obstacles to reuse can come from management through lack of support, incentives, and interest in outside help—the "not invented here" syndrome. Obstacles also come from economic considerations. Reusable software costs more to develop than normal software. It must have better documentation and testing, and it must be designed with a more general use in mind. Maintaining and cataloging reusable software also increases its continuing costs (see Figure 10.1). There are also considerations such as the need to interface with legacy systems that hinder the deployment of reusable software. It is often felt that software at the subroutine or class-library level will require so many changes in response to new hardware, operating systems, and programming languages that it doesn't pay to plan for reuse. Finally, reuse makes sense only if the software is likely to be reused. In many in-house developments, most software will exist only in one program, and replacement programs will have all new software. The current state of software reuse is presented as Fayad's law of software conservation, as shown in Figure 10.2, "Old programs never die, they just move to secondary storage."

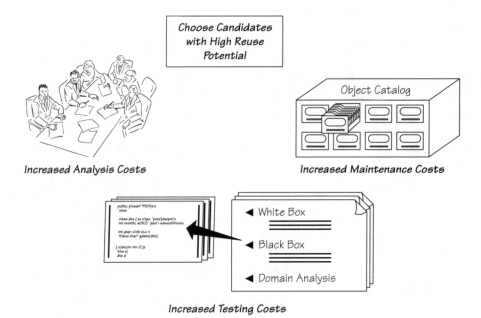

Figure 10.1   Caution: Reuse is not free.

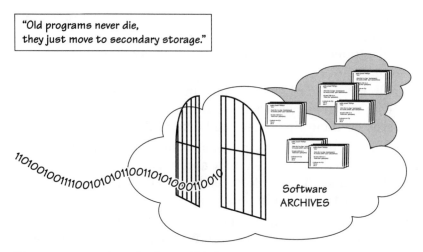

"Old programs never die,
they just move to secondary storage."
110100100111100101010110011010100011001
Software
ARCHIVES

Figure 10.2 Fayad's law of software conservation.

Strategic management is key to successful reuse [Schmidt-Fayad97], as shown in Figure 10.3. Successful companies will be the ones that achieve high levels of reuse by the following methods.

- Maintaining a long-term perspective. Software reuse makes sense only if software can be reused. And a long-term view of software as an asset is the way to plan for reuse.
- Creating reuse groups. The problems of cataloging, advertising, and maintaining reusable software may be ameliorated by creating software reuse groups that perform these activities. The reuse groups can provide projects with information about soft-

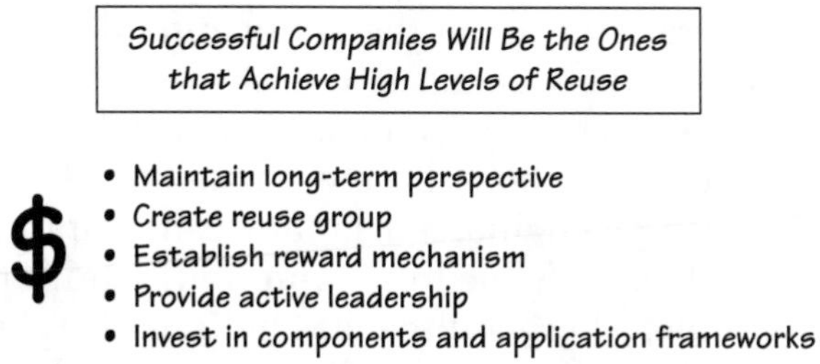

Successful Companies Will Be the Ones that Achieve High Levels of Reuse
$
• Maintain long-term perspective
• Create reuse group
• Establish reward mechanism
• Provide active leadership
• Invest in components and application frameworks

Figure 10.3 Strategic management is key to successful reuse.

ware that already exists within the organization that pertains to their application domain. They can also identify outside products that offer functionality less expensively than the cost of development.

◆ Establishing reward mechanisms. In larger organizations where project pressures overwhelm other considerations, explicit rewards for including reuse can be helpful.

◆ Providing active leadership. Reuse is unlikely to happen on its own. As stated, it is more costly and time-consuming to develop and keep. Therefore, leadership that makes reusability a high priority can aid in reuse.

◆ Investing in components and application frameworks. This is possibly the best strategy. Components have greater functionality and higher reuse potential. Application frameworks dramatically reduce the time and effort required to create an application or a family of applications.

10.2   Engineering Adaptability

If you want a system to be flexible, you usually have to engineer the flexibility into the system, to solve tomorrow's problems as well as today's. This is called going beyond the problem domain. It is important to look for relationships and generalizations that transcend the current problem domain by asking wider questions about the specific domain and what it is in general. Finding a more general domain and accommodating it in the analysis and design models can greatly increase adaptability.

In addition to generalizing about the application domain, it is important to speculate about likely changes in future versions. The changes can come from probable technology advances, user requirements, competition, and a changing customer base with new needs. The analysis and design models can be engineered so they can adapt to these likely changes. The goal is to satisfy the (often implicit) requirement that the software be changeable. These approaches help realize the three primary requirements of building good software as described in the following [Fayad96]:

Build the right thing means validation. The requirements must be accurately understood. There continues to be a great deal of effort spent to try to figure out what the right thing really is. The reality, however, is that the definition of *right* changes between the time when the perceived customer says "this is what I want" and the time the software is actually delivered. Therefore, the only way to build the *right thing* is with changeability.

Build the thing right is the notion of verification, correctness, and defect rate. Markets are increasingly ready to refuse products that do not have an adequate level of robustness and general correctness. Because the breadth of the market has increased, the average customer is actually less technical. This new influx of software users are not as forgiving of technical issues like technical errors and technical complexities. Also, core business functions are increasingly controlled by software. These forces combine to produce a big push toward simplicity of the software, and toward correctness.

Support the next thing. There are several approaches to make the software that we build today support building the next thing. One approach is the reuse approach where we build reusable parts, and these Lego parts get snapped together later to build something that's completely different. That works in the small (e.g., with little class libraries), but it doesn't appear to work in the large. What does work is to engineer changeability into your current system. Here are a few ways systems have to be changeable as shown [Fayad96]:

- ◆ Extensions mean changing the system's capabilities in amount, but not in kind. For example adding another graphical device to a system extends its functionality but doesn't fundamentally change it.

- ◆ Flexibility means changing the system's capabilities in kind. For example, taking a graphical system and making it sensory or sound-based makes the system more flexible. Flexibility is harder to achieve than extensibility.

- ◆ Performance tunability can be thought of as a change activity where the system design allows the system, after it has been constructed, to be enhanced without significant cost. Unfortunately, changing software performance may require some fairly deep changes (e.g., if the architecture demands a certain database structure implicitly), which causes a great emphasis on up-front performance engineering work. It is important to do up-front performance engineering work, but no one can guess it all; and, therefore, the system needs to allow some changeability at the back end.

♦ Fixability means the ability to fix one thing without breaking something else. This is surprisingly difficult in large systems. It requires, among other things, separation of interface from implementation and specification.

Changeability versus Reuse

Reuse is one way of getting changeability, but it's not the only way. For example, reuse of parts requires building little reusable parts that can, in turn, be used to build new things. That is a way of getting changeability, but it's very difficult to achieve it in a way that is reusable across different problem domains. Within a given problem domain, you can get some reuse of the parts. A better way of looking at changeability is the reuse of the whole architecture. As long as your system supports some reasonable amount of change, you will then have a system that's flexible, extensible, tunable, and fixable.

Changeability is the real goal and low-level reuse is a way of getting there—but it's not the best way, because trying to build reusable parts that are independent of a context implies that you're going to have to put a nearly infinite amount of flexibility into the parts. There's tension between flexibility and power. That is, the more flexible something is, the less powerful it can be.

10.3   Levels of Reuse and Corresponding Effort

Figure 10.4 shows the following three levels of reuse:

1. Reusing code by cutting and pasting source code. This level corresponds to reengineering.

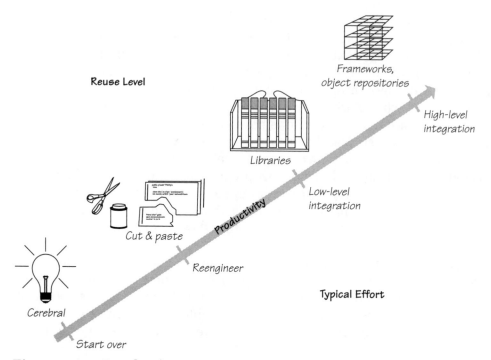

Figure 10.4   Levels of reuse.

2. Reusing libraries by including source code text from libraries. This level corresponds to low-level integration. Examples of libraries reuse are function and class libraries.

3. Reusing repositories of software components, such as design patterns [Gamma95; Siemens96; Pree94; Fayad95], and application frameworks [Fayad97].

Design Patterns

A pattern is a recurring solution to a standard problem. When related patterns are woven together, they form a language that provides a process for the orderly resolution of software development problems [PLoP2]. Design patterns help developers communicate architectural knowledge, help people learn a new design paradigm or architectural style, and help new developers ignore traps and pitfalls that have traditionally been learned only by costly experience [Schmidt96]. Gamma [Gamma95] provides an excellent reference on the types and uses of design patterns.

Patterns have a context in which they apply. In addition, they must balance, or trade off, a set of opposing forces. The way we describe patterns must make all these things clear. Clarity of expression makes it easier to see when and why to use certain patterns, as well as when and why not to use these patterns. All solutions have costs, and pattern descriptions should state the costs clearly. From one point of view, there is nothing new about patterns since, by definition, patterns capture experience. It has long been recognized that expert programmers don't think about programs in terms of low-level programming language elements, but in higher-order abstractions. What is new is that people are working hard to systematically document abstractions other than algorithms and data structures.

Most design patterns exist to support some kind of change. Each provides a specific axis of change, a specific hinge, where the system will be flexible. Very generally speaking, use a design pattern wherever you need such a hinge. If a system needs to be changeable, it is helpful to have some notion ahead of time which axis it's likely going to change along.

Application Frameworks

Object-oriented (OO) application frameworks are a promising technology for reifying proven software designs and implementations in order to reduce the cost and improve the quality of software. A framework is a reusable, semicomplete application that can be specialized to produce custom applications [Johnson88]. In contrast to earlier OO reuse techniques based on class libraries, frameworks are targeted for particular business units (such as data processing or cellular communications) and application domains (such as user interfaces or real-time avionics). Frameworks such as MacApp, ET++, Interviews, ACE, Microsoft's MFC and DCOM, JavaSoft's RMI, and implementations of OMG's CORBA play an increasingly important role in contemporary software development.

Classifying Application Frameworks

Although the benefits and design principles underlying frameworks are largely independent of the domain to which they are applied, we've found it useful to classify frameworks by their scope, as follows:

- **System infrastructure frameworks.** These frameworks simplify the development of portable and efficient system infrastructure such as operating system [Campell93] and communication frameworks [Schmidt97] and frameworks for user interfaces and language processing tools. System infrastructure frameworks are primarily used internally within a software organization and are not sold to customers directly.

- **Middleware integration frameworks.** These frameworks are commonly used to integrate distributed applications and components. Middleware integration frameworks are designed to enhance the ability of software developers to modularize, reuse, and extend their software infrastructure to work seamlessly in a distributed environment. There is a thriving market for middleware integration frameworks, which are rapidly becoming commodities. Common examples include ORB frameworks, message-oriented middleware, and transactional databases.

- **Enterprise application frameworks.** These frameworks address broad application domains (such as telecommunications, avionics, manufacturing, and financial engineering [Birrer93]) and are the cornerstone of enterprise business activities [Fayad98]. Relative to system infrastructure and middleware integration frameworks, enterprise frameworks are expensive to develop and/or purchase. However, enterprise frameworks can provide a substantial return on investment since they support the development of end-user applications and products directly. In contrast, system infrastructure and middleware integration frameworks focus largely on internal software development concerns. Although these frameworks are essential to rapidly create high-quality software, they typically do not generate substantial revenue for large enterprises. As a result, it is often more cost-effective to buy system infrastructure and middleware integration frameworks rather than build them in-house.

The Strengths and Weaknesses of Application Frameworks

When used in conjunction with patterns, class libraries, and components, OO application frameworks can significantly increase software quality and reduce development effort. However, a number of challenges must be addressed in order to employ frameworks effectively. Companies attempting to build or use large-scale reusable frameworks often fail unless they recognize and resolve challenges such as development effort, learning curve, and maintainability, which are outlined in the following as shown in [Fayad97]:

◆ **Development effort.**   While developing complex software is hard enough, developing high-quality, extensible, and reusable frameworks for complex application domains is even harder. The skills required to produce frameworks successfully often remain locked in the heads of expert developers.

◆ **Learning curve.**   Learning to use an OO application framework effectively requires considerable investment of effort. For instance, it often takes 6 to 12 months to become highly productive with a GUI framework such as MFC or MacApp, depending on the experience of developers. Typically, hands-on mentoring and training courses are required to teach application developers how to use the framework effectively. Unless the effort required to learn the framework can be amortized over many projects, this investment may not be cost-effective.

◆ **Maintainability.**   Application requirements change frequently. Therefore, the requirements of frameworks often change, as well. As frameworks invariably evolve, the applications that use them must evolve with them. Framework maintenance activities include modification and adaptation of the framework. Both modification and adaptation may occur on the functional level (i.e., certain framework functionality does not fully meet developers' requirements), as well as on the nonfunctional level (which includes more qualitative aspects such as portability or reusability). Maintenance of frameworks requires deep understanding of the framework and its application domain.

◆ **Cost estimation.**   Cost estimation, which has been well-developed since Boehm [Boehm81] described the COCOMO model, is not very advanced with respect to frameworks. The difficulties include the markets for frameworks, their increased documentation and reusability requirements, and their life-cycle characteristics. In addition, customers need models which will help them understand the economic trade-offs in buying, building, and adapting frameworks.

◆ **Investment analysis.**   This is an area which needs development. Lim [Lim94] describes the use of *net present value* (*NPV*) for both costs and time savings by reusing software. Net present value is the difference between the benefits and costs of an investment based on the time value of money. In Lim's analysis on smaller reuse modules, break-even periods were generally on the order of a year or two. For frameworks, however, the standard NPV calculation rarely shows a benefit. The reasons for this are the costs, the time frames, and, most importantly, the assumption of business as usual. Favaro [Favaro98] suggests that a new way of calculating value, *value-based reuse investment* (*VBRI*), which is similar to stock option valuing, is a considerably better investment analysis model for frameworks. In order for this model to work, the sources of framework value must be understood, both in terms of direct return and future opportunity. In addition, a framework investment strategy must be developed and it must be based on managing framework projects in a business context using appropriate financial modeling.

Software Components

Software components are higher-level objects that supply functionality. In general, they are more complete than a class library and may have multiple levels of integration. Typical component systems run the gamut from OLE to full-blown application frameworks. Ralph Johnson suggests that frameworks are forms of components that are composed of smaller components and patterns [Johnson97]. Reusable components have to be identifiable and self-contained and have clearly specified functionality, clear interface and hide details, and appropriate documentation. In some applications, components can add significant functionality with little effort. In some environments, such as Microsoft Windows, there are thriving markets for smaller components.

10.4   Budget for Reuse

We concentrate our discussion to economic issues in the development and use of frameworks because they provide the greatest potential for reuse and their economic models present the greatest challenges for understanding. Given their cost, determining their return on investment (ROI) is more involved than for smaller approaches to reuse.

Object-oriented enterprise frameworks (*OOEFs*) address broad application domains, such as telecommunications, avionics, financial services, and manufacturing. Enterprise frameworks are expensive to develop and/or purchase, relative to system infrastructure (i.e., GUI and Choice Operating Systems) and middleware integration frameworks (i.e., ORBs). However, enterprise frameworks can provide a substantial return on investment since they directly support the development of end-user applications and products [Hamu-Fayad98].

System infrastructure and middleware integration focus only on internal software development concerns. These are important aspects of an information system and are essential to the rapid creation and modification of high-quality software, but they typically do not contribute to revenue generation for large enterprises.

Even though well-architected information systems can yield a strategic advantage, an organization's information system does not directly generate revenues. As a result, it is often more cost-effective to buy an enterprise framework with a built-in system infrastructure and middleware framework rather than engaging in large-scale in-house development projects [Hamu-Fayad98]. Hamu and Fayad describe the budgetary, technical marketing, and managerial advantages in detail [Hamu-Fayad98].

Enterprise frameworks make the issue of data collection and reuse metrics more applicable. Since enterprise frameworks are reusable, semicomplete applications, there is greater emphasis on reuse. In fact, enterprise frameworks are real reuse. With an enterprise framework, the organization can enjoy the ability to collect data against a system which, by definition, is the cornerstone of any organization, and one can measure and estimate the following:

1. The cost and benefit of reusing framework components versus the cost of building from scratch

2. The percentage of reused and un-reused code for every application

3. The stability of the framework over time

4. The ratio of customizable components (business objects) to the number of industrial objects

5. The number of reused elements utilized the most in every application generated

6. The cost of extending a given enterprise framework

7. The cost of integrating several frameworks to build applications

8. ROI from extending the framework to an application or several applications and rank alternative framework extensions

9. Savings by collecting data to identify the cost drivers

Furthermore, the organization can apply several approaches to investment analysis, such as net present value (NPV), average return on book value, and profitability index.

Economic Impact

While early adopters of enterprise frameworks will have to pay a premium for these products and services, the framework economy will ensure that even very complex solutions will be deployed in a turnkey fashion, and, while hourly and capital costs may increase, lengthy implementation schedules will be compressed from years to months and months to weeks or even days.

10.5   Summary

We believe that the information systems space will be dominated by application and enterprise frameworks well into the next century. This will result in the establishment of a framework marketplace which will have a measurable economic impact. While the short-term cost of entry for application and enterprise frameworks is higher than traditional alternatives, the life cycle costs are less and return on investment is greater due to the ability to rapidly deploy and extend application and enter-

Tips and Practical Advice

Lesson 10.1   To support change, the system needs to have it built into the system.
Changeability is not accidental. It is the result of analysis and design.

Lesson 10.2   The whole notion of changeability must be a fundamental business decision.
Because changeability requires extra effort and possibly extra design features, it must be explicitly defined as a business decision. Its cost is most properly understood as being amortized over the system's whole life cycle.

Lesson 10.3   Do not expect huge gains from the first reuse effort.
The first reuse effort may not even break even, especially if reuse groups are formed and other startup costs are factored in. The real benefit comes over multiple revisions and multiple products.

Lesson 10.4   Designing for reuse requires extra effort.
As previously stated, reuse takes planning, analysis, and design. It requires greater initial cost and greater continuing costs, such as documentation. It may be worth it, but it doesn't come by accident.

Lesson 10.5   Reuse is not free.
Taylor [Taylor91] claims that standard, reusable objects will be the fundamental building blocks of future software. However, the development of reusable software modules may take more effort than application-specific modules. This effort will be more than worth it in the long run when the use of these reusable components can help produce finished software in a fraction of the time required with conventional techniques.

prise frameworks. Thus, the technical benefits of this approach to systems engineering are compelling. However, the benefits extend beyond the technical aspects of this methodology. Specifically, adopters of application and enterprise frameworks will realize additional budgetary, managerial, and market benefits resulting in bottom-line improvements [Hamu-Fayad98].

References

[Barnes91] Barnes, B. and T. Bollinger. "Making Software Reuse Cost Effective." *IEEE Software* (January 1991).

[Birrer93] Birrer, Eggenschwiler T. "Frameworks in the Financial Engineering Domain: An Experience Report." *ECOOP '93 Proceedings, Lecture Notes in Computer Science nr. 707,* Springer-Verlag, 1993.

[Boehm81] Boehm, B. W. *Software Engineering Economics.* Englewood Cliffs, New Jersey: Prentice-Hall, 1981.

[Campbell93] Campbell, Roy H. and Nayeem Islam. "A Technique for Documenting the Framework of an Object-Oriented System." *Computing Systems,* 6, no. 4 (Fall 1993).

[Favaro96] Favaro, John. "Value-Based Principles for Management of Reuse in the Enterprise." *Proceedings of Fourth International Conference on Software Reuse.* (Murali Sitaraman, ed.) Orlando, Florida, April 23–26, 1996.

[Favaro98] Favaro, John M. and K. R. Favaro. "Maximizing Economic Value in Application Framework Investments." Chapter in *Object-Oriented Application Frameworks,* Mohamed E. Fayad, Douglas Schmidt, and Ralph Johnson, eds. New York: John Wiley & Sons, 1998.

[Fayad95] Fayad, M. E. and M. Cline. "Object-Oriented Design Patterns." Course Notes, 800 pages, 1995.

[Fayad96] Fayad, M. E. and M. Cline. "Aspects of Software Adaptability." *Communications of the ACM,* Theme Issue on Software Patterns, guest eds: D. Schmidt, M. Fayad, and R. Johnson, 39, no. 10 (October 1996): 58–59.

[Fayad97] Fayad, Mohamed E. and Douglas Schmidt. "Object-Oriented Application Frameworks." *Communications of the ACM,* 40, no. 10 (October 1997).

[Gamma95] Gamma, Erich, Richard Helm, Ralph Johnson, and John Vlissides. *Design Patterns: Elements of Reusable Software Architecture.* Reading, Massachusetts: Addison-Wesley, 1995.

[Hamu-Fayad98] Hamu, David S. and Mohamed E. Fayad. "Achieve Bottom-Line Improvements with Enterprise Frameworks." *Communications of the ACM,* July 1998.

[Johnson97] Johnson, Ralph E. "Frameworks = (Components + Patterns)." *Communications of the ACM,* 40, no. 10 (October 1997): 39–42.

[Lim94] Lim, W. "Effects of Reuse on Quality, Productivity, and Economics." *IEEE Software* (September 1994).

[PLoP2] Coplien, J. O., J. Vlissides, and N. Kerth, eds., *Pattern Languages of Program Design,* vol 2. Reading, Massachusetts: Addison-Wesley, 1996.

[Pree94] Pree, Wolfgang. *Design Patterns for Object-Oriented Software Development.* Reading, Massachusetts: Addison-Wesley, 1994.

[Schmidt96] Schmidt, D. C., M. E. Fayad, and R. E. Johnson. "Software Patterns." *Communications of the ACM,* 39, no. 10 (October 1996).

[Schmidt-Fayad97] Schmidt, Douglas C. and Mohamed E. Fayad. "Lessons Learned: Building Reusable Object-Oriented Frameworks for Distributed Software." *Communications of the ACM,* 40, no. 10 (October 1997): 85–87.

[Siemens96] Buschmann, F., R. Meunier, H. Rohnert, P. Sommerlad, and M. Stal. *Pattern-Oriented Software Architecture—A System of Patterns.* New York: John Wiley & Sons, 1996.

[Taylor91] Taylor, D. *Object-Oriented Technology for the Manager.* Reading, Massachusetts: Addison-Wesley, 1991.

PART FOUR

OBJECT-ORIENTED PROJECT MANAGEMENT ACTIVITIES

Part 4 contains six chapters and describes how to manage a new OO development.

Chapter 11 covers modeling and prototyping. Object-oriented models and prototypes are a cost-effective way to study software designs. Software models approximate the target resource requirements, such as CPU scheduling for a software part, without implementing any functionality. Software prototypes, on the other hand, are functional approximations of some aspect of the actual target system. These complementary approximations can be generated to evaluate alternative software designs. Eventually, these prototypes evolve into rules of thumb to help guide future design decisions. It is important not to overdesign models or prototypes. These tools should be used to estimate resource utilization or iron out design issues. Once this is done, the models and prototypes should be considered disposable.

Chapter 12 covers project tracking and control. Large software projects require accurate and detailed tracking systems to provide insight into development progress. Using the tracking system, managers can ascertain the current performance against schedule, and project personnel have access to the latest development data. Deciding what information and how much information to track depends upon how the system will be used. This chapter describes an OO tracking system that identifies, estimates, allocates, and tracks the software objects.

Chapter 13 discusses process orientation. Defining and documenting the development process is an important step. The processes must be defined that tailor the OO technique to *our* project. The processes transform the theories of the textbook into the real world. Documented processes enable the development team to consistently apply and benefit from the new OO technique.

Chapter 14 discusses metrics. While documented processes provide the framework for improvements, metrics provide the ruler that measures success or failure. Software metrics are an important part of managed development, especially when the effort introduces a new OO development technique.

Chapter 15 covers software inspections. Software inspections substantially improve product quality and help to keep new OO development on track by reducing defects and decreasing overall cost.

Chapter 16 covers software documentation issues. Documentation may be the most visible sign of software quality. It exposes not only the construction, but also the logic behind the physical connections. Mapping an OO technique to documentation standards can be difficult.

chapter eleven

Analyzing, Modeling, and Prototyping

11.1   OO Analysis and Modeling Techniques

Object-oriented (OO) development places a much heavier emphasis on analysis and design than the functionally oriented approach does. The reason for this is to create good models that can be expanded into implementation-specific designs, mapped to programming languages, and coded, as shown in Figure 11.1. With good models, the up-front cost of analysis is offset by reduced integration, testing, and maintenance costs. Future enhancements can more easily be added because there is some assurance that the existing system is an implementation of its model and that system functionality can be traced back to system requirements. To put it another way, the analysis phase produces a model that is used for design, and the design is a model of expanded detail that is used for the code.

Tracing requirements in a large project is one of the most basic and, at the same time, difficult needs of development. In function-based programs, a requirement must be mapped to a set of functions in the design that satisfies the requirement. This mapping is nonobvious. Tracing back from the functions in the design to the requirements is not easy. Functions also commonly satisfy many separate requirements, and assuring that a change to a particular multiuse function doesn't violate some other requirement can be exceedingly difficult. While moving from functional design to code isn't nearly as bad, there are still significant problems involved in making sure a particular function is available to every caller who needs to use it.

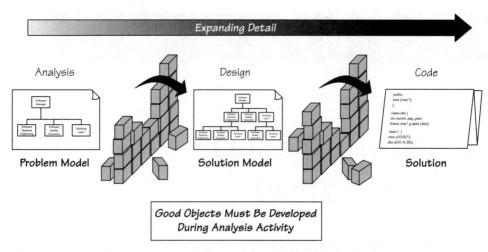

Figure 11.1 OO developments build upon models from previous activities.

A major advantage of object-oriented development is that each phase can be seen as a more detailed version of the previous model. A very high level analysis model may be the one used to define requirements with the user. A more detailed analysis model, but one which clearly includes the higher-level model, is used to define lower-level classes, objects, and associations. This model then becomes the basis for a yet more detailed design. Since object-oriented languages have some implementation of classes and objects, the code can be traced back to the design. Thus, even at the code level, an object can be traced back to its requirements. Moreover, everyone associated with a project can use some level of the same model for their particular needs, as shown in Figure 11.2.

A requirements traceability matrix is used in both traditional and OO development. The difference, as already stated, is that the OO model is easier to verify [Fayad97]. Figure 11.3 shows a simple example of a requirements traceability matrix and the two major streams of development that use it. The software development stream moves from requirements to code, while the software validation stream uses the same information to

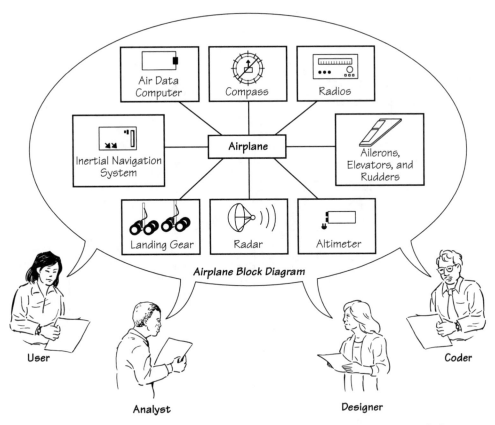

Figure 11.2 Common problem/solution model enhances traceability.

produce a test plan and test cases. As objects are integrated and unit tested (a function which may be performed by developers rather than testers), the software quality assurance (SQA) group validates the objects to make sure they match the requirements and then tests them to make sure they work as specified. As we said earlier, it is considerably easier to perform the validation function when objects and classes can be traced to requirements, and it is therefore easier to develop test cases for objects once they have been validated.

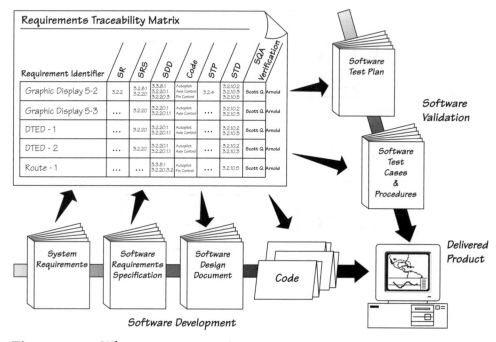

Figure 11.3   Where to trace requirements.

11.2   Prototyping

Even with good analysis performed by competent people, it is possible to develop a product that the user finds unsuitable. There are good reasons for this. First, customers tend to focus on what the system will do for them, not on detailed relationships in system functionality. Second, the behavior of even simple systems can be extremely complex. For example, a user interface decision may have negative ergonomic impact, but this is very difficult to foresee without being able to try it. If a user tries a finished system and finds that it's hard or impossible to use the first time, the cost of rework can be devastating. The obvious solution to this problem is to build inexpensive prototypes and base analysis, and design decisions on the results of using them.

For a transition project, analysis can be confusing. There may be cases where two object models appear to be equally valid, and there may also be cases where there appears to be no object model that works. In both cases, a good prototype can elicit information about the objects and their relationships that other approaches obscure.

Building a prototype reduces risk by providing analysis and design information that would be too expensive or technically too difficult to obtain otherwise, as shown in Figure 11.4. Prototypes can range from simple mock-ups of user interfaces to small systems that test throughput. In any case, unlike a full system, a prototype doesn't require the same level of effort in producing specifications, designs, and other documentation. In general, a limited object model is the most that is required. This takes less time and a smaller resource allocation than trying to forge stubbornly on with analysis and design.

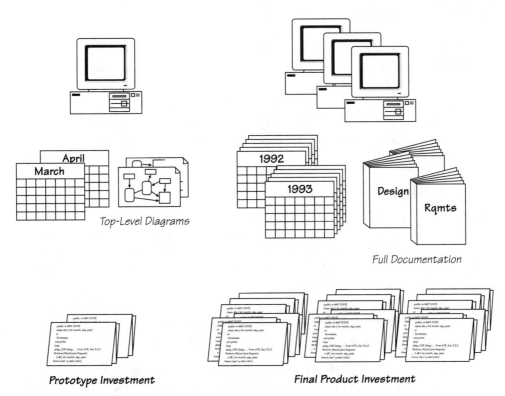

Figure 11.4   Prototypes save money by reducing risk.

11.3   When to Build a Prototype

When to Build a Requirements Prototype

Analysis is designed to elicit the requirements for a project, but it often leaves questions open. When specific questions arise during analysis, it is quite possible that the users haven't thought about what is being asked and may not know exactly what they want. Asking a user about various project details and behaviors may involve many "I don't know" or "I haven't thought about that situation" answers. These are not the sorts of things one usually considers when thinking about a system. In many cases, the complexity of a question may be great enough that nobody is likely to have a ready answer. Although this is normal, if the question has significant impact on the analysis, then an answer must be developed. This is where a prototype may be used. An iterative three-step approach is used, as shown in Figure 11.5.

1. Analysis is done and class/object models are created.
2. Where questions arise, either from a question that the users can't answer or one that comes up in more detailed examination by the developers, a prototype is developed.
3. The prototype is reviewed with the user, the object model is updated, and, if necessary, step 2 is repeated with the new information.

When to Build a Design Prototype

The usual purpose for design prototypes is to test the viability of design decisions. In a new or dramatically changed system, performance cannot be determined in advance. While algorithm analysis can identify a poorly designed module, it cannot guarantee that a well-designed one will work acceptably in a particular system. Therefore, other methods must be employed to assure the adequate performance of the system. Prototyping is a good technique for testing design performance.

The most common areas of performance testing are the following.

♦ **Throughput and performance.**   In OO development, message passing can create greater overhead, and some designs that appear robust in the object model can have excessive message-passing rates. In addition, language implementations can have

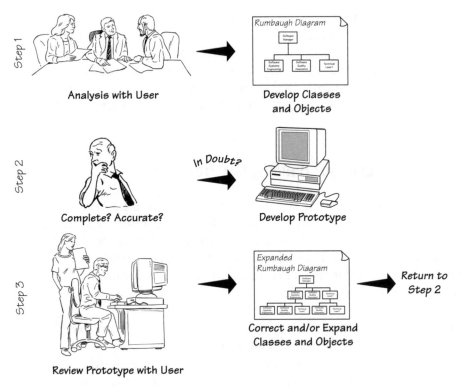

Figure 11.5 When to build a requirements prototype.

nonobvious impacts on OO performance. For example, virtual C++ functions do not cause serious performance problems, but sometimes the overhead can be unacceptable in objects that are called with great frequency.

◆ **Memory and storage.** It may be hard to assess the baseline memory and disk usage of a particular scenario that involves a number of object instances and messages between them. Therefore, information about how well the system scales up must be determined by simulation or prototyping. In addition, OO implementations usually create more object instances and messages, thus requiring more memory.

◆ **Prototype.** The best way to tell if I/O facilities are adequate for a project is to create a prototype that simulates I/O loading.

Although I/O loading may possibly be predicted from the design and the expected maximum amount of I/O transactions to be performed in a time period, the physical hardware and operating system can dramatically affect the system's performance. A prototype will give a more useful answer than the calculation. Again, OO, especially in distributed environments, will increase I/O demands.

11.4   Key Factors for Building OO Prototypes

Like every other aspect of system development, it is possible for the prototyping process to get carried away and become a model of the whole development project. Boehm refers to this approach as the build-it-twice approach [Boehm81]. This, of course, defeats the purpose of prototyping. In order to keep prototypes from having too much functionality, the following rules should be observed.

- Develop class and object definitions and interactions, but do not concentrate on object behavior.
- Develop the classes and objects that interface with the user. For prototypes that are modeling design issues such as throughput and capacity, the user may be sending and receiving objects.
- For classes and objects not visible to the user, implement the minimal functionality necessary to give the user a sense of the functionality. Don't make it too perfect; it won't pay off. In design prototyping, the equivalent rule is to implement the least functionality that can affect the targeted performance behavior. If the prototype doesn't give the user enough information, the prototype can be incrementally enhanced so that the user can evaluate its operation and decide if the new version produces the desired behavior.

11.5   How to Schedule OO Prototype Efforts

As shown in Figure 11.6, prototyping is a normal part of the development process and should be part of the schedule. As we say in Chapter

Tips and Practical Advice

Lesson 11.1   OO analysis and design dramatically enhance requirements traceability.
The objects defined by OO analysis bear a clear resemblance to the programming constructs in the target object-oriented language. This makes tracing requirements easier in both directions. In contrast, function-based languages force an awkward mapping from requirements to a very different programming language implementation of coded functions.

Lesson 11.2   Reduce risks by using prototypes early in the development phase.
Prototyping can answer questions, especially those that involve user interaction, more effectively than other analysis methods. Prototyping capacity and performance design issues can not only save money but avert system failure.

Lesson 11.3   Prototyping provides better and more accurate feedback for user interaction.
User interaction issues, especially those areas involving usability and ergonomics, are too complex to understand without the aid of prototypes.

12, meaningful estimates rely on the output of analysis. Estimating without analysis is just guessing. However, requirements prototypes are created purely because the analysis cannot be firmed up. This may make project managers nervous. In fact, prototyping of unclear objects and relationships can be done in parallel with analysis of lower-risk objects. By having prototyping experts available, and by using work packages, a reasonable amount of control can be maintained. Moreover, by explicitly scheduling the prototyping effort, the ratio of prototyping to conventional analysis and design can be easily seen. If the ratio is too high, it may indicate that some development teams are using prototyping to avoid the effort of learning object-oriented approaches.

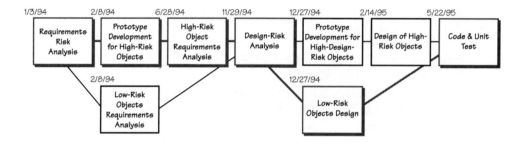

• Prototype efforts should be inserted in regular development schedule
• Prototypes do not eliminate the need for formal requirements and design

Figure 11.6 How to schedule prototyping efforts.

11.6 Summary

A major advantage of object-oriented development over earlier methods is the close and natural mapping that continues from the analysis phase through the coding phase. Object-oriented languages implement classes and objects which relate closely to the objects specified in the design. And the design objects look like more-detailed views of the objects specified in the requirements analysis documents. The OO approach avoids the inherent mapping difficulty of the function-based development approach.

The trade-off of OO is that this more obvious mapping requires much greater up-front effort in analysis and design. Good objects must be created in order to capitalize on the downstream benefits of object orientation. If too little effort goes into the early phases, the analysis and design will remain unstable, and it will diminish the value of the object model.

One way to make sure the object model is stable is to employ prototyping. Object-oriented prototyping helps clarify analysis problems that other analysis approaches leave unclear. Prototyping saves time and money in both the definition of requirements and the modeling of performance issues at the design level. Prototyping is an integral part of iterative development methodologies.

References

[Boehm81] Boehm, Barry W. *Software Engineering Economics.* Englewood Cliffs, New Jersey: Prentice-Hall, 1981.

[Fayad97] Fayad, M. E., W. T. Tsai, and M. L. Fulghum, "Transition to Object-Oriented Software Development." *Communications of the ACM,* 39, no. 2 (February 1996): 108–121.

chapter twelve

Effective Project Tracking and Control

12.1   Differences in Object-Oriented Tracking and Control

In order to be effective, experienced managers should be aware of the basic differences in the management and control of object-oriented projects, as shown in Figure 12.1. We list the most important ones here.

- Iterative development must be handled to prevent project *thrashing.* At any time, different parts of the system will be in different stages of development. While one object is in the analysis phase, another will be in the design phase, and yet another will be tested. In addition, the same object or group of objects will go through multiple iterations of analysis and design. If the development method is not understood, then it will appear that the project is in chaos. Further, people both inside and outside the project will be tempted to add just another feature or change a few requirements because, "after all, it's still in the analysis phase."

- Object-oriented projects will require access to support systems earlier in the project. Because objects are developed in parallel, it may be necessary to start testing, prototyping, and doing execution simulation earlier. This will require the appropriate hardware and staff.

- Cost sensitivities are different from functionally structured programs. The greatest costs in an OO project come up front, both in terms of resources needed and time spent in analysis and design.

IS PLANNING FOR OO DIFFERENT?

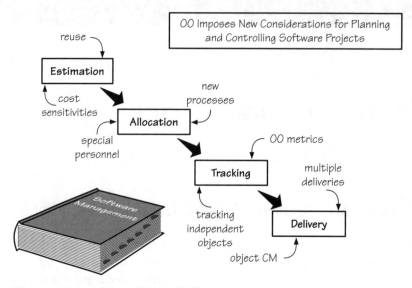

Figure 12.1 How OO is different.

To compensate, integration and testing costs are lower. Moreover, staffing and training costs occur at the start of the project. The result is that some OO projects may not appear to pay for themselves. But once the startup costs are amortized, the recurring costs, including maintenance and enhancement, are substantially lower. OO development then has a significant payoff. Reuse in its many forms also changes the cost and benefit equation.

◆ OO projects often have multiple deliveries of parts of the system rather than the traditional single delivery. Both the nature of objects and the use of prototyping make it possible and desirable to deliver projects in stages, each stage implementing part of the project's total functionality.

◆ New processes will be implemented. Some of these may be OO specific, such as dealing with class libraries and object configuration management, and some will be traditional, such as inspection and status reporting. In most cases, however, the documentation of processes will be different.

♦ Training and staffing must be more carefully structured for the transition OO project. In order to make it worthwhile (and to maximize the benefits), the whole team must be trained at once. This means that training time and cost must be factored directly into the project schedule. Staffing, likewise, requires that certain new positions be filled before the project can get underway.

These differences must be understood and the project tracking and control mechanisms must be adapted to deal with them.

12.2   Project Tracking

Large software projects require accurate and detailed tracking systems to provide insight into development progress. Tracking systems become even more indispensable for OO development because several software parts typically coexist in various life-cycle stages. Using a tracking system, managers can ascertain the current performance against schedule, and project personnel always have access to the latest development data.

Deciding what and how much information to track depends upon how the tracking system will be used. A system used solely to chart progress will contain less information than one used to plan future work. A system used for management overview may contain significantly less data than one used for future cost estimation. It is more efficient to decide what we want out of a system before we decide what to put in.

A tracking system identifies, estimates, allocates, and tracks the software objects or work packages as shown in Figure 12.2. We think of work packages as individual orders for which we contract and measure work. Work packages exist for requirements, design, code, and testing/integration. We identify sufficient information with each assignment to allow an external contractor, knowledgeable about the specific application and processes, to execute the assignment.

Work Packages

The typical work package allocates about one person-week of work. We found that this level of detail is sufficient to adequately estimate

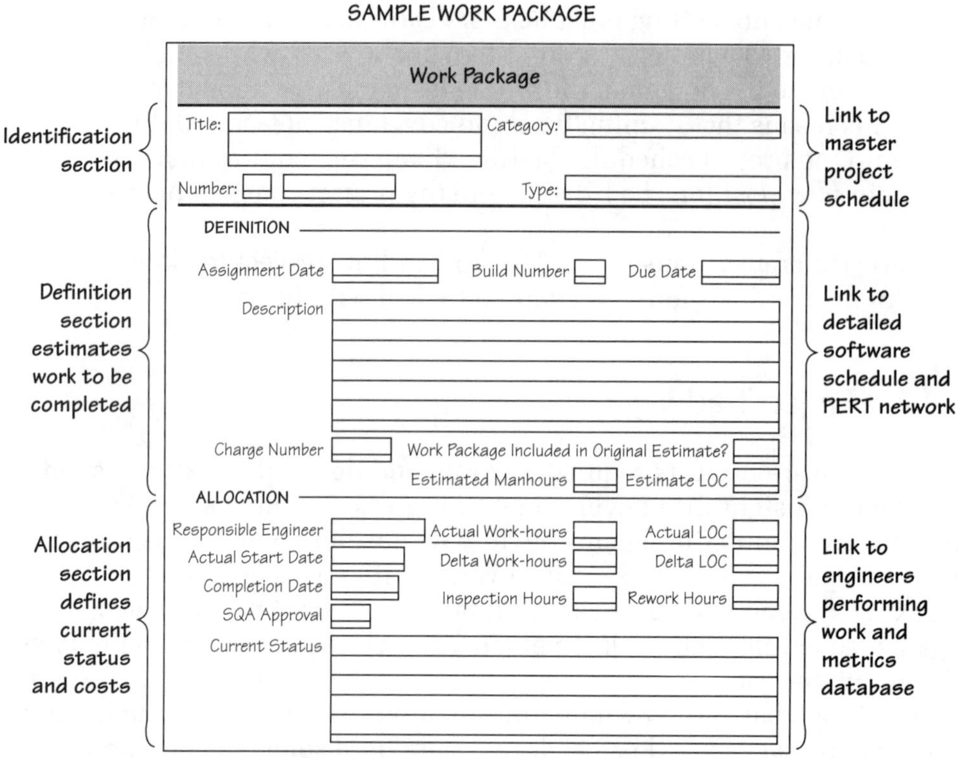

SAMPLE WORK PACKAGE

Identification section

Definition section estimates work to be completed

Allocation section defines current status and costs

Work Package

Title: _____   Category: _____

Number: [_]_____   Type: _____

DEFINITION _____

Assignment Date _____   Build Number [_]   Due Date _____

Description _____

Charge Number _____   Work Package Included in Original Estimate? [_]
                          Estimated Manhours [_]   Estimate LOC [_]

ALLOCATION _____

Responsible Engineer _____   Actual Work-hours _____   Actual LOC _____
Actual Start Date _____   Delta Work-hours _____   Delta LOC _____
Completion Date _____   Inspection Hours _____   Rework Hours _____
SQA Approval _____
Current Status _____

Link to master project schedule

Link to detailed software schedule and PERT network

Link to engineers performing work and metrics database

Figure 12.2   Work packages.

the work without being unmanageable. These typically identify several subsystems' requirements to define and prototypes to implement. This initial set of work packages recursively spawns additional work packages to complete the system. For example, design, code, test, and integration work packages are created for sufficiently decomposed software objects.

Additionally, we estimate the required effort and resource utilization for each new work package. Required effort is usually estimated in the form of person-hours or lines of code. Resource utilization estimates the required access to development facilities, such as unique test stations. The tracking system maintains these estimates to help establish and maintain realistic system development and integration schedules.

Work Packages and Earned Value

The work packages must be closed after satisfactory completion. The process mandates that the authenticating agent, usually *software quality assurance (SQA)* or system engineering, close the work package. Closure typically involves a formal review of the work, documentation of actual resources used or created (such as lines of code), and collection of appropriate quality metrics. Inspections provide an excellent way of certifying the completion of a work package. The closure of work packages earns value for the project, as shown in Figure 12.3.

In measuring progress, only completed work packages count. The 90 percent complete syndrome that plagues so many projects can be effectively eliminated by this. A useful way of measuring progress (and progress versus cost) is by assigning value to work packages. As Boehm points out [Boehm81], costs often run somewhat ahead of earned value, but generally the correlation between earned value and costs is good

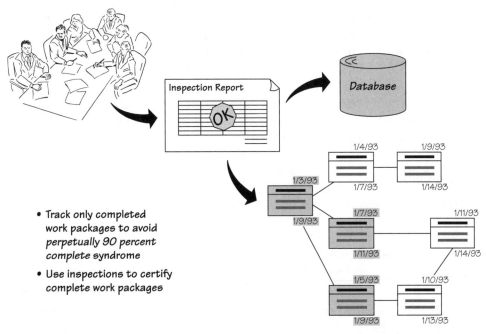

- Track only completed work packages to avoid perpetually 90 percent complete syndrome
- Use inspections to certify complete work packages

Figure 12.3 Projects earn value as work packages are completed.

enough to detect problem areas. Projects as a whole earn value as work packages are completed.

Work packages must be specific and limited. The initial work packages, as previously mentioned, will recursively spawn new work packages. While the number of spawned work packages cannot be absolutely determined (and in fact will only be known at the end of the project), historical data can be used to provide order-of-magnitude estimates.

Additionally, since the initial work packages are usually concerned with analysis (feature points, class/object, etc.), the second or third generation of work packages will generally include reasonably accurate estimates of the number of work packages in the project.

Work Packages Help Prevent Feature Creep

Work packages should describe tasks that take between 40 and 80 hours to complete. This granularity is small enough to provide good tracking, yet large enough to discourage micromanagement. Small time increments of work packages leave little room for unplanned extras. New features need new work packages, with prior approval for inclusion in the project and formal certification when complete. Developers, managers, and customers use the system to quickly view project status. Developers can identify what new work is available and how their completed pieces fit into the big picture. Managers can review the recently completed work, compare progress to schedule, and compare actual to estimated metrics. The customer with a limited access to the system can review the up-to-date schedule and quality metrics.

Tracking Considerations

Consider the following ideas before implementing a tracking system.

- ◆ Incorporate tracking system updates directly into the existing software development processes. The software development processes should specify what, when, and how to update. Complete compliance is imperative for tracking system usefulness.

- ◆ Make the tracking system readily available and easy to use. People naturally resist tedious systems, and resistance is the enemy of compliance. It is worth spending up-front time to ensure that the tracking system is as easy and helpful as possible. Automate key features, including extensive use of default or boilerplate data, and template data is always appreciated. Time invested in tracking system simplification is always well spent.

◆ Establish trust in the tracking system. The faith that is placed in the system must be visually obvious and unwavering. Set high quality standards and expect no less. The development team must clearly understand the importance of the tracking system and the potential results of neglect. This attitude will become contagious and spread through the group. Ensure the system works—and trust it.

12.3   Project Control

OO Project Control Is an Active Process

While the dangers of both micromanagement and lax management are well known, effective control must exist between these extremes. OO projects require more detailed tracking and control than non-OO projects because the former typically consist of many more modules for the same size project. In addition, OO technology allows various portions of the project to exist in different life-cycle stages. This is especially true during early development when the project will probably go through several cycles of analysis, prototyping, and design. While OO technology provides many benefits, it also adds complexity to the project management process, which, if not effectively dealt with, can lead to project failure.

There is no single best project management method for all projects. Just as projects vary widely in size, staffing, technology, and customer expectations, so must the methods for tracking and control vary. And just as organizations have different structures and core capabilities, the management needs from a system can vary widely. Therefore, each organization should plan to establish its own tracking system. This does not suggest that the whole system should be developed from scratch, but rather that analysis be undertaken to establish baseline standards for what must be measured and tracked, as shown in Figure 12.4. Except for very small projects with only a few developers, an automated tracking system should be considered.

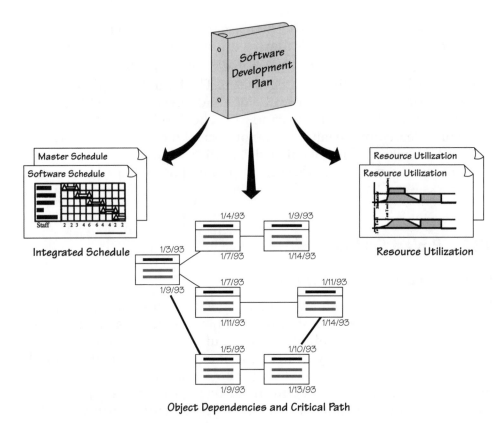

Figure 12.4 Establish a baseline plan for measurement.

Much of the project tracking needed is not specific to OO projects. As previously mentioned, any nontrivial OO project without tracking has an excellent chance of failure. Among the constituents of a tracking system are the scheduling system, resource utilization estimates, and analysis and design methods. Of these pieces, the only OO-unique portions are likely to be the analysis and design portions. This suggests that organizations already using project-tracking methods will find this part of the transition process relatively easy. Conversely, organizations without such existing discipline will find the transition substantially harder.

OO projects require more tracking and controlling in order to progress. At the design and programming level, the discipline enforced by OO, encapsulation, and data hiding, for example, must be preserved or the program structure will be destroyed. The result will be neither object-oriented nor procedural but will have the worst characteristics of both methods. Thus, the interfaces must be carefully controlled.

The basic feature of project control is to keep up with continuous assessment and respond quickly and appropriately to changes. A measurement plan using the tracking system must be implemented. The first part of implementation is setting up a baseline plan for measurement based upon the software development plan (SDP). From this, the project's master schedule, activity networks, and resource utilization metrics can be coordinated. The baseline plan includes original estimates and subsequent revisions. Note that all the estimates and revisions should be kept for later review during the postmortem.

Among the issues in OO project control are dealing with iteration, dealing with risk, and dealing with the inevitable changes any project incurs.

Dealing with Iteration

One special concern of iterated development is the fact that parts of the project may go back and forth between analysis, design, and prototyping as a normal part of the development methodology. The problem with this for a manager is to differentiate this normal iteration from lack of progress associated with thrashing. Williams [Williams96] gives some guidelines that help. If useful progress is occurring, then later iterations focus more on class details, and the identities and relationships of the classes becomes more stable. In effect, the iteration is moving more toward design and away from analysis.

Dealing with Risk and Change

One of the biggest project risks is losing time. To paraphrase Brooks [Brooks95], a project becomes a year late a day at a time. Response to slippage should be in proportion to the slip. Using work packages gives a way to assess the magnitude of the shortfall. If the project is set up with hard milestones made far in advance, then the risk of missing the milestones is high. By making milestones correspond to completion of certain sets of work packages, progress reporting becomes more meaningful. This is the use of an earned-value method. Incomplete work packages are worth nothing. Complete work packages have value. This eliminates the

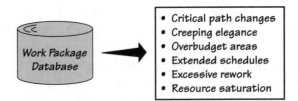

Figure 12.5   Monitor progress with
work packages.

80 percent complete syndrome (in which the last 20 percent of the work
takes 80 percent of the time).

Work-package monitoring also provides a way to identify and correct
other progress impediments, as shown in Figure 12.5. By making a chart
of work-package dependencies, critical paths of development can be
monitored at a reasonable level. Changes in the critical path can then be
identified, and if necessary, assignments can be changed. As stated earlier, the work package is short enough in time to discourage developers
from adding extra features, and people who want "just small additions"
to the project must have new work packages created, approved, and
added to the dependency charts. These steps help stem the *creeping elegance* problem. If areas are over budget, the delay can be traced to a
particular set of work packages and appropriate action (including refore-
casting) can be done. Excessive rework also shows up as a product of the
work package certification process. Additionally, resource saturation
shows up by analyzing critical path dependencies.

No method prevents changes, and rigid development processes are not
generally desirable, but using these methods gives an effective way of
understanding the impact of project changes.

12.4   Size, Cost, and Time Estimation

As stated earlier, object-oriented development offers a number of advantages that make its use desirable, along with challenges that make its
adoption problematic. For any project, time and cost estimates are critical management parameters. In assessing an OO transition project, time
and cost are even more important and even harder to assess. In this section, we discuss approaches to OO project software estimation.

Note that large software systems incur extra cost penalties. In addition to the greater planning, configuration management, and tracking requirements, the communications overhead increases nonlinearly for large projects. The traditional big bang integration method where modules and subsystems are integrated near the end of the development cycle becomes increasingly difficult (and therefore riskier) as the size of the project increases. Object-oriented development helps with both the communication overhead by enforcing encapsulation and with the integration by encouraging incremental integration steps. As stated before, since OO technology works poorly without proper tracking and configuration management, the OO project will have these features as well.

The actual cost of a project is a function of its size and the productivity of the development team. In order to use this information, it is necessary to determine the total software volume. Of course, determining software volume and team productivity are complex tasks. Before software size can be calculated, an analysis of requirements is necessary. Then, with requirements in hand, a variety of methods exist to estimate software size. Team productivity depends on the environment, team experience, and team member skill.

Fayad's Law

One of the authors offers his law of project estimation: "Successful projects have schedules equal to six months," as shown in Figure 12.6. A six-month time horizon is long enough to do significant work but short enough to allow meaningful progress measurement. For very large projects, incremental deliveries should be made at six-month intervals. Projects with longer time horizons encounter many hazards. First, both development software and hardware are evolving so fast that longer projects must assume that the development and target systems will be different from the ones they started with. Second, longer projects without intermediate deliverables impose far greater risks on the customer. (They encourage the 90 percent complete syndrome.) A failure of a multiyear project, almost always discovered very late in development, can be disastrous. In addition, only the most ruthlessly disciplined longer projects can avoid feature creep, a sure method of introducing many delays. A six-month project has a far greater chance of avoiding feature creep.

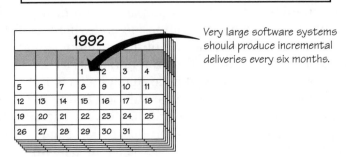

Successful projects have schedules equal to six months.

Very large software systems should produce incremental deliveries every six months.

Figure 12.6 Fayad's Law of Successful Projects.

Software Size Estimation

One of the oddities of software development is the tendency to estimate the size of the system before anything is known about it. "We want to put a database back end on our ABC system," states the marketing VP. "How much will it cost to ship by January?" The answer is expected on the spot, or at most in a day or two. Software managers are regularly asked to estimate time, cost, software volume, hardware, development resources, and personnel costs based on such nonspecifications.

The results of these estimates—guesses really—are wildly unreliable. In order to have any validity, software size estimates should be directly traceable to the project's requirements. In order to have such traceability, one of two general methods must be employed: a top-down estimate based on mapping requirements to an estimating method such as function points, or a bottom-up estimate of lines of code (LOC) based on historical information for a similar project. Both approaches are based upon the completion of requirements analysis, as shown in Figure 12.7. LOC estimations can, of course, be based purely on the assumption that the target project is a lot like the previous project (thus avoiding analysis), but the obvious conclusion is that the old project is just being reimplemented!

We discuss these various estimating methods in more detail.

Lines of Code (LOC)

Lines of code (LOC) projections have long been used as a tool for development estimates, as shown in Figure 12.8. While they have some value,

ESTIMATING SOFTWARE SIZE FOR OO
PROJECTS

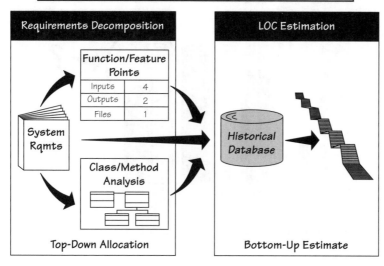

Figure 12.7   Estimation methods.

there are a number of reasons why they do not correlate well with object-oriented projects. First, LOC estimates become less meaningful for higher-level languages [Jones96]. Second, LOC measures are not standardized even in traditional development environments. Humphrey provides a good discussion of issues involved in developing a LOC measure [Humphrey95]. And new development environments can supply large amounts of code. For example, using Microsoft Visual C++ to write a Microsoft Windows *hello world* program results in the generation of thousands of lines of source code. In OO developments, LOC metrics are more complex since subclasses use superclass code.

Second, what historical data exists indicates that OO projects often have more lines of code than the equivalent non-OO project but, even so, cost less to develop. This apparent paradox is explained by the fact that object-oriented programs usually have many more modules, each of which is simpler and smaller than its non-OO counterpart. The source overhead involved in creating more modules will result in more lines of code for a given functionality.

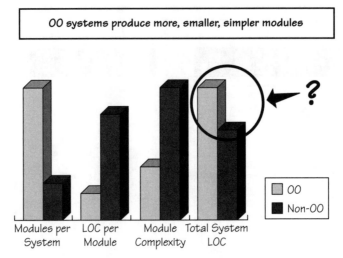

OBSERVATIONS OF LINES OF OO CODE

OO systems produce more, smaller, simpler modules

Modules per System | LOC per Module | Module Complexity | Total System LOC

OO
Non-OO

Figure 12.8   The OO-LOC paradox.

COCOMO

Estimation models such as COCOMO [Boehm81] have not been extensively calibrated to object-oriented development projects, so the built-in 20 percent uncertainty has additional uncertainty added based on the unfamiliarity of the method, the project type, and the lack of historical information available. Goldberg and Rubin [Goldberg-Rubin95] suggest an increase of 10 to 25 percent over what would be needed for a traditional project. Booch [Booch96] suggests similar estimate adjustments. Among the obvious factors in a COCOMO model that affect the project are the analysts' experience, programmer capabilities, experience with the target programming language, and the development practices, as shown in Figure 12.9. For an organization making the transition to object-oriented development, each of these factors will necessarily have a larger impact. In addition, at least two new factors, reusable part development and integrated project tracking, add to the impact.

Function Point Estimation

Function point analysis (FPA) is a different sort of estimating technique. The function point metric, rather than trying to estimate total code, mea-

ESTIMATING OO ENVIRONMENTAL PRODUCTIVITY DRIVERS

COCOMO model with basic OO extensions

	V. Low	Low	Nom	High	V. High	X High
Product Reliability	0.75	0.88	1.00	1.15	1.40	
Database Size		0.94	1.00	1.08	1.16	
Product Complexity	0.70	0.85	1.00	1.15	1.30	1.65
Execution Time Constraint			1.00	1.11	1.30	1.66
Main Storage Constraint			1.00	1.06	1.21	1.56
Virtual Machine Volatility		0.87	1.00	1.15	1.30	
Computer Turnaround Time		0.87	1.00	1.07	1.15	
Analyst Capability	1.46	1.19	1.00	0.86	0.71	
Application Experience	1.29	1.13	1.00	0.91	0.82	
Programmer Capability	1.42	1.17	1.00	0.86	0.70	
Virtual Machine Experience	1.21	1.10	1.00	0.90		
Prgm Language Experience	1.14	1.07	1.00	0.95		
Modern Dev. Practices	1.24	1.10	1.00	0.91	0.82	
Use of Software Tools	1.24	1.10	1.00	0.91	0.83	
Requirements Volatility		0.91	1.00	1.19	1.38	1.62
Integrated Tracking System	1.20	1.06	1.00	0.96	0.85	
Developing Reusable Parts			1.00	1.10	1.30	1.50

Figure 12.9   The COCOMO model.

sures a group of software attributes that are more meaningful for the customer. After analyzing requirements, determining the program type (a new development being different from an existing system), and determining what functionality is visible to the user, five separate counts are taken: number of inputs, outputs, inquiries, interfaces to other applications, and logical files. These counts correspond to operations and results that would be visible to a user of the system. Having acquired these measures, along with complexity assessments of each element counted, a function point total is calculated. This total can then be related to the size of the program based on historical information. A standards group, the International Function Point Users Group (IFPUG), has published definitions and complexity tables to help standardize the use of function point analysis. For non-OO projects, FPA is reasonably well defined and seems to provide consistent and scalable results.

Using historical data, both industrywide and organization-specific, it is possible to come up with estimates of function points per staff month.

Industrywide estimates are based on a number of factors, including language choice, project type, and industry sector. According to Software Productivity Research [Jones96], the gross U.S. productivity is 1.55 function points per staff month. But individual organizations vary widely in characteristics such as group experience, project complexity, and resources. The organization-specific historical data, then, will be far more accurate than the industry averages. This highlights the need for organizations to keep historical data and to continuously refine and expand their measurement databases. We talk more about this in the section on metrics.

For OO projects, however, the application of FPA is not definitive and not enough historical data exists to calibrate function points to size and effort. For example, in OO systems, if transactions are rated by how many classes they access, the complexity measure may be higher than is reasonable. On the other hand, transactions through aggregate classes may generate a lower complexity number than is justified. Booch indicates that function points may be equated with scenarios, which provides some consistency in OO projects [Booch96].

Note that function points relate indirectly to lines of code: for high-level languages, a function point comprises relatively few lines of code; for lower-level languages, function points comprise many more lines of code. For example, assembly language averages 300 statements per function point, while Smalltalk averages fewer than 25 lines per function point.

Feature Point Estimation

Feature point analysis, an extension of function point analysis, uses the same counts as FPA but with somewhat different weightings, see Figure 12.10. In addition, it adds one more count, the number of algorithms, to the analysis. In part, this was done to overcome the limited range of complexity measures in FPA. The FPA model limits the most complex component to no more than twice the complexity of the simplest component.

Class/Method Estimating

Class/method estimating assumes that analysis has proceeded to the point where the system's classes and methods have been fully specified.

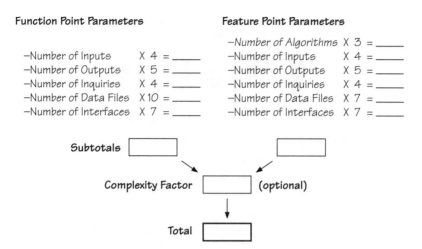

Figure 12.10   Function points versus feature points.

Then, based on some assumptions about the size and complexity of classes in the target programming language, an estimate of the development effort and cost can be made. One of the assumptions is that individual methods are relatively short and have no complex side effects. This assumption embodies good OO programming style. Similarly, it assumes that the analysis has not produced macho classes. A *macho* class is overly complex and usually controls too much behavior, too much data, or both data and behavior. Such classes are the result of poor analysis.

Class/method estimation has not been widely standardized, so using this approach requires that each project must develop a mapping to convert object counts to effort estimates. In addition, deciding how to deal with abstract classes that don't have program counterparts and dealing with parameterized classes adds to the complexity of this method. Nevertheless, with mappings based on data from previous projects, this approach may be the best match for object-oriented programs.

Specific Cost Issues

Large software systems pay cost penalties, as shown in Figure 12.11. Larger systems presumably deal with more complex problems than smaller systems, and therefore require greater analysis and planning efforts. In addition, since size itself increases complexity, the analysis and planning phases do not scale linearly. Communication between vari-

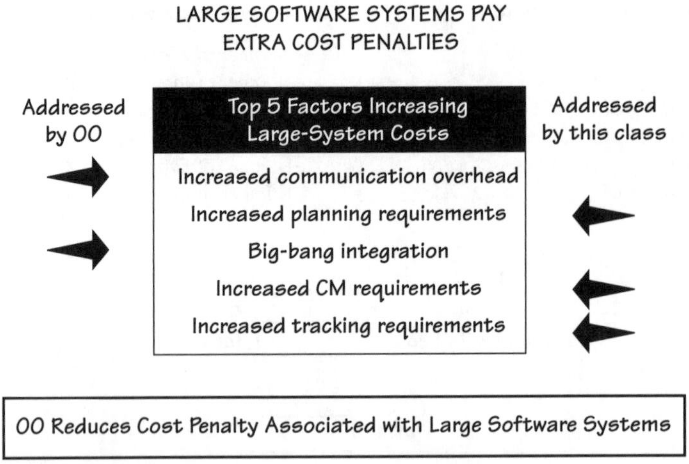

LARGE SOFTWARE SYSTEMS PAY
EXTRA COST PENALTIES

Addressed by OO	Top 5 Factors Increasing Large-System Costs	Addressed by this class
➤	Increased communication overhead	
	Increased planning requirements	◄
➤	Big-bang integration	◄
	Increased CM requirements	◄
	Increased tracking requirements	◄

OO Reduces Cost Penalty Associated with Large Software Systems

Figure 12.11   Extra costs of large systems.

ous modules in a system is likely to be very involved. Likewise, larger systems make greater logistical demands on organizations. As the number of groups working on a project increases, the communication between them becomes more complex. Configuration management systems must deal not only with larger bases of code, but since larger projects have longer time horizons, they must also handle more versions of both development and production systems. Project tracking also becomes more complex for the same reasons that configuration management does. In non-OO developments especially, system integration tends to be more demanding since the number of components is so large and their interactions not always well behaved.

Object-oriented software development does not address all the problems of large projects, but it does help in a few important ways. First, the communication overhead is limited by the nature of objects. Object interfaces are specified and fixed early in the project so that teams can program to them. Since objects are by design self-contained, a person or team working on one object should not have to worry about the development details of objects being worked on by other teams. This reduces the amount of interaction required between groups. Obviously, modifying interfaces requires interacting with everyone, but that is why interface definition is done early to reduce modification. Second, because design, implementation, and testing of objects can occur in parallel, the massive integration testing of traditional programs is avoided. The big-bang test phase can be extremely time-consuming and, in function-oriented programming, is the place where many late-term design changes are made. By reducing this aspect of development, OO programming reduces the large system cost penalty.

12.5 Issues in Tracking and Estimating

There is no way to avoid the fact that moving to the first OO project has an inherently higher risk of failure for a group just becoming acquainted with the technology. However, in most projects, the causes of problems tend to be depressingly predictable, and the majority of them can be put under two major categories: inadequate planning and inadequate management.

Inadequate Planning

- **Unrealistic plans.** One huge contributor to inadequate planning are the almost bizarrely unrealistic expectations that customers, management, and developers have about the time, effort, and cost of software development. Unlike other engineering efforts, software estimates are expected to be done without extensive groundwork, and the figures the estimates report are usually deemed too long and costly. As DeMarco [DeMarco82] states, "An estimate is the most optimistic prediction that has a non-zero probability of coming true." It is fascinating to observe that environments where the pressure is intense to be overly optimistic, even experienced developers and managers may succumb and agree to irrational estimates.

- **Lack of clear goals.** Although the cost of developing software can be very high, companies often are not sure about the goals of the project, and different departments have differing ideas about the project's necessary direction. This fuzziness legitimizes continual changes and delays in the project. Requirements gold plating can run rampant. The final project is likely to satisfy none of the stakeholders. Without clear goals, adequate buy in of all the project stakeholders is unlikely. This is also a manifestation of inadequate management.

- **Inadequate resources.**   Part of the planning process should be to identify the necessary resources for the project. These include development software and equipment, staffing, funding, and time. Note that other resources can be substituted for time only to a point. Brooks [Brooks95] points out that adding staff to an already-late project will make it later. As McConnell [McConnell96] clearly shows, there is also a minimum time for any project.

- **Reliance on unproven technology.**   New technology is essential for advancement, but even in the current frenetic pace of development, technology must be adopted carefully, with as much understanding of its inherent risks as possible. New technology takes time to adapt to and to work out bugs. Even if it pays off in the long run, there are up-front costs and risks. Many project failures can be attributed to uncritical incorporation of new technology [Glass97].

- **Overlooking necessary tasks.**   It is common to focus on analysis, design, implementation, and testing on a project, but to ignore other tasks. Because these tasks are so demanding, even experienced project managers sometimes overlook the many other tasks required to deploy a product. In mass market software, these peripheral tasks consume a large part of the development effort.

- **Inadequate planning.**   Inadequate risk assessment, unrealistic goals, lack of goals, gold plating and requirements deficiencies, overlooking necessary tasks, overestimated results (profits, performance), inadequate resources, inadequate staffing, and lack of buy in.

Inadequate Management

- **Lack of requirements management.**   Allowing requirements creep, feature creep, accepting unrealistic requirements, and requirements gold plating are all management failures that result in troubled projects.

- **Risk management failure.**   Not identifying obvious risks and scenarios for their resolution is a common reason for project trouble. Not every risk can be forecast, but certainly the most likely risks are relatively well known. In some failing projects, the risks are identified but no real response has been developed. In other cases, when identified risks become reality, political or other pressures cause projects to ignore them.

- **The catch up syndrome.**   Ever optimistic, managers assume that time lost early in the project can be made up later, so no schedule changes are made. In reality, if the schedule slips, the project will never catch up. Nonetheless, the catch up syndrome is almost universal.

- **Overcommitment of staff.**   This can happen from unrealistic expectations, attempting to compensate for lack of staff, and not providing adequate tools or training for development. Two common forms of overcommitment are assigning people to a new project before their current one is finished, and temporarily taking senior people off another project to help a troubled project.

- **Tracking failure.**   In some organizations, project tracking becomes a surreal exercise in denial. As the project drifts away from its original estimates, the tracking information continues to reflect the plan. Managers start believing in the catch up syndrome, definitions of complete are fudged, and finally, the whole thing disintegrates into a technical and political disaster. As things start to drift, fewer people are allowed to look at the project management information for fear that they will blow the whistle on the project.

- **Failure to enforce development standards.**   When things get tight, it's easy to give up on object-oriented standards (at least in transition projects), configuration management, documentation, and testing and review. All of these activities are essential for product quality, but they all take time. The price gets paid during the end of the project or in maintenance.

- **Ignorance of appropriate practices.**   Of course, it's entirely possible for management changes to place someone in charge of a project who has no understanding of software development. Such people are likely to allow destructive practices such as unrealistic estimation, reducing testing, or letting standards be ignored. There is no technical solution for this problem.

12.6 Postmortems

There is little time for thoughtful examination of the whole project while it is in progress, and, especially in the final phases, where all the organization's resources are concentrated on finishing, there will be no time at all for reflection. While much data is captured in a good tracking system, there is vital information that is captured only in the minds, and sometimes the notes, of the project team. Therefore, immediately after the project (within two weeks) conduct a postmortem session to review what worked and what did not.

In order to make the postmortem successful both technically and motivationally, a few rules should be observed. First, get out of the office. A nonconfrontational atmosphere without the normal distractions and temptations of the office is essential to make the session productive (see Figure 12.12).

Second, the postmortem is not a time for finger pointing. While it's proper to be hard on the project's processes, identifying a person or

Figure 12.12 Conducting postmortems.

group as the cause of problems is not appropriate and virtually never accurate. If the project encountered a great deal of conflict, consider using a facilitator from an outside organization to moderate the session. Be sure to include all the project's participants; otherwise, scapegoating becomes an inviting prospect. As an introduction to the session, reiterate the point that processes, not people, are the targets of the postmortem.

Third, prepare for the postmortem by bringing project data for review. Keep in mind that the sort of statistics to be reviewed are those that provide insight about how well or poorly aspects of the project worked. Among those that are worthwhile are size and cost estimates versus actual, defect discovery over time, interface changes, and late project changes. These statistics will provide a basis for review, but even more important is the need to bring out project experience acquired by the participants.

Fourth, examine qualitative feelings about the project. Do the participants feel the project was successful or not? If different groups have widely differing views of the smoothness or success of the project, examine the discrepancy. Encourage participants to evaluate how effective the organization seemed. Organizational problems may point out deficiencies in communication or in allocating authority commensurate with responsibility. Poll the participants to see how well prepared they felt so that a sense of overall training and experience can be ascertained.

Fifth, concentrate on what made some solutions effective and what made others difficult or unsuccessful. Identify, for example, difficulties in analysis and see how they affected estimates. Find out if there were design or analysis methods that were regularly not used or ignored. Remembering that the object of the session is to find out why methods weren't used rather than criticizing those who didn't use them, probe deeply into why. In some cases, it may be found that the methods did not fit the problems or not enough time was allocated to do the methods correctly. In other cases, it may be that insufficient training, inadequate tools, or inadequate management support existed. It is most often the case that noncompliance to a method is a symptom of procedural problems rather than staff rebellion.

Finally, and most importantly, document the postmortem findings and distribute them to the participants and management. Better still, review the postmortem document at an early stage in the next project

---

Tips and Practical Advice

Lesson 12.1   Avoid wishful thinking for project estimates.
Software is not trivial and it takes significant effort and resources to create. Exhortations and incentives, either positive or negative, cannot make an unrealistic schedule achievable.

Lesson 12.2   Estimates must come after analysis.
Competent planning requires realistic estimating based on requirements analysis. Estimation itself takes time. Trying to estimate without analysis is just guessing, and the results will be highly variable.

Lesson 12.3   Pay attention to interfaces.
In an OO project, development advantage is gained by having teams code to class interfaces and not to details of other classes. If the interfaces remain unstable, then much of the advantage is lost. A high priority of analysis and design is to firm up interfaces and then to drastically limit modifications later.

Lesson 12.4   Conduct a postmortem.
A properly conducted postmortem provides tremendous opportunities to improve methodologies and processes, as well as gives the project's participants an opportunity for some emotional release. But be warned: conducting a postmortem and then ignoring its outputs is destructive.

---

so that pertinent insights can be incorporated. Not only is there no point in taking the time and effort to hold a postmortem session if the results are not used, but the resentment and cynicism bred by ignoring the accumulated experience of the participants is almost impossible to eliminate.

For long projects, consider having minipostmortems at the end of significant project phases (at least every six months). This is soon enough to keep significant issues fresh in the minds of the team and to allow worthwhile suggestions to be implemented into the next development phase.

12.7   Summary

Let us repeat the most important ideas of this chapter: Estimation without prior analysis is guessing; competent project management is critical to project success; work packages make project control tractable; and postmortems are a valuable addition to the development cycle.

Poor estimation, a cause of many software project woes, is a sign of the industry's immaturity. Nobody would estimate the cost of developing an office building with the nonchalance standard in software, so why, especially when moving to an unfamiliar building technology like OO, would anyone expect casual estimates to be valuable?

Without competent project management, a large development effort risks failure. While there are many problems that a project encounters, most of them can be classified as a combination of bad planning and management failure. Obviously projects can encounter technical and natural disasters or can be cancelled for other reasons, but eliminating these causes reveals that the majority of problems are internal. For the transition project, managers must also be aware of the inherent differences in OO development.

The work package approach confers two benefits that make it worth adopting in any software development environment. First, it curtails the fuzzy reporting common in projects. With its all-or-nothing completion requirement and completion certification—usually as a result of successful inspection—it avoids the 90 percent complete syndrome. Second, it reduces the common tendency to micromanage project pieces. Even in large projects, some people equate good project management with tracking progress down to hour increments. The work package's natural size limits this. In addition, if used wisely, it can reduce that scourge of developers: meetings. The all-or-nothing rule suggests strongly that meetings should convene no more frequently than the average length of work packages.

Finally, postmortems can be an especially valuable tool not only for improving technical performance but also for dealing with organizational and people issues. The postmortem, done while issues are fresh in everybody's mind, gives feedback on processes and methodology that can't be found otherwise. Moreover, every project will have conflicts at many levels, and a properly moderated postmortem provides an opportunity to address these conflicts in a positive way.

References

[Boehm81] Boehm, B. W. *Software Engineering Economics.* Englewood Cliffs, New Jersey: Prentice-Hall, 1981.

[Booch96] Booch, G. *Object Solutions: Managing the Object-Oriented Project.* Reading, Massachusetts: Addison-Wesley, 1996.

[Brooks95] Brooks, F. P. *The Mythical Man-Month, Anniversary Edition.* Reading, Massachusetts: Addison-Wesley, 1995.

[DeMarco82] DeMarco, T. *Controlling Software Projects.* Englewood Cliffs, New Jersey: Prentice-Hall, 1982.

[Glass97] Glass, R. L. *Software Runaways.* Upper Saddle River, New Jersey: Prentice-Hall, 1997.

[Goldberg-Rubin95] Goldberg, A. and K. S. Rubin. *Succeeding with Objects: Decision Frameworks for Project Management.* Reading, Massachusetts: Addison-Wesley, 1995.

[Humphrey95] Humphrey, W. S. *A Discipline of Software Engineering.* Reading, Massachusetts: Addison-Wesley, 1995.

[Jones96] Jones, C. *Patterns of Software System Failure and Success.* London: International Thompson Computer Press, 1996.

[McConnell96] McConnell, S. *Rapid Development: Taming Wild Software Schedules.* Redmond, Washington: Microsoft Press, 1996.

[Williams96] Williams, J. D. "Managing Iteration in OO Projects." *IEEE Computer* (September 1996).

chapter thirteen

Defining and Documenting
the Development Process

13.1 The Manager's Roles and Responsibilities
in the Object-Oriented Software Process

Throughout this book we have been emphasizing the link between object orientation (OO) and controlled development. Object-oriented (OO) techniques by themselves do not include progress reviews, extensive documentation, or bidirectional requirements traceability, although such features are necessary to make any significant development successful. To address such topics, we need detailed, repeatable documentation that can guide and control our work. The process is the fundamental way of implementing that control. A process is a description of the steps required to implement some goal, usually part or all of a method. Processes transform textbook theories and method descriptions into real-action steps. Documented processes enable the development team to consistently apply and benefit from the application of OO techniques. It is essential to realize that processes are codified steps that describe a particular organization's way of achieving development goals. This means that processes cannot be acquired off the shelf, but rather must be developed over time [Fayad97a]. As shown in Figure 13.1, detailed processes are dependent on the application area, object-oriented methods, tools, and languages in use.

Fayad points out that, "Management must support the move to process-based development. This implies that process must not be abandoned when schedule pressures loom or process costs initially slow some

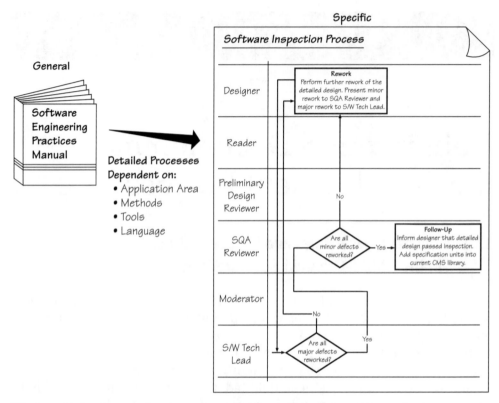

Figure 13.1   General processes must be tailored to your projects.

development phases. Processes are especially important for new OO development teams. Even in a well-organized group, new methods and tools introduce confusion. Individuals will often perceive themselves as less skilled than before, and the routines they had established with others will certainly change. Management must make sure that establishing process-oriented development will allow team members to contribute positively. It is management's job to show how processes will help achieve the overall goals of the organization and how each team and its members fit into the big picture. But perhaps the hardest challenge management has in promoting processes is to make sure that people do not view processes as weapons to be used against them. Promoting this view requires a change in management's thinking from the individual as the basic unit to the team, and from individual performance measurement to process measurement. Process measurement will highlight problems and errors in the process. If these measurements are used for performance reviews rather than process improvement indicators, the process is doomed to fail" [Fayad97a].

Measure Processes Rather than People

Process orientation has developed a somewhat tarnished reputation because of the way it has been implemented. The goals of process orientation are to improve reliability and efficiency, thereby increasing quality. Too often, organizations try to *install* quality by the use of techniques such as processes. With the increased emphasis on process as technique, problems may arise [Laitinen98]. Process paralysis and losing sight of the goal of creating products are common traps. Attempting to use off-the-shelf processes, devaluing skill and experience in favor of processes, and putting *experts* in the position of defining and imposing processes all contribute to the failures that have damaged the reputation of quality management. Having installed processes, some clever management types often decide to speed things up by setting goals above the current statistical average for processes. This is destructive. The only way to improve goals is to change the process. Processes are tools that, if done with a sincere organization-wide approach, can help improve work quality and increase productivity [Laitinen98].

If management succeeds in creating a process-oriented approach, the next logical step is to base management on the use, improvement, and measurement of processes. This is a radical step, and we cannot do full justice to the idea in this short section. We refer the reader to sources that expand upon this idea [Deming86; Latzko95; Senge90]. We lay out the basic idea by reiterating that effective development is a team effort. Just as the misuse of process data will cause people to subvert error reporting, a system of processes that allow one part of the system to succeed at the expense of another will also be destructive. Processes help organizational systems run effectively, and to do that, processes cannot be viewed in isolation. When we suggest a different approach to managing people and processes, we do not mean that traditional issues such as absenteeism and personal responsibility should be ignored. Rather, by focusing on the process, a fairer evaluation of people can be made. And because coordinating people to reach a goal that cannot be met by individual action is one of the prime tasks of management, measuring processes is an excellent measure of management itself [Laitinen98].

13.2 The Top Five Excuses for No Process Documentation

Process orientation is hard to adopt. Processes are commonly seen as extra bureaucracy that only serves to make a project less effective. In far too many cases, this perception is correct, and process adoption is resisted. Even if the organization is sincerely committed to adopting a process-oriented approach, many excuses will be offered at first. We list a few in Figure 13.2 and discuss them in detail in Fayad [Fayad97a]. Many others will require much effort to overcome. While there may be some truth in the excuses, they are still excuses rather than valid reasons for lack of documentation. The emphasis must be made to move forward.

Our short answers for these excuses are that undocumented procedures are not scalable or transferable. Using repeatable processes reduces avoidable mistakes and frees developers up for more creative, less routine work. Processes are meant for the people who implement and use them. Other uses are usually, and rightly, considered busywork, and such processes

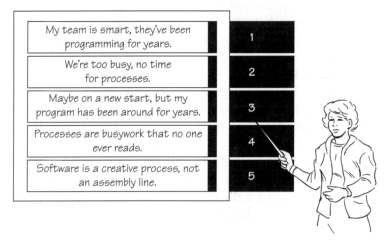

Figure 13.2 Top five excuses for no process documentation.

will end up buried on shelves, unread, and unused. There is no ideal time to start implementing processes, but documenting processes while performing them gives them the best chance of being accurate and useful.

13.3   Where to Start and How?

Very few organizations have established a set of defined processes for software development. Those groups having processes often have not spent the time and money to do real process assessment and improvement. It is common, in our experience, to see *processes* that are merely lists of rules in a somewhat arbitrary order. In many organizations, especially those trying to conform to the Software Engineering Institute's (SEI's) Capability Maturity Model (CMM), turning everything into a process has become a goal in itself. We believe this is the wrong approach. Software development organizations exist to develop software rather than processes [Fayad97a]. The intent of the SEI [Paulk95] and other process improvement programs is not to change focus from developing software to developing processes, but instead to use processes and process improvement to better develop software.

The Trouble with Process Assessment: Process Improvement Models

Software process improvement programs begin with assessment. This activity is intended to give a development organization a sense of where it stands in terms of software production skills. In most assessment models, the organization evaluates its development capability against a set of *best practices* that are supposed to be found in effective organizations. The number of practices, their mastery, and their level of integration into the development organization determine the organization's assessment score. There are a number of process improvement initiatives, of which the best known are SEI's CMM, SPICE, the United States Department of Defense SDCE, ISO 9000, and ISO/IEC 12207. Some programs allow self-assessment while others require outside certification.

The SEI's CMM is one of the best known and most widely discussed software process improvement models. It defines five levels of organizational maturity, from initial or chaotic to optimizing. Each increasing

maturity level, starting at level 2, has associated with it a set of key process areas. For example, level 2 includes (among other things) requirements management and project planning as key areas. Level 3 includes
training and peer reviews. Levels 4 and 5 include software quality management and defect prevention, respectively. Each level also includes the
process areas of its lower levels.

Software Process Improvement and Capability Determination (SPICE)
was developed as an international metastandard under ISO/IEC, which
doesn't aim to replace other standards but to provide a benchmark for
current and future process improvement initiatives. SPICE assessment
recognizes two categories of software engineering practices: base practices, which are essential practices of specific procedures, and generic
practices, which are applied to any process. It lists five process areas of
concern: customer–supplier, engineering, project management, support,
and organization. Capability levels for base practices range from 0 (not
performed) to 5 (continuously improving).

ISO 9000 is a set of international standards that mandates the existence
and use of written procedures and requires assessment for certification
by an outside organization. The idea of the standard is to produce written
processes that are consistently followed and can be continuously
improved. ISO 9000 certification is widely used in Europe and is becoming increasingly a minimum requirement for doing business there.

ISO/IEC 12207 is a relatively new standard that provides software life
cycle process definitions. Although it does not require outside assessment or certification, it has strong influences from the United States
Mil-Std 2167a and 498. Therefore, it may be assumed to be used as a
basis for contractual agreements between suppliers and customers.

Problems with Assessment

One difficulty with assessments is their cost. According to El Emam and
Briand [El Emam97], the initial assessments can be costly. Reports for
CMM assessments and improvements range from $100 per person to
many times that. The average time required for an organization to move
from level 1 to level 2 was 30 months and from level 2 to level 3, 25
months. The average cost in time for SPICE assessments was 110 person
hours, but it varied up to 824 person hours. For ISO 9000 certification,
the studies indicate a varying person-month effort based on the number
of people in the organization and the degree of preexisting compliance

with ISO 9001. The least effort reported was 13 person/months of effort for an organization that was 85 percent compliant. While the organizations listed in the study all reported improvements, only companies that had positive outcomes were included. Currently there is little data that verifies assessment and improvement always work. Assessments, then, are expensive, and in an immature organization the results of such an assessment are likely to be meaningless. For example, if a department does not use configuration management to keep track of product versions, there is no process to assess. Until configuration management is put in place and used for a while, assessment of this facet of development will have a significant cost but will not even serve as a baseline for further measurement. Time and effort could be better spent in acquiring and implementing a configuration management system. Even in more mature organizations, it is not necessarily valuable to do such assessments. For smaller organizations the cost may be prohibitively expensive, and the results point not at specific issues that will help the organization improve, but rather at ways in which the organization falls short of meeting CMM standards [Fayad97b].

The SEI's CMM is a valuable theoretical model of levels of maturity in an organization. One problem with it, however, has been its general acceptance as a meaningful standard for progress. As of this writing, a decade after the CMM was published, most development organizations are still at level 1, the bottom level, and only two organizations in the world are accepted to be at level 5. Most of the world's best known commercial software is produced by organizations at or below level 3. And yet, despite this apparent lack of progress with respect to the CMM, nobody would want to move back to the software of a decade ago. Given this somewhat dismal correlation between the CMM and the state of software development, it is surprising that organizations are being encouraged (or required) to be certified at CMM level 3 to get government contracts [Fayad97b].

There is a certain orthodoxy about placing organizations in various levels that does not reflect the reality of software organizations. As reported by El Emam, many organizations find the early adoption of certain processes, such as change control and code reviews, more effective than adopting them in the recommended sequence [El Emam97]. Bamberger reports that when she works with clients, she helps them look more at the essence of the ideas of the CMM rather than the explicit maturity levels involved so they can get control of their software projects [Bamberger97]. At lower levels then, getting a start in controlling projects is more important than orthodox progression through levels of maturity. Further, few level 1 software organizations believe they are at level 3 or above. While they would like to be more mature, as the SEI defines the concept, gaining such certification should not be a primary goal.

Another problem with process improvement orthodoxy (and not just for CMM) is that there is still no causal evidence that software process improvement initiatives (SPIs) always work [ElEmam97, Jones96]. As stated above, the preponderance of success stories to date only proves that organizations are not especially willing to report on costly failures. Even more interesting is the possibility that other factors may be involved. Candidate factors include improvements in software tools, the *start-up effect,* in which new initiatives get much more highly qualified and motivated people than standard projects and the idea of *heroic efforts* [Bach95]. We suspect, however, that as more studies come out, a slightly different perspective will emerge. In the past, for example, various worthwhile programs such as total quality management (TQM) and quality circles have been adopted and subsequently discarded. Upon analysis, the programs didn't fail; it was their application and the expectations that people had for them. Total quality management doesn't work as a technique; it only works as a fundamental approach to quality. Quality circles, likewise, are worthless without other enabling organizational changes. In the same way, SPI as technique may prove to be of little value. However, if processes are looked upon as tools, and if the effect of process improvement is to see how work is done and how tools might be used to improve the work, then SPI, we predict, will have a positive effect [Fayad97b].

Small- and medium-sized companies have been put off by the presentation of software assessment and SPI. There is no question that assessment can be costly, and for a small, lean organization, the overhead involved in meeting and verifying CMM or ISO 9000 criteria can be prohibitive. ISO 9000, for example, lists dozens of conditions and types of documentation required for certification. For these groups, if ISO 9000 certification is required, they may elect to buy an off-the-shelf solution that meets the letter but not the spirit of the requirements. And for a small group, the CMM level 3 requirements of training programs and peer reviews might be nonsensical. As Bamberger notes, the way CMM is presented often makes smaller organizations feel it offers them no value [Bamberger97]. Moreover, smaller organizations cannot afford the two- to three-year duration it normally takes to reach CMM level 3. If CMM certification becomes required for contract awards to subcontractors, then rather than fostering improvement, it will more likely become a meaningless regulation [Fayad97b].

Process improvement, then, must be tailored to the organization and with the goal of improving systems. The best part of assessment with respect to various standards is that a smart organization can use the assessment as a framework to evaluate how projects are done. And then, by conscious analysis rather than slavish adherence, the organization can plan and take steps that will improve its operation. We feel that the focus on the existence of processes, at least in the way that many people apply CMM and ISO 9000 assessments, tends to overvalue the technique at the expense of the goal. As we stated earlier, processes are tools that help with solutions rather than solutions themselves [Fayad97b]. Fayad discusses several problems with assessment models in detail. The *Communications of ACM's Forum,* April 1998, has several responses to a number of questions related to this issue [Forum98].

Process Paralysis

Because of the hype and pressure to improve processes, it is easy to move into *process paralysis.* Process paralysis, as defined by Yourdon [Yourdon87], is when the project team can become thoroughly overwhelmed by the new technology and gradually end up spending all of its time (1) trying to understand the new technology, (2) arguing about the merits of the new technology, or (3) trying to make it work. At the microprocess level, this paralysis can cause groups to forget that they are developing software rather than processes. Part of these problems can be attributed to a misunderstanding of what a process is [Laitinen98].

13.4   How to Use Processes as a Baseline for Improvement

A baseline is a formally agreed upon specification that then serves as the basis for further development [IEEE87]. The baseline is used as the measured starting point of each of the documented processes. Baselines provide indicators for major milestones. Milestones can be described as major development events, and baselines are major milestones [Bennatan92]. The baseline identifies the weaknesses and strengths of each of the existing processes. A complete baseline includes all the improvable facets of documented and tracked processes (see Figure 13.3).

13.5 Software Process Hierarchy

We categorize process hierarchy in two ways: the organizational level and the process granularity. We can identify a software process hierarchy in three major levels: the industry/government level, the company level, and the project level, as shown in Figure 13.4. The industry level includes the well-known government and commercial standards for process definition. For example, the SEI's CMM describes process models applicable to the whole software development community. It is much more of a description of a way to view the software process than a description of how to do processes. Government standards, in contrast, tend to be more prescriptive. The new standards, MIL-STD-498, J-STD-

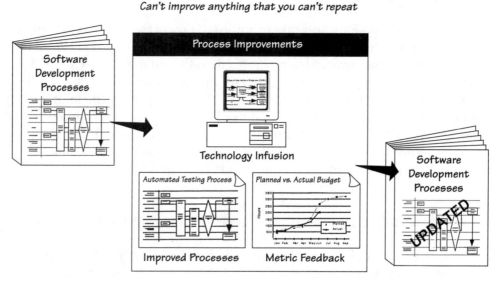

Figure 13.3   Defined processes are baselines for improvement.

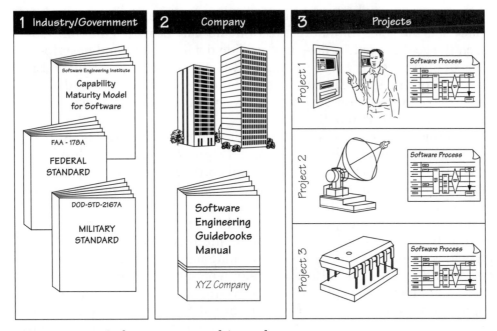

Figure 13.4 Software process hierarchy.

016, and the U.S. Commercial Standard 12207 (ISO/IEC 12207) describe which processes should exist at the macrolevel and what components the software life cycle process should (or must) consider. Naturally, these standards do not spell out step-by-step details.

Humphrey [Humphrey89] uses yet a different classification: universal, atomic, and worldly. The universal describes basic process steps at a general level, such as the spiral or waterfall models. The atomic level might include the object-oriented method used, and the worldly includes the specific and detailed level of tasks.

At the company level, the processes spelled out in detail are usually those that concern compliance with regulations and similar legal matters. Most company-wide processes will be relatively general, stating how divisions or departments will interact and what general life cycle issues will be observed. The company's software engineering objectives will be spelled out at this process level. In some cases, processes at the company level will essentially be policy statements.

There is a significant difference between a policy and a procedure. A policy sets the goals for an organization and may provide guidelines to reach the goals. A policy does not provide detailed steps and descriptions of operations. Since it is a high-level statement, it generally doesn't undergo continual revision and modification. A process is more detailed, has expected inputs and outputs, and is used as a tool to achieve the goals of the applicable policy.

The project level processes are specific to individual projects. At this level, processes tend to be specific and the proportion of microlevel processes is much higher. This level contains processes identifying groups and project duration. Many processes will be customized to specific projects with their own particular personnel and equipment.

Since there is no unequivocal standard for the hierarchy, we somewhat arbitrarily arrange processes into macro-, mini-, and microlevels. Macroprocesses cover the whole software development life cycle. A macroprocess would include the software development methodology, like the waterfall model or the spiral model. It would also cover the fundamental approaches used, such as the OMT or unified development. A minilevel process would include the methodology used to do analysis or design or a process existing in a phase of the development cycle. An example of this might be the OMT analysis method. A microprocess is one that covers a specific task and lasts for a short period of time within a project phase. Examples of microprocesses include defect tracking, object identification, or risk assessment. All processes describe *who, what,* and *when,* but lower-level processes also have more on *how.*

13.6 How to Document the Processes and How to Tailor General Processes to Your Project

First Steps

Defining and documenting processes is neither quick nor cheap. For an organization without a great deal of experience, the costs and disruption of implementing processes can be a risk. However, it is difficult to improve development capabilities without using well-defined processes. We recommend a slow start, documenting existing operations and reviewing any written processes that exist.

Defining a suitable format for process documentation is an important first step (refer to Figure 13.5). We have found that a combined graphical/text format was easy to understand, communicate, and maintain. The graphics provide sufficient abstraction and decomposition for easy communication with developers, management, and customers. The textual descriptions complement the graphics by providing additional details. Section 13.7 gives more details on a symbolic notation for process documentation.

A process describes a series of tasks to be done to achieve a specific goal. It tells who does what, when the tasks are done, and how to do them. The task descriptions list conditions required to start and continue, and the criteria for task completion. They describe measurements taken during the process for the purpose of control and reporting. Processes exist at different levels, from detailed descriptions of short-term, single-person tasks to high-level descriptions of the development process. The purpose of defined processes is to have a repeatable and verifiable way of achieving a goal.

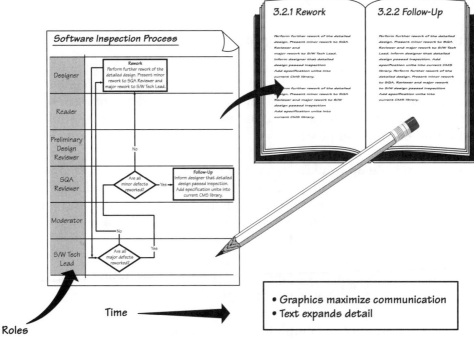

Figure 13.5 Integrated graphical/textual documentation recommended.

Microprocesses, those that describe specific, detailed tasks, look much like cookbook recipes, while macroprocesses, which describe operations and interactions of larger systems, cannot be as specific. For example, your software development process may be based on the spiral model. The documentation of that process will not contain detailed steps and interaction.

The process's definition concentrates on what and when software products are required. For example, what level of documentation is required for a preliminary design review? Which graphics are incorporated into our requirements specification? What is the exit criterion for object-level testing? We found that by precisely defining the software products required for each development phase, each developer can maximize individual contributions and still maintain system consistency.

The software process must be defined with sufficient detail that any competent developer outside the scope of the current project could correctly answer the question, "What's next?" Specifically, the process defines the intent, techniques, entry and exit criteria, and appropriate quality standards for each step of the development. Figure 13.6 shows appropriate process details.

Recommendations for Documenting Object-Oriented Processes

Having stated general principles, we now suggest items to remember when documenting OO processes. First, specify entry, exit, feedback, task (who, what, when) measurement, and approvals. These are essential components of any process documentation. Then review the following list for other essential pieces.

- ◆ **Concentrate on tracing inputs to outputs.** Traceability is one of the most important traits of successful analysis and design. One of the ways to ensure it is to make sure that inputs and outputs are connected in some understandable way. It is not sufficient to merely list inputs and outputs.

- ◆ **Identify all reviews.** According to the development method you choose, reviews will be part of the process. You should be able to identify in your processes the points at which reviews take place. Part of the review process is to define the expected products. These may be completed work packages or more significant items. There is usually no point in having a review unless

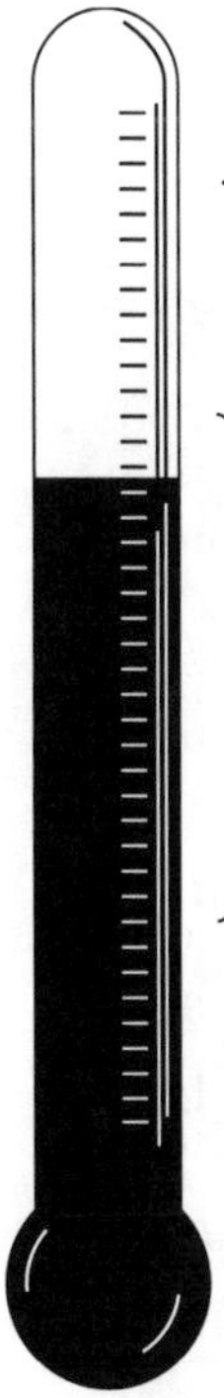

Figure 13.6 Identifying appropriate process detail.

its outcome indicates some action to take. This may be to proceed to the next step, redo the previous step, or to add another step to the process. In any case, the approval authority required to take action must be defined in the process documentation.

- **Identify where configuration management occurs.** Configuration management defines versions, revisions milestones, and components of a project. These are all items to be documented in the development process.

- **Consistently specify all roles involved.** Developers, Software Quality Assurance (SQA), testers, customers, marketing, sales, and management will have functions in any project, although not all phases will include all groups. A consistent method of identifying the roles will make the process documentation more understandable.

- **Map method products to each software activity.** Object-oriented development will have many outputs: graphics, tables, text, configuration management object, code, and other repositories. Documentation should identify what product is used in what software development activity. For example, object interaction diagrams would be mapped to the design phase and would contain graphic depictions of message flow between objects.

- **Identify what/when from CASE tools.** Computer-aided software engineering tools, to be useful, must produce output that is integral to the process. Interface descriptions, for example, may be one of the outputs. These should be identified in process documentation. If some action depends on the output of a CASE tool, this should also be described.

- **Identify appropriate OO notation for documentation.** Having decided on an OO development method, it is essential that the documentation describe the method using the same notation as is used in analysis and design. Output from CASE tools may be the way to get this notation into the documentation.

- **Specify what level of coordination must exist between objects.** This information may be documented with the help of interaction diagrams, object flow diagrams, state transition diagrams, and interface descriptions. Again, CASE tool output may provide these items.

13.7   Process Documentation

Symbolic Notation

We present here an introduction to a symbolic notation for process documentation. The advantage to a symbolic notation is that it is easier to follow than the equivalent textual description. Detailed text items can be attached to the symbolic notation for further clarification, if necessary. Missing or overly complex steps tend to show up quickly in symbolic notation, as do unintended loops and other bottlenecks. Figures 13.7a and 13.7b show a notation scheme that will aid in reading the process. Appendix A has complete examples using the following notation to illustrate several processes.

Roles		Input description—process inputs (i.e., tools and information)
Roles 1		
Roles 2		**Process Step Name**
	Participant's Chart	
• •		Output description—process inputs (i.e., tools, manual, and information)
Role N		Transition Arrow ➔

Figure 13.7a Process symbolic notation.

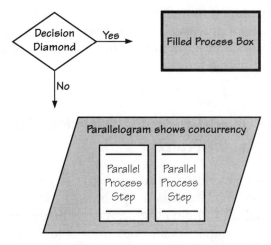

Figure 13.7b Process symbolic notation.

◆ Participant's Chart identifies roles where the persons performing the process are showing between the horizontal lines.

◆ Process Step Name contains three components: (1) input description that describes process inputs, such as tools and information; (2) name of the process step and a procedure; and (3) output description that describes process outputs such as products.

◆ Transition Arrow indicates the transition from one process step to the next.

◆ Decision Diamond indicates that a decision must be made before the next step.

◆ Filled Process Box decomposes further to subprocesses or describes a step of a procedure that has further detail provided at the lower level.

◆ Parallelogram contains two or more process boxes. These process boxes may be concurrent or may be performed in any order.

Template

The following template (Figure 13.8) gives a layout for documenting the essential elements of a process. It can be used along with the symbolic notation to document a process fully. Appendix A has a complete example of using the following template.

13.8 Impact of Object-Oriented Development Processes on Managing the Project

For an organization just starting the move to process-oriented engineering, the effort can be significant and the impact can be disconcerting at first. One of the major problems with any significant change is reorienting the experience of managers and developers to the new norms. We especially expect management to understand trouble signs in a project, but both the ramp-up of learning new methods and the changing types and duration of the methods make trouble spotting difficult. One thing

Item	Description
Process title	Defines process name, such as Software Inspection Process
Process #	Process number for software configuration management
Date	Creation or last modification date
Created/modified by	Person/group/department name
Definitions	Defines all the special concepts and roles in the process
Rationale	Identifies the *what* part of the process definition. What is this process for? You need to state only the ultimate reason for the process to exist.
Roles and how	Identifies the *who* and the *how* of the process definition, such as the process participants and their responsibilities. This section identifies also the following process steps: 1. Known inputs to the process (the things required to start the process step or the entire process) 2. Known outputs to the process (the product of the process step or the process) 3. Known steps in the process of substeps of each single step of the process
When	Identifies the *when* part of the process. This section answers the following question, "When should the process be applied?"
Regulations	Defines all the constraints related to this process. This section also describes the major process properties.
Checklists	(Optional) Defines guidelines for applying the process
Forms	Identifies and documents the process findings and collects data for process measurement.
Notes	Lists problems encountered and participants' suggestions

Figure 13.8   Process documentation template.

is certain for object-oriented development: more time will be spent in analysis than in traditional development. Generally, the design phase is also longer. While we expect these costs to be offset by lower overall development time and reduced maintenance time, the cost changes must be understood.

We describe in Chapter 8 training approaches that can help the transition to OO development. While training is often regarded as an extra cost item or an employee benefit, we feel that there is so much to absorb in moving to object-oriented processes that formal training is absolutely necessary. In fact, training should be considered a strategic advantage of the organization. The down side, of course, is that training is expensive, both in direct cost and in personnel availability, and it must be conducted over an extended period.

One of the firm requirements of significant object-oriented development is that analysis and design artifacts (for example, the interfaces between objects) be firmly defined and controlled. For significant development, CASE tools must be employed to help ensure such control. We discussed CASE tool selection in Chapter 6, so we only mention here that the cost of the tools and time of selecting and learning them is a significant project impact. In fact, it is unlikely that integrating CASE tools into the development process is a one-time cost. Each project will have different needs and hence different object modeling requirements. As experience grows with a modeling method, the CASE tools will be used differently.

The use of iterative development models (necessary for OO) will change the need, character, and frequency of reviews. As an example, it may be reasonable for an analysis artifact that has gone through multiple iterations to have a more limited inspection than one that is just starting out. As discussed in Chapter 15, new technology makes it possible to change the number of people participating in inspections, so that larger, more complex objects may be inspected by more people than would be possible in a conventional inspection meeting.

We have talked at length about the impacts of object-oriented development methods on the management of the project. Here we state again that moving to OO methods will take time, effort, and money. Moving to a process-oriented software engineering will be similarly costly. If there were no advantages to process improvement and OO development, then it would be extremely foolish to undertake the changes. But experience has shown that process improvement and object-oriented development have substantial long-term benefits, once they're mastered, throughout the life cycle of the projects. Object-oriented development helps fulfill the fundamental goals of software engineering. As Figure 13.9 details, OO development provides formal mechanisms to address such principles as:

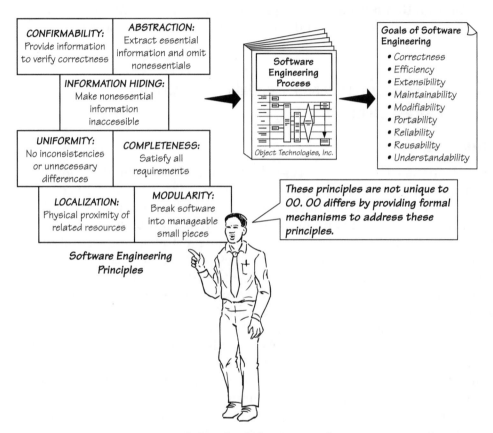

Figure 13.9 Incorporate OO principles into software processes.

Confirmability. By providing information in the model to verify correctness

Abstraction. At various levels of detail, to extract only essential information about the system

Uniformity. Elimination of inconsistencies and unnecessary differences

Completeness. Assuring that all requirements are satisfied

Localization. Assuring that related resources are in proximity

Modularity. Software is divided into manageable portions

Information hiding. Limiting access to information to those functions that require it, and then only by well-defined access means

13.9   Process Criteria and Essential Object-Oriented Process Elements

Macroprocesses

Organizations new to iterative development and OO technology should probably not develop elaborate macroprocesses in advance. (This does not imply that you should develop without a software development plan.) Whether the software process swirls in a spiral or spurts like a fountain is far less important than developing a strategy for estimation and control. The work package concept, estimating tools, and a way of assessing progress and necessary change should be documented and modified as development progresses. Some of these areas may never achieve a cookbooklike level of repeatability. For example, the spiral model shows prototyping and risk analysis at every full turn of the spiral, but the order in which these actions occur is usually not critical, and trying to specify the order in the process is most likely a waste of time. This does not mean, however, that macroprocess actions should be ignored, undocumented, or not measured for improvement. Macroprocesses tend to control most or all of a software life cycle and almost always extend across functional boundaries of the organization.

Miniprocesses

Object-oriented analysis, design, and development require experience to master. As you progress on a project, attempt to capture the phase-level processes used and review regularly to see how they are changing. Do not attempt to codify the process too soon, especially analysis and design, since they will be evolving as experience with it grows. This does not suggest that you have a haphazard approach to analysis or design. The analysis and design methods must be in place before you begin; appropriate training must have taken place; and an object/method expert must be available to help keep analysis on the right track. However, the details of using the methods and the sequence of work will vary as experience grows. This same advice is true of all the miniprocesses of development. If you are new to OO methodology, the way you use it will be changing rapidly. It will already be expensive enough to take the time and effort to capture the processes used without trying to formalize them too soon. At first you may want to develop usage notes or other less formal guides. Similarly, avoid gathering too many metrics at early stages. Not only are they expensive and disruptive, but since a new process is hardly likely to be in statistical control, all but the grossest measurements will have little or no meaning.

Microprocesses

Attending to microprocesses may be every bit as important as the higher-level processes: they form the day-to-day systems that take most of the time and effort in development. Because "everybody knows how to do microprocesses," and they tend to cover unglamorous tasks, they are often the most overlooked and least organized portion of the process hierarchy. Besides, people are doing these tasks regularly, as part of their normal activities, even if the tasks are not formally documented. In fact, documenting and improving microprocesses can dramatically smooth the development operation and allow more resources to be focused on the new features of OO engineering. A good microprocess gives specific steps to accomplish a task. Each task should have a clear set of preconditions for starting the task and clear indications of task completion. Using a schematic approach to documenting the process can help avoid gaps, redundancies, and unintended loops.

Be especially sensitive when creating microprocesses to the level of skill required to perform it and the fragility of the process tasks. If performing a routine task requires expert skill, then the process should be analyzed to see if it can be simplified. Note that some processes legitimately require high skill levels to execute, but sometimes the process is unnecessarily complex. By fragility, we mean the likelihood that a person familiar with the process can perform tasks incorrectly (thus causing serious delay) or can perform the tasks incorrectly without clear error indications. An example of a fragile task might be a data entry procedure in which a single keystroke error requires starting the task over from the beginning. Another example might be a program build task in which a syntax error in a source module doesn't stop the build but merely prints an error message on scrolling output. This latter error might not be discovered for some time if the previous version of the executable is in the location where the updated executable was to go.

While the warnings about formalizing processes too quickly don't usually apply to microprocesses (they should be specific), process paralysis and overprocessizing should be avoided. The benefit of turning some actions into a process, or the liability of not codifying some set of actions, should be compared with initial and continuing costs of having the process.

Who Does the Process?

The people performing the process must own the process. While a process group may be essential in helping to capture a process or analyze a process, it is the group using the process that is likely to have the best understanding of its purpose and appropriate use. In fact, we recommend forming a process team to document exactly how to apply OO techniques. This team should consist of members from all phases of software development: systems analysts, designers, programmers, quality assurance, and testers. The team should meet regularly to determine what, how, and when to document. Obviously, the people who will perform the processes should be included in the meetings.

There are a number of issues regarding who does the processes. First, processes do not usually eliminate the need for skill and experience. For example, if defect tracking has been done on an ad hoc basis with software developers doing the work, implementing a process would not necessarily allow the task to be done by clerical staff. The judgment of the developers would still be required, but the reporting functions could be done by others. (In some relatively rare cases, where the use of highly trained people compensates for a total lack of process, defining and implementing a process can allow less-experienced people to do the same work.)

Second, it is important to recognize that the people performing a task may well know what they are doing. The knowledge of the people doing tasks must be used as the basis for defining the new process. This suggests that when process specialists or team members from other groups are brought in to help define the process, they should not assume a superior attitude. The process must also work for the group doing it, not just for an idealized group with skills and attendance rates that don't match reality. A corollary to this is that process *experts* should not create the processes in isolation: experts tend to create processes so complex and fragile that they can't be used by mere mortals.

13.10   How to Measure Progress by Using Object-Oriented Software Development Processes

Process Improvement

Implementing a process will probably result in an initial reduction of performance for the obvious reason that people will be adapting to new procedures. (Why this perennially shocks everyone is one of the mysteries of organizational life.) We must watch, however, for process paralysis. If we detect it, we must get the project back on track by emphasizing that our goal is a product rather than a process. Consultants and outside process improvement teams may help with mired groups. Remember that processes, once defined, will undergo incremental evolutionary change and that changes in the volume of work to be handled, or the technology underlying the process, may cause fundamental changes in the process. For example, a process for defect tracking on a small project might be wholly inadequate for a large project. As we stated above, we fully expect the minilevel processes to change as we learn more about object orientation and about the project itself. With process evolution or changes in environment, the whole process hierarchy should be examined for improvement possibilities. The project's process group should coordinate with the company's process improvement group.

When working on process improvement, remember that reactive change will make things worse rather than better. In most cases, people are impatient with the time it takes to make a process better, and they identify every variation in process operation as a problem to be fixed. The result is chaos. A cycle of change, measurement, and evaluation must instead be followed. Deming makes this point forcefully [Deming86].

Process Metrics

People tend to invest mystical properties in statistics that are sent to managers. "We just collect it and let management decide," is often the attitude. Managers, on the other hand, feel compelled to ask for statistical data, even if they don't use it or methodically review it. They somehow feel they aren't doing a proper job—or think they appear to be uninterested—if they don't ask for and save piles of data. This just proliferates the collection and generation of useless data. Certainly in microlevel processes, statistics should be more oriented toward informing the people doing the process so they can control and improve it. Moreover, at the microlevel, some data measurement may come and go as needed [Laitinen98].

13.11   What You Should Look for and What Actions to Take

What a Process Is and Is Not

Let us first describe what a process is not. A process is not a replacement for experience or skill. It does not turn untrained personnel into effective workers. Process development is not a make-work project for incapable employees. It does not solve all operational problems, and *processing* a development quickly will not result in improvement. It is not, in itself, the goal of a software development organization. A process does not guarantee error-free development, nor does it prevent false starts or dead ends. A process is not a code word for a set of rules that management imposes upon subordinates. In fact, it is not merely a set of written rules. Having said this, we can begin to examine the properties of object-oriented processes.

Process Properties Related to Object-Oriented Methods

Philosophy. Any software system has three different perspectives: structural, functional, and behavioral (or data, transformation, and control). The structural perspective concerns the decomposition of the system into a set of interacting and/or nested components and the allocation of data, functions, and behavior related to these components. The functional or process-oriented perspective is the transformation of data without concern for where (structure) or when (behavior) the transformations occur. The behavioral or control-oriented perspective is the system's response to external events, the propagation of control through the system, and the scheduling of work items (functions). This criterion examines the ability to model process for each of the three different perspectives.

Simplicity. This criterion covers those attributes of the OO technique that provide various modeling aspects of the problem domain in the most understandable manner. This criterion measures technique complexity in terms of number of process steps, notational aspects, constraints, and design rules. In addition, this criterion is also concerned with the familiarity of the modeling notations of the technique to the developer (user).

Tailorability. Tailorability is the customizability of a technique to a domain. Aspects of the object-oriented technique can be altered to tune the technique to fit a particular purpose, organization, individual need, or a particular problem domain. This property is very useful if the OO technique can be consistently extended or tailored to fit a particular domain. Extensions are either notational changes or process modifications that incorporate development expertise or implementation needs. This criterion addresses implicitly three other criteria: scalability, decomposition, and incremental growth. Scalability addresses reducing or increasing the technique's notation and process according to the problem size. Decomposition is a special case of scalability where decomposition addresses breaking the problem into manageable components. Incremental growth has two aspects: (1) the ability to produce models that allow the development of the product in increments, and (2) the technique should have the ability to produce increments of its own deliverables allowing delivery of pieces of the OO analysis or OO design.

Measurability. Measures are quantities that can be evaluated to determine whether a software process meets a particular criterion or to evaluate the degree to which a software process exhibits a certain characteristic, quality, property, or attribute.

Repeatability. If two groups come to the same set of models (output) for the same problem domain, this is repeatability.

Testability. Testability is the extent that one can identify an economically feasible technique for determining whether the developed software products (requirements specifications, design, operational software) will satisfy the specification. To be testable, requirements specifications must be specific, unambiguous, and quantitative wherever possible [Boehm84].

Reusability. Reusability is the degree to which one project's software development products can be reused on another development project. Reusable items include requirements specifications, design artifacts, codes, test cases, plans, and so forth. Then reusable software products are software products developed in response to the same requirements for one application that can be used, in whole or in part, to satisfy the requirements of another application.

Traceability. Traceability is a measure of how well implementation traces to design artifacts and to satisfy a certain set of requirements. Traceability has five elements: (1) the document in question contains or implements all applicable stipulations of the predecessor document; (2) a given term, acronym, or abbreviation means the same thing in the software documents; (3) a given item or concept is referred to by the same name or description in the software documents; (4) all the material in the successor document has its basis in a predecessor document (that is, no untraceable material has been introduced); and (5) the two documents in a traceability relationship do not contradict one another [DOD88-STD88].

Maintainability. This criterion refers to the ability of the OO technique work products to accommodate changes (for corrective maintenance), to adapt the product to a changed environment (for adaptive maintenance), or to add new requirements (for perfective maintenance). Information hiding or abstraction and precise, up-to-date documentation increase flexibility and play major roles in overcoming the maintenance problem. This criterion examines: (1) if the object-oriented technique employs information hiding and abstraction, and (2) if the technique provides documentation aids.

Abstraction. Abstraction is a representation of something that identifies the essential details while omitting nonessential details. Abstraction can exist in many different levels. High-level abstraction focuses on general characteristics of the abstract thing, and low-level abstraction reveals more details of the abstract thing. There are many types of abstractions: functional abstraction, data abstraction, behaviors abstraction, process abstraction, object abstraction, and others.

Information hiding. Information hiding focuses on making certain details of an abstract thing inaccessible [Parnas72]. Information hiding is the deliberate hiding of information to promote: (1) abstraction and readability (e.g., by suppressing detail until the appropriate time); (2) modifiability (e.g., by preventing the unauthorized use of private information that is subject to change without notice); and (3) portability, reusability, and extensibility (e.g., by limiting the impact of change). A better choice of words for information hiding would be *information protection,* the concept that information should only be granted on a need-to-know basis.

Verification. Verification is a process of confirming or substantiating that implementation meets the requirements. This process involves demonstrating that the models are consistent within and across phases. Verification is the act of reviewing, inspecting, testing, checking, and comparing. Verification also is the formal proof of program correctness. This criterion refers to technique processes used to determine the degree to which work products fulfill the requirements.

Validation. Validation is a process of confirming or substantiating that development meets the needs of the customer. Validation answers the question, "Am I building the right product?" [Boehm84]. Then, this criterion assesses the degree to which the OO technique provides for demonstrating that the end system (product) satisfies the user's requirements.

Degree of formality. The formality of the technique depends on the formality of three major aspects of the technique: (1) the notations (notation formality), (2) the relationship between phases (relationship formality), (3) and the verification of this relationship (proof formality). The formality of notations is the most obvious to satisfy.

Performance Engineering. Performance engineering addresses the ability of a computer system to perform its functions, for example, response time, throughput, and number of transactions. Then the goals of performance engineering are to: (1) ensure timely response to externally generated events, (2) guarantee periodic processing, and (3) maximize system throughput without sacrificing the system reliability and maintainability. Issues related to performance engineering are resource allocation, throughput bottlenecks, processing delays, communication delays, time constraints, and others. Performance engineering must begin in the analysis phase of the software development (performance analysis). Performance engineering techniques fall into two categories: (1) ad hoc, such as prototyping; and (2) formal performance estimation using analytical models, simulation, and mathematical proof.

Process Capture

Capturing existing processes can be very difficult. The danger is that one will record too little relevant data (assuming that everyone knows all the steps) or that one will record far too much data, making the essential features of the process murky. The questions one must ask include, "How do you know when to do it?"

- Are there variations in priority that affect the sequence of steps?
- What critical factors are there in the process? For example, are there tasks that are easy to do incorrectly, hard to tell if they have been done correctly, or that if done incorrectly can cause the failure of this or downstream processes? For example, in building software for production, if development and debug flags are not turned off, it may not be recognized immediately, but security can be compromised and performance or even operation can be degraded for customers.
- How do you know if you've done the task properly? How do you know when to start?
- Process versus heuristic versus policy versus plan. Is this really something that should be a process? For example, in debugging

there are a number of heuristic techniques used, but usually there is not a step-by-step method that guarantees finding a proper analysis of the defect. Consider not turning it into a process. As a corollary, what benefit accrues by turning something into a process? Is it useful or does it merely increase bureaucracy? (Just because it was a process on another project does not mean it should be one on this project.)

◆ How do outputs vary? They vary by volume, type, and so on. Are there different outputs? Following the process must yield the same output each time or the process is ambiguous. It may be that the process is not understood at the proper level.

◆ What are the upstream processes that feed into this process? Are any upstream processes skipped sometimes? Are there more than one that feed in? Are there multiple processes that can start this process?

◆ What are the downstream processes that this feeds into? Is there a fan-out? Are there different processes that can be started by the same output? Are there cases where a following process will be skipped depending on the output of this process?

◆ Basic metrics—How often is this process done? How long does it take?

◆ How scaleable is this process? For example, can you double the process and still use it? A tenfold volume increase? Can more people be added to do this process, or does another group have to be formed? Can you easily have others do it, or does it require specialized skill? How do you know when the process is overloaded?

◆ Can this process be meaningfully extended? This question should be reformulated to ask how general the process is. For example, a source code inspection process can be extended to do document inspections, but what each type of inspection looks for and what metrics are kept will be different. At a microlevel, they might be considered two different processes. At this point, it makes more sense to ask, "Is this microprocess part of a family of similar processes, and if so, are they coordinated as much as possible?"

13.12   How to Manage Multiple Processes

In "The Art of Managing Multiple Processes," Fayad discusses the following two approaches in detail [Fayad98]:

Complete Uniformity Is Not Always Desirable

The fact that different groups have a number of similar processes leads to the ideas that each group's process work should be made absolutely uniform and that each group should have the same number of processes. This is not necessarily correct. Different groups may be in different phases of transition to new development methods which would suggest different procedures [Fayad98].

Suboptimization

One of the major concerns when dealing with multiple processes is suboptimization, that is, simplifying a process or making it more efficient at the expense of up- or downstream processes. It is common between different functional groups. The classic example of software suboptimization is cutting corners during development to meet schedule, thus dramatically increasing the work needed during testing. This tactic still works all too often [Fayad98].

13.13   Summary

Effective use of object-oriented development requires strong coordination at every phase of development. At the macroprocess level, an iterative approach brings out the advantages of object technology, while a more staged waterfall-like approach obscures its advantages. A major portion of the transition to OO technology is the adoption of miniprocesses, such as choosing methodologies for analysis, design, and development. In many cases, implementation of minilevel processes will signal the most radical departure from the previous development environment. Much of our book has been devoted to the evaluation and acquisition of the tools and methodologies that miniprocesses will organize. The costs and risks

Tips and Practical Advice

Lesson 13.1 The development process must be documented. More specific detail is needed than what is included in the published technique. You must also describe how the process has been adapted to your project. The project's level of detailed decisions should be recorded. The project process should provide "what's next?" to the team members.

Lesson 13.2 Use a project process team.
Using a team with members experienced in creating processes is important. They will assist in producing a workable process, but they do not dictate the process to the development team. The development team should own and enforce processes.

Adapting a new development technique will undoubtedly change the way developers do their jobs, and a documented development process helps them understand what is expected of them during each development phase. It is also important that team members buy into the new development technique. The manager must insure that they understand the development technique and how it has been adapted to their specific project.

Lesson 13.3 Measure processes rather than people.
Processes make a framework that defines appropriate action and efficiency. Effective execution of a process is usually easier to measure and more accurate. It reduces opportunities for an employee to look good at the expense of coworkers. Intergroup conflicts can often be traced to conflicting expectations and requirements. A process-oriented evaluation can show that the conflict is built in. Measuring processes does not mean that individuals no longer have responsibility for performance, and it does not suggest that managers can overlook traditional personnel issues. It does, however, provide a clear path of action when employees identify process failings.

(continued)

Lesson 13.4   Software development processes map the abstract theories of the object-oriented technique into concrete and repeatable actions.
A well-defined process is essential. Our experience in applying a new OO technique emphasizes the importance of having a well-defined software process. Software development processes insure that the software products have a consistently high quality, and using an unfamiliar development technique makes them even more important.

Lesson 13.5   Processes cannot be acquired off the shelf but must be developed over time.
Trying to buy a package of processes virtually guarantees a bad fit, with more work required to adapt the processes than is gained by the purchase. Process experts may help, and for any meaningful measurement, statistical expertise is a must, but the process must reflect what its users do and must reflect the environment in which it is used. Process prototyping and analysis can help process development. Work flows, state transition diagrams, and even Petri nets may aid in process analysis [Holdsworth94].

Lesson 13.6   Warning: poor process use is crippling.
Processes are tools, nothing more. Too often they are used in place of effective management or even as punishment ("Keep those programmers in line!"). Installing process orientation does not cure most organizational problems. Be cautious about trying to use processes as a tool for replacing experienced people with less experienced (and less costly) workers. It usually doesn't work. Processes can, however, be a very useful tool for training less experienced workers.

   Process paralysis can destroy the organization's focus and can drive out the most productive developers.

   Too many processes at the wrong level trade suffocating bureaucracy for chaos; too few processes overlook critical areas and encourage suboptimization; wrong processes stunt efficiency and hurt morale.

(continued)

> **Lesson 13.7** Process-oriented development lets team members contribute effectively.
> One of the most important functions of a process is to make the team members think about what should be done and how to do it. A process should not be a set of rules imposed from the outside and passively followed. Process improvement lets the team take a bigger role in shaping work. It helps them understand the work of other team members. Interestingly enough, process orientation can also help management better understand and more appropriately value the roles all team members play.

of these new tools and methods are high, and considerable attention must be paid to embedding them into processes that make them assets rather than threats. At the macro- and minilevel, process improvement is as often process implementation.

Some of the greatest inefficiencies in an organization exist at the microprocess level. The repetitive tasks that consume so much of any software development project are often wells of frustration for the people that must perform them. We feel that some of the greatest gains can be made by analyzing and improving microlevel processes. At the microlevel especially, process improvement asks the people who do everyday tasks to look at their work with the mandate to make it more efficient and less frustrating. Providing expert help to analyze and guide process improvement can reduce the conflicts that characterize suboptimization.

Finally, adopting a process orientation implies thinking about how the organization works. When this is done, it creates an environment for process innovation with its opportunity for dramatic improvement. As object-oriented technology advances, it provides the basis for new modes of development, such as reusable components (often in the form of third-party class libraries), use of design patterns, and more radically, application frameworks. We are just beginning to see the impact of these new development modes. But to take advantage of them, we must have an understanding of how we work, and the best way to get that understanding is by looking to processes.

References

[Bach95] Bach, J. "Enough About Process: What We Need Are Heroes." *IEEE Software* 12, no. 2 (February 1995).

[Bamberger97] Bamberger, J. "Essence of the Capability Maturity Model." *IEEE Computer* 30, no. 6 (June 1997).

[Bennatan92] Bennatan, E. M. *On Time, Within Budget: Software Project Management Practices and Techniques.* UK: McGraw-Hill International, 1992.

[Boehm84] Boehm, B. W. "Verifying and Validating Software Requirements and Design Specifications." *IEEE Software* 1, no. 1 (January 1984): 75–88. [Reprinted in R. H. Thayer and M. Dorfman (eds.). *Tutorial: System and Software Requirements Engineering.* Washington, D.C.: IEEE Computer Society Press, 1990.]

[Boehm88] Boehm, B. W. "A Spiral Model of Software Development and Enhancement." *IEEE Computer* (May 1988).

[Davenport93] Davenport, Thomas. *Process Innovation: Reengineering Work Through Information Technology.* Boston, MA: Harvard Business School Press, 1993.

[Deming86] Deming, W. Edwards. *Out of the Crisis.* Cambridge, MA: MIT CAES, 1986.

[DoD-STD88] Department of Defense. *Defense Systems Software Development, DoD-STD-2167A.* Washington, D.C.: Department of Defense, 29 February 1988.

[El Emam97] El Emam, Khaled, and Briand, Lionel. "Costs and Benefits of Software Process Improvement." In *Better Software Practice for Business Benefit: Principles and Experience.* Washington, D.C.: IEEE Computer Society Press, 1997: 10.

[Fayad97a] Fayad, M. E. "Software Development Processes: The Necessary Evil!" *Communications of the ACM* (Sept. 1997).

[Fayad97b] Fayad, M. E., and Laitinen, M. D. "Process Assessment: Considered Wasteful." *Communications of the ACM* (November 1997). 40, no. 11, 125–128.

[Fayad98a] Fayad, M. E. "The Art of Managing Multiple Processes." *Communications of the ACM* (April 1998): 41, no. 5, 103–105.

[Forum98b] Fayad, M. E., and Laitinen, M. D. "Readers Thinking Objectively." *Communications of the ACM* (April 1998): 41, no. 4, 22–26.

[Holdsworth94] Holdsworth, Jacqueline. *Software Process Design: Out of the Tar Pit.* London: McGraw-Hill, 1994.

[Humphrey89] Humphrey, W. S. *Managing the Software Process.* Reading, Massachusetts: Addison-Wesley, 1989.

[IEEE87] IEEE Standard 1058.101987. *Standard for Software Project Management Plans.* IEEE, Computer Society Press, 1987.

[Jones96] Jones, C. *Software Systems Failure and Success.* Boston, MA: ITP, 1996.

[Laitinen98] Laitinen, M. D., and M. E. Fayad. "Surviving a Process Performance Crash." *Communications of the ACM* (Feb. 1998): 41, no. 2, 83–86.

[Latzko95] Latzko, William J., and Saunders, David M. *Four Days With Dr. Deming.* Reading, MA: Addison Wesley, 1995.

[Parnas72] Parnas, D. L. "On the Criteria to Be Used in Decomposing Systems Into Modules." *Communications of the ACM* (December 1972): 5, no. 12, 1053–1058.

[Paulk95] Paulk, M. C., et al. *The Capability Maturity Model.* Reading, MA: Addison-Wesley, 1995.

[Senge90] Senge, Peter M. *The Fifth Discipline.* New York: Doubleday Currency, 1990.

[Yourdon87] Yourdon, E. "A Game Plan For Technology Transfer," (a tutorial on software engineering project management). Washington, D.C.: IEEE Computer Society Press, 1987, 214–217.

chapter fourteen

Applying Software Metrics

14.1   Introduction

Software development measurement serves many functions: assessing progress, keeping activities within prescribed limits, controlling software development and maintenance, and predicting future efforts and future defects. Measurements, or metrics, are an important part of managed development, especially when the effort introduces a new object-oriented (OO) development technique. They are used in that context to measure the impact and success of moving to a new technology, assuming a history exists with which the new system can be compared. While documented processes provide the framework for improvements, metrics provide the ruler that measures process success or failure. Carefully selecting measures indicating application of the process will help to prove a growing proficiency. The collection of valuable software metrics should be integral to and permanently engrained in each software process. However, with all the benefits of measurement, adoption of metrics also carries some significant problems (see Figure 14.1).

Quantification is a double-edged sword: it allows us to compare outcomes to assess progress or assure constancy, but it also invites us to trade numbers and graphs for thoughtful analysis. Being able to quantify some outcomes is important: it's extremely difficult to accurately determine how well things are going without quantifiable measures. But there is usually no set of measures that's good enough, complete enough, or accurate enough to satisfy all questions that stakeholders might have. There is never enough information to completely determine a project, and even if there were, it wouldn't be possible to analyze such an enormous amount of data. For example, we tend to think that if we could only identify every

Rank potential metrics, then limit collection to those with high potential for process improvement.

Figure 14.1 Choosing metrics.

possible risk factor for a project, then we would effectively eliminate any chance of failure. Or, if we specify every requirement then we can accurately predict how long the project will take. This leads us to gather even more data. Additional metrics seem desirable because they provide more data. The difference between, say, 30 metrics and 31 is small, so we add another. Soon we have a huge set of metrics to deal with.

We can, however, process only a very few different variables before we become lost. If each variable describes an attribute, we have a poor ability to figure trade-offs between different attributes. Even with powerful statistical multivariate analysis, understanding trade-offs between different outcomes is hard for us to visualize. Hence, we try to simplify. We have two competing trends: getting more information to make more accurate analyses and simplifying the data we do get down to one or two numbers. Given our 31 metrics, we try to simplify them into one measure. A number of things happen then. First, we develop an intricate web of metrics that feeds into other metrics, and changing or eliminating any part of our web will result in many downstream changes. Second, we develop an organizational accretion where data consolidation, once handled by a single person, must now be done by a half dozen. Undoubtedly the metrics are more sophisticated, but their greater value to the organization is questionable.

In any company there will be some who are enamored with numbers, graphs, and complex manipulations of collected data. Unfortunately, too many of these people will pay more attention to the output than to the usefulness of the information. The result is that projects start mutating to improve the metrics output rather than the metrics being first validated, then analyzed, and then used to improve the processes. Some people make this point more strongly. Steve McConnell states, "What you measure gets optimized . . ." [McConnell96]. DeGrace and Stahl call this "chasing the indicators," after the tendency of inexperienced airplane pilots to focus on a single instrument rather than the whole panel, and thereby either move off course or continually overcompensate [DeGrace93]. Relying too much on the results of a few metrics or worse, the values of a single metric, guarantees that people will work to optimize the metric rather than the activity it is supposed to measure. You can provide metrics for anything—prediction, management, employee skills, even attitudes. However, you must remember that metrics, like processes, are tools, and tools are the means to a product, not the product itself. By relying too much on measurement tools, you run the very real risk of skewing your efforts away from getting work done and toward making the organization fit or justify your metrics.

Another interesting feature of metrics mania is the raising of DeMarco's famous dictum, "You can't control what you can't measure" [DeMarco82] into a prime organizational directive, as shown in Figure 14.2. We start believing that only quantifiable measures are worthwhile and activities that interfere with measurement are bad. For example, the direct relationship between training and job performance tends to be hard to measure, and time spent training reduces short-term productivity by taking time away from regular activities. Does this suggest that training is bad? If one looks at the metrics, then the answer is "yes." If one looks at longer-term variables, such as increased capability, the answer is "no." In fact, many activities can be controlled without being measured. Most would agree that the ability to work together is an important function of group effectiveness, yet there is no easy way to measure this ability. Managers do, however, effectively get groups to work together.

We have mentioned before that measuring processes is more important than measuring people. Here we point out that developing metrics to

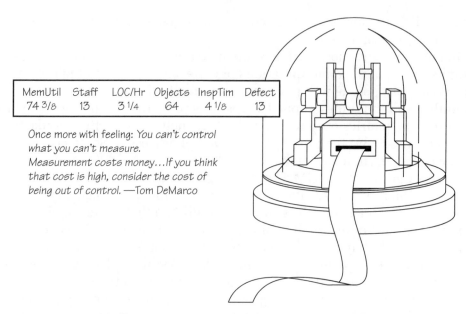

MemUtil	Staff	LOC/Hr	Objects	InspTim	Defect
74 3/8	13	3 1/4	64	4 1/8	13

Once more with feeling: You can't control what you can't measure.
Measurement costs money...If you think that cost is high, consider the cost of being out of control. —Tom DeMarco

Figure 14.2   Collecting project metrics.

measure people is very dangerous if done improperly. The act of measuring human processes is personal and disruptive. The risks range from offending the software developers to eroding valid, long-standing values. When using metrics to measure people, the effect of optimizing the metric rather than the activity it purports to measure will be excessive. The most well-known example of mismeasuring people is using lines of code (LOC) to measure individual performance. It virtually guarantees code padding. But there are more examples.

Imagine that we start recording the number of errors found during module inspections along with the developers' names and we provide this as a statistic for management. Imagine further that we also measure the average time individual developers spend on finding and resolving problems. The predictable result is, first, that managers will assume a strong correlation between individual performance and the number of defects generated and found. Second, realizing the information is being used against them, developers will find ways to subvert the measurements or will refuse entirely to cooperate. Here are some of the problems associated with these metrics:

- The point of inspections, besides finding defects, is to train developers. Less-experienced developers may well have higher defect levels, while less-experienced inspectors are likely to make more errors—either missing or erroneously finding mistakes. Using the information for personal performance evaluation penalizes learning.
- The complexity of the module, errors in requirements or design, or late design changes can affect the number of defects in a module. Such errors are not attributable to the efforts of the individual programmer or are out of the programmer's control.
- Sometimes a troublesome module will be reassigned to a more experienced programmer for repair. If the metrics only list the last person to work on a module, then the more experienced person will appear to be less reliable as a developer.
- For the metric of the average time to find and resolve a defect, more senior developers may be assigned to exceptionally difficult errors that involve dynamic conditions, and thus take much longer on average to resolve. Such a metric only penalizes them.

Such concerns about metrics misuse may seem paranoid or cynical, but they tend to be common errors. An unfortunate tendency is to use data with less regard than we should have for its suitability to the task. It is not surprising that managers, when faced with what appears to be clean statistics regarding employee performance, might seek to use them. And while it may be depressing, most people who have worked in industry have encountered a number of occasions when data has been taken out of context, overanalyzed, or oversimplified.

14.2 Collecting Software Metrics

Finding potential software metrics is easy. We provide some samples later in this chapter, and there are references to many sorts of measures. But collecting meaningful software metrics requires effort. What makes them meaningful? Consider the following suggestions: gather metrics only in support of specific, predetermined objectives and evaluate the measures in that context. Figure 14.3 shows the software metrics collection process.

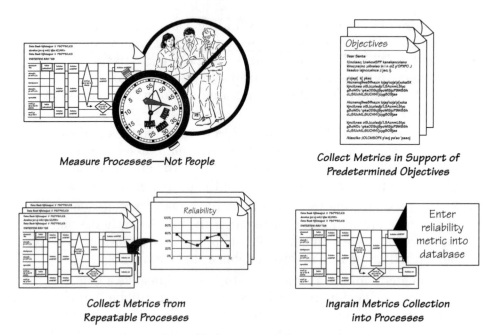

Figure 14.3   Process for collecting useful metrics.

Measures of planned versus actual class or object reuse, or costs of designing for reuse help guide follow-on projects. Measures of object quality, such as coupling or cohesion between classes or objects, provide insight on how well developers are applying object-oriented technique concepts.

Before measuring any process, rank the metrics based on the potential value they add. Also, the act of measuring some processes alters what we are measuring. With all of this at stake, we make sure that we only collect metrics for high-value, repeatable processes. Collect metrics on processes, not people.

Six Characteristics of Good Metrics

We offer here six characteristics that any software measurement should have. When thinking about adopting a metric, check to see if the measurement can meet all six tests. If not, either rework or abandon the measurement.

1. Software metrics must be useful for measurement in multiple areas.
2. Software metrics must be comprehensible and explicit.
3. Software metrics must be economical and must be tied to your major goals and objectives.
4. Software metrics must be timely (or just-in-time).
5. Software metrics must be practical and testable. Beware of theoretical software metrics that have never been applied in practice.
6. Software metrics must be the base for process improvement.

14.3   Classes of Software Metrics

There are a number of ways to classify software measurements. These classifications are neither canonical nor mutually exclusive, but rather are intended to suggest how and where the metrics might be used. We will cover the first two metric classifications: (1) organizational and (2) products, processes, and resources; and we will mention management metrics.

- ◆ **Organizational-level metrics.**   Organizational metrics are defined based on organizational boundaries, organization, project, teams, and sometimes by personnel.

- ◆ **Products, processes, and resources metrics.**   Product metrics measure any artifacts, deliverables, or documents that are produced by the processes. Process metrics measure related process issues, such as organization, techniques, tools, and processes used to develop software products. Resource metrics measure inputs of all types to the processes.

- ◆ **Function metrics.**   Function metrics measure certain functions or tasks with respect to reliability, performance, or completion. Measures that test actual software capabilities against a list of expected capabilities are function metrics. Such metrics may be based on functional requirements of the project, or they may rely on expected performance norms.

- ◆ **Management and quality metrics.**   Management metrics measure progress against the plan. Quality metrics measure the desired quality factors, such as performance and reliability.

◆ **State, predictive, and improvement metrics.**   A state metric measures the state of some key issue. A predictive metric aids in predicting the state of a key issue. An improvement metric aids in improving key issues. A case of a state metric might mean time between failures. Predictive metrics include schedules and cost estimates.

◆ **Quantitative and qualitative metrics.**   Quantitative metrics measure the quantitative attributes (most likely internal attributes) of a process, product, or resource, such as size, time, speed, price, and number of incidents of a specified type, such as classes, functions, and requirements. Qualitative metrics measure quality attributes (most likely external attributes), such as reliability, usability, quality, and stability.

◆ **Time-oriented and timeless metrics.**   Time-oriented metrics measure with respect to time. Person-hours expended per month and defects detected per week are examples of time-oriented measures. A timeless measurement does not directly reference time. Lines of code and defect counts by type would be considered timeless.

◆ **SEI's Five-Level Capability Maturity Model (CMM).**   The CMM has metrics related to each level's key process area (KPA). Software size, software staffing, and requirements volatility are instances of level 2 metrics. Defects found and defect-distribution-by-types metrics are shared by level 2 and level 3.

Organizational Classification

Categorization by organizational level might include management, project, team, and in some cases, personnel. At the management level, there are common measures such as estimation, staffing, and project control. Project measures might include some of the management metrics plus defect tracking, inspection metrics, and work package completion. Team metrics might include various software measures such as object size, object volatility, and items relating to complexity.

Metrics in this section should be based on customer satisfaction and company satisfaction at various organizational levels. Customer satisfaction is usually measured at either the company or project level and can be further categorized into four major areas: performance, price, features, and product quality. Performance measures include such measures as software size, speed, and defects found. Price includes both cost and schedule measures and can be augmented by metrics affecting cost and schedule. Defects found, implementation progress, and staffing are metrics that affect cost and schedule. Product quality measures can include inspection coverage, requirements verification, risk evaluation, and test progress. It should be noted that customers in many cases will not be reviewing measures related to customer satisfaction, but the metrics relate directly to goals that affect satisfaction.

Company satisfaction can be measured at all organizational levels and includes business performance issues such as return on investment (ROI), personnel capabilities in both skill and availability, and overall cost structures. The efficiency with which a company can develop software and the extent to which it can keep maintenance costs low affect the performance of the company. Cost and quality are the main issues in such measurements. Factors such as reuse, component development, and framework development affect these areas as well and may factor into ROI metrics.

Watts Humphrey introduced the notion of a Personal Software Process (PSP) that requires rigorous efforts and meticulous record keeping [Humphrey95]. The extensive measurements required constitute a serious personal metrics program. While PSP sounds promising, there is not yet much evidence regarding its acceptance by and effect upon practicing professionals. The PSP might be compared with a home gym, such as those advertised endlessly on television. The results they report are clearly achievable and significant, but the work involved, even spread out over time, is so substantial that the majority of purchasers give up within a short time. Humphrey suggests that a minimum of ten exercises, each requiring five to ten hours, be done for acquisition of basic skills, in addition to the time required to read and understand the underlying software and statistical basis of the program. He further states that organizations supporting the process be at CMM level 2, give the participants one day a week to work on the PSP, and that trying to use work-related projects instead of the exercises will not work. We suspect that few companies will support such a significant drain on resources, regardless of the potential value it may have.

Product, Process, and Resources

Another way to look at measures is by classifying them according to how they apply to processes, products, and resources. Many object metrics, such as inheritance depth or code size per process, are product measures. Metrics that assess overall product quality, such as mean time before failure (MTBF), are also product measures. Defect density, defect rates, and object identification rates might be considered process measures. Cost or time per object would be examples of resource measurements. The point of process measures is to improve the process and thereby improve the products. Process measures generally extend over time and show trends.

Product Measurements

We can further break down product metrics into those that assess attributes seen by the customer and those that assess attributes seen by developers. We sometimes talk about all measures as supporting customer satisfaction, and in some sense that is true. However, few users of a product really care about metrics such as object inheritance depth or even defect density. They are interested in overall reliability, usability, cost, and performance. Pretending that the customer is the primary beneficiary of such internal product metrics may distract us from their proper use, which is to help development and maintenance.

Later in this chapter we list various metrics and suggest how they fit into this classification.

Process Measurements

Process measurements are used to assess and control processes, and thus are central to any improvement efforts. Among the best sources for process metrics are inspections (see Figure 14.4). We already gather product and process information during inspections, and identifying a set of metrics based on the output is a natural choice.

The other obvious phase to gather process metrics is testing. Testing takes a significant portion of the time and effort in any project, and finding a small set of suitable measures to identify the effort, efficiency, and to predict test completion should be a goal.

It's desirable to have a baseline measurement for process metrics, but experience shows that metrics are even rarer than formal processes in software development. This will be especially vexing when senior man-

Software size

Productivity

Defects by activity, type and severity

Cost of rework

Inspection time

Figure 14.4 Inspections provide an ideal opportunity for metrics collection.

agement asks for proof that the efforts to move to object-oriented development are cost-effective and faster. Our best suggestion is to admit up front that only the sketchiest of baselines exists for previous work, but to assure management that a significant benefit of the transition to object orientation will be considerably better metrics.

Control Charts One of the principal examples of a process measure is the control chart. A control chart, as in Figures 14.5 and 14.6, shows

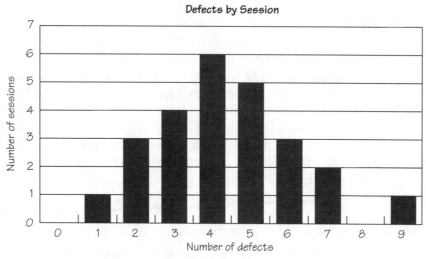

Figure 14.5 Distribution-of-defects chart.

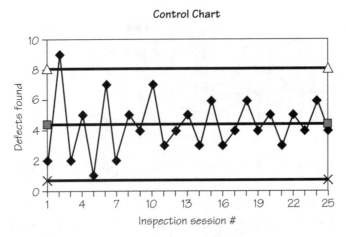

Figure 14.6 Control chart of the same data.

change over time and variation, both of which are important to understand for a process. For example, if you were starting to implement software inspections, the data showing numbers of defects found in each session would vary significantly. The most common analysis of such data would be a distribution chart, as indicated hereafter. A chart of the variations just tells us in this case that we are finding between zero and nine defects per hundred lines of code per session, but it doesn't give us any idea if this is changing over time or if such a wide variation is meaningful. By using a control chart instead, we can see how defect discovery is changing over time and whether the process is settling in. The control chart shows that initially the inspections vary widely in the number of defects that are found per session, but as time progresses, the inspections tend to be more consistent, finding an average of 4.4 errors per session. The two horizontal lines above and below most of the points are called control limits—they indicate the range of normal variation in the process. Only the second session's defect find is outside the control limits. The important points of the two charts are that:

◆ Graphical representation of metrics is useful.
◆ The same data can be represented in various ways and can provide differing amounts of information.

- The control chart tells how things are changing over time and what amount of variation is normal.
- The control chart also gives clues about how to improve the process.

What are those clues? By looking at the chart, we see that reducing the variation is important. In fact, it is happening just by virtue of the increased experience the inspectors are gaining. In this example, of course, we are assuming that errors per hundred lines are reasonably evenly distributed throughout the code, an assumption that often is not true. The other clue we have is that the object of inspections is to find defects and trouble spots, so presumably, we would like to increase the average number of defects found per hundred lines of code in each session. While the average values could have been inferred from the distribution chart, the control chart gives us a much clearer view of what's going on.

Resource Measurements

Resource measurements have great value in assessing the progress and cost of projects as a whole and project parts such as work packages. At the project level, headcount, schedules, and development resource costs are obvious measurements. The cost of development tools, which will likely be upgraded in the duration of the project, can add significantly to the cost of development. Resource metrics that include such costs can help identify the real efficiency of development.

At a lower level, resource measurements include such items as calculation of development time and cost per object. Especially in a new object-oriented project, the time and cost expenditure for object development will be higher and should decline over time. Using a control chart or other time-based resource measurement, there should be a steady progression of lower costs per object. If there is no cost decline, then analysis of the cost can be undertaken. Possible reasons for continuing high resource costs include inadequate training, overly ambitious schedule requirements, and poor analysis or design. The point of the measurement is to identify how resources are being used and how they change.

Management Metrics

Management metrics are used for estimation, resource allocation, and project control. The most common type of metric is one that compares the actual state of some part of a project against its original and current plans. The purposes for keeping such measurements include improving estimating and planning skills and ensuring that the project or some part of the project is not out of control. We discuss the metrics for tracking and controlling projects in a separate chapter, so here we mention some of the other management measures.

A number of checks help identify whether a project is in control. With iterative development, a project may go through analysis and design on the same part of a system a number of times. System volatility measures help tell whether the iterations are converging to a firm analysis and design or if they are diverging. Requirements, design, and interface volatility can be tracked, as can process volatility. A project starting the transition to OO development will probably see considerably higher volatility. These measures will also be useful in detecting and curbing creeping elegance. More traditional management measures include staffing levels, staffing profile by discipline, and planned versus actual staffing levels. These measures help in estimating plan versus actual progress. Checks such as objects integrated and number of interfaces help chart programming progress.

An important aspect of an object-oriented transition is avoiding relapsing to previous ways of working. Interface stability, information hiding, coupling, and cohesion metrics help identify whether the project is keeping to OO principles. Checking process adherence and team productivity help keep the team on the program. To measure the cost of object-oriented development, metrics such as activity cost per object, rework costs, overhead costs, and cost-versus-complexity measures are useful. Clearly, metrics such as productivity and work completed per time period will be lower at the beginning of the transition. It is important, however, that these metrics show a rising trend at some point (otherwise, the transition is not delivering the expected results). Tracking projects by activity can help find trouble spots and identify team and process weakness.

Test and integration charts, along with configuration and release management measures, are also essential, especially as the project nears completion. If these metrics don't show convergence toward stability, then the project is in trouble. Note, however, that adapting to new methods and languages will generate a significantly higher level of rework. By checking rework items such as time spent correcting defects, not only can maintenance efforts be estimated, but team effectiveness and training applicability can also be assessed. Inspections, as stated, offer many areas of management information. As inspectors become more experienced, inspection time should be reduced. If inspections show high levels of certain categories of errors, then methods and training can be used to reduce their incidence. It may be useful as a sales tool for upper management to track software defects by phase. Using the rule that errors cost more the later in the development cycle they are found, showing significant results from analysis, documentation, and design inspections can help show the value of new methods.

Reusability metrics identify those items that support reusability and, by extension, improved future efficiency. Among the more important reusability measures are portability, independence, domain suitability, self-descriptiveness, and reuse potential.

Performance and reliability metrics are key indicators of system success. Mean time before failure (MTBF), throughput, memory utilization, I/O utilization, and performance benchmarks are all measurements that may be useful for the management of the project.

Figure 14.7 shows some useful software management metrics.

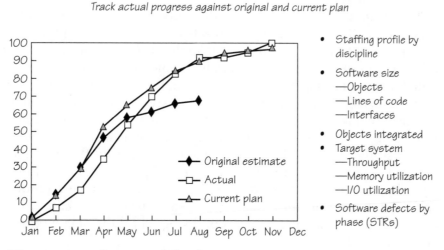

Figure 14.7   Some useful software management metrics.

14.4   Issues in Defining Metrics

We mentioned at the beginning of the chapter that metrics should not be used to measure individuals. The results will be detrimental to the company. We also mentioned that a metric tends to take on a life of its own in which it, rather than the attribute it's measuring, becomes more important. We tend, as well, to discount the value of processes and activities that don't lend themselves to quantification. This, too, is an example of measurement misuse.

There are other problems as well. Metrics, even automated ones, are expensive. It takes time, effort, and computing resources to collect and analyze data. Collecting metrics tends to be distracting, irritating to developers, and in many cases invasive. It requires a change of attention and flow from other development activities to one of data collection and analysis. There is no easy way to make the collection of metrics easy or cheap. This means that some potentially desirable measurements will not be made (at least not regularly). Even if we use measurements that come from automated tools, they still take time to collect. A compiler that takes 10 percent longer to add some metrics is a major impact for a large system. But more importantly, metrics must be analyzed, stored, and acted upon. Analysis is rarely a task for automation, and far more often than not, neither is storage and retrieval.

If measurements are collected from developers but not shared with them (as is too often the case with project-level metrics), then they will resent the distraction and usually not take the collection of information seriously. Exhortations and threats are bad remedies. Rather, severely limiting the amount of measurement, sharing the results of the measurement and analysis, and taking the data seriously are better management approaches. By taking the data seriously, we mean that clear indicators must not be ignored or fudged. For example, if the measurement indicates a schedule slippage, then management must accept that fact and reestimate the project. If lower-than-anticipated performance is indicated from testing, the problem must be faced. If management insists on unreasonable schedules or decides to change the measurement data to look better, it will guarantee the same sort of disregard for the data by the development staff.

Another problem that plagues metrics is that they are easier to collect than to use properly. Coming up with a measurement does not mean that it correlates with the attribute you are trying to measure. For example, complexity measures, which have been used for over two decades to predict reliability and maintainability, are still controversial, especially in object-oriented languages. Jacobson and Booch make this point [Jacobson92; Booch94]. Using a weighted-size-per-class measure to predict object quality may correlate poorly with actual object quality.

In the analysis of metrics, multiple problems exist as well. It is easy to combine data sets in ways that render the information useless. Zuse [Zuse97] provides an example of combining data sets in different ways to get significantly different results with implying very different interpretations. Overnormalization, trying to force the data to look like a normal distribution for example, is another easy but information-destroying activity. We need a model to create predictive metrics, and this model should use local data for calibration. It does no good to rely purely on the data provided by other organizations for prediction (although sometimes that's what we must start with). At the other extreme, we must be careful not to try forcing our data to match the model, eliminating data that doesn't fit, and modifying calculations to get more model-like results. If the model doesn't match the data then the model is at fault.

We reiterate that a few metrics with some analysis are far more valuable than a mountain of metrics covering every aspect of a project. For example, Muller [Muller97] offers a 90-page on-line text supplement, *Unified List of Operational Objectives,* that includes hundreds of metrics for every project stage. While the measurements might be useful in various situations, attempting to use more than a small portion of the listed metrics would be counterproductive. Although it might be tempting to use every possible metric, it is important to take a minimalist approach to measurement. The reality is that a project cannot be thought of as just the totality of its metrics any more than an automobile repair shop can be thought of as the totality of its tools and repair manuals. Having a metric for every activity, every process, and every product does not guarantee success by a long shot.

When going beyond basic collection and analysis, engage someone with expertise in statistics and their appropriate use. With today's spreadsheets and analysis programs, powerful statistical tools are readily available, but the experience to use the tools properly is far rarer. It's unfortunate but true that a well-formatted presentation will make an impression disproportionate to the soundness of the underlying statistical analysis. Therefore, it is particularly important to get an expert to define the appropriate analysis techniques before the data gets in the wrong hands.

Other common and related problems are reading too much into measurement data and being too sensitive to variations. In the former case, we take precision to ridiculous extremes, assuming, for example, that there is a meaningful difference between software inspection rates of 1.2 and 1.3 defects found per hour. We read a recommendation that C++ methods should be about 12 lines long, and we take it as an absolute commandment. In the latter case, we attempt to micromanage normal variation. In the control chart example shown above, values falling between the upper and lower control limits are normal variation. If we decided to take corrective action after each inspection session to ensure the next session's defect detection rate was at or above the average, we would not only fail, we would make the rates worse. Deming makes this point painfully obvious [Deming86].

There are also transition considerations, the first of which is the learning curve. This will manifest itself in many ways, and if there are metrics from pretransition projects, they most likely won't compare too closely with the new measurements. In an object-oriented development, far more time is spent on analysis and design than in traditional approaches. In addition, progress will be slower as people learn both object-oriented techniques and implementation details of the new programming languages. Measuring initial OO efforts against traditional development at its highest point will make the new approach look dismal. This point must be made explicitly and constantly repeated, or the new approach will look like a failure from the start. (The corollary, of course, is that over time the new approach must improve dramatically and the improvement must be reflected in the metrics).

Another transition issue is that the metrics themselves will change over time. If there are preexisting metrics based on designs by functional decomposition and nonobject languages, they will have to be replaced by more appropriate measures. Moreover, the initial set of measurements will evolve over time. Remember that metrics are tools, and they can and should be replaced by more suitable tools as the environment changes. Do not be afraid to discard measurements that are no longer used. This is especially important at the team level. Teams should have the ability to try measurements for assessment and process improvements, and then to discard them. In some cases, these measurements should not be made available outside the team membership, and if they are, they should be done with the clear understanding the information will not be provided after it outlives its usefulness to the team itself. Otherwise, if teams are forced to provide data that they no longer need, they will be unwilling to experiment as they need.

14.5   Documenting Software Metrics

Software metrics must be documented for analysis, review, record keeping, and presentation. We introduce a generic template for documenting software metrics (see Table 14.1). The template contains nine items: metric title, metric number, metric description, general requirements,

TABLE 14.1   Metric Documentation Template

1. *Metric Title:* Define the metric name.
2. *Metric Number:* Define the number given to the metric by the software configuration management.
3. *Description:* Provide a brief description of the metric and its applications.
4. *General Requirements:* Has two requirements:
   - The first item identifies if the metric is required, substitutable, optional, or special case?
   - The second item identifies if the metric is required by the customer, by the model (SEI, CMM, or ISO), or by the company or the division?
5. *Required Data/Computation:* Identifies all the required data and all the required equations or computation.
6. *Graph Attributes:* identifies four attributes:
   - Usage Period: Identifies the useful duration of the graph.
   - Graph: Describes the graph.
   - Graph Per: Identifies the measured item, such as class, component, or project if applicable.
   - Min Update Frequency: Identifies how often this graph must be updated.
7. *Use of Data:* Identifies the usefulness of the data and specifies the results and explains how to interpret the results.
8. *Control Chart or Example Graph:* Shows a graph.
9. *Actions:* Lists all the actions taken or indicates no action taken.

required data/computations, graph attributes, use of data, a control chart or an example graph, and actions taken.

We show hereafter two examples of metrics documentation: an inspection coverage measure and a staffing metric (see Tables 14.2 and 14.3). Figure 14.8 shows the graph associated with the inspection coverage metric. Figure 14.9 shows the graph associated with the staffing metric.

14.6 Metrics Examples

We provide hereafter some samples of useful metrics in a variety of contexts. The fact that these measurements have proved useful in some situ-

TABLE 14.2 Documentation Template for Inspection Coverage Metric

Template Items	Descriptions
Metric title	Inspection coverage.
Metric number	DPM5.2.
Description	This metric tracks the portions of object-oriented requirements specifications, object-oriented design, code, test cases, and user documentation that has been formally inspected.
Requirements	Required.
	The customer and SEI level 3.
Required data/ computations	Profiles of portion of object-oriented requirements specifications, object-oriented design, code, test cases, and user documentation inspected. See graph.
Graph attributes	Usage period: software project through completion.
	Graph: profile of percentage inspected versus time.
	Graph per: project.
Minimum update frequency	Monthly.
Use of data	This metric tracks the inspection coverage. Ideally, inspection coverage should be 100 percent, but that may not be practical in some projects.
Actions	No actions.

TABLE 14.3 Documentation Template for Staffing Metric

Template Item	Description
Metric title	Staffing.
Metric number	DPM5.2.
Description	The staffing allows project managers to monitor staffing needs and available resources.
Requirement	Required.
	The customer and SEI level 2.
Required data/ computation	Actual staff profiles will be compared with the project plan. Modifications in the planned staffing will also be specified. In addition, the monthly loss rate will be presented.
	Monthly loss rate = Number of people left/Staff at start of the month.
Graph attributes	Usage period: Software project through completion.
	Graph: people versus time and percentage versus time.
	Graph per: project.
Minimum update frequency	Monthly.
Use of data	Failure to meet the planned staffing profile will threaten the project schedule. A high monthly loss rate is an indicator for turnover. High turnover can be a potentially major problem for the project.
Actions	We are hiring right now.
	We are working closely with human resources division and in the process of inviting a few potential candidates for two positions.

ations does not make them universally applicable. As we stated above, the metrics should be adopted for specific, predetermined purposes and the results evaluated in context. Merely adopting some subset of these metrics, based on their publication here, will make the effort wasted. Figures 14.10 and 14.11 show a number of useful metrics.

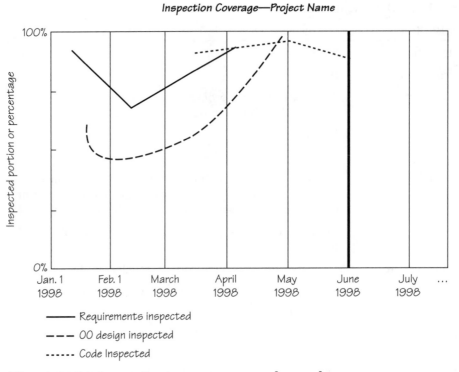

Figure 14.8 Inspection coverage example graph.

14.7 Summary

Metrics are an essential part of effective software development. Without them, it is impossible to assess progress on any significant project. It is important to use metrics sparingly, because they are expensive and disruptive to collect and expensive to analyze. That means you must prioritize what is most important to measure and limit the metrics accordingly. Automating as much of the data collection and presentation is important, but analysis still must be done by a human and will be time-consuming. It's the human analysis, however, that gives measurement its value. If an analyst is effective, his or her output will help the development team advance the project, improve its own efficiency, and identify problems before they threaten the project. If the analyst is ineffective, the project

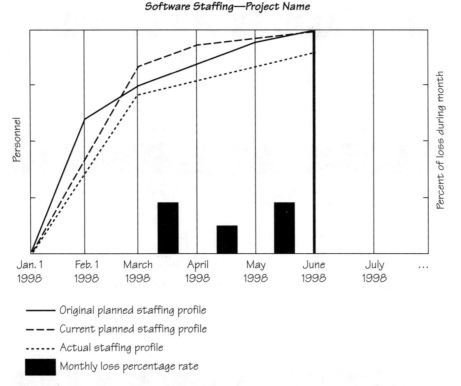

Figure 14.9 Staffing metric graph.

will be subject to an endless stream of meaningless charts and numbers given to the wrong people. At best, the activity will be irritating; at worst, it will be seriously misleading.

To summarize our advice, identify the goals for the metrics you use, and document the metrics and processes they measure before you start collecting data. Concentrate on the repeatable aspects of development, and don't analyze something that can't be repeated. Lack of repeatability suggests that the wrong thing is being measured. Finally, the goal of the project is to deliver a product. Discard metrics that detract from that goal, that don't correlate to actual development realities, or that provide no useful information to further the delivery of the product, no matter how much the company has invested in them.

Requirements Volatility	Team Productivity
• Track requirements versus requirements changes • Identifies creeping elegance and technical greed • Useful to track interface volatility	• Track work completed over time • Expect lower than usual initially • Track by activity to identify weak processes
Time Spent in Inspections	Software Rework
• Track for each inspection type • Time should decrease as participants understand roles • Use results to fine-tune inspection checklists	• Time spent correcting defects • Should decrease as team gains experience with method • May identify activities requiring additional training

Figure 14.10   Useful metrics for projects using new methods.

Reliability	Reusability
• MTBF • Simplicity • Anomaly management	• Portability • Independence • Domain suitability • Self-descriptiveness
Maintainability	Software Cost
• Modularity • Information hiding • Coupling • Cohesion	• Activity cost per object • Test and integration costs • Rework costs • Configuration and release management • Overhead

Figure 14.11   More useful metrics.

Tips and Practical Advice

Lesson 14.1   Metrics provide the ruler that measures success or failure.

- Collecting useful software metric requires effort.
- Collect metrics on processes, not people.
- Don't let metrics take on a life of their own and don't chase the indicators.
- Don't be afraid to discard metrics that have no meaning.

Lesson 14.2   Metrics provide a means of measuring process quality and identifying potential bottlenecks.

Lesson 14.3   Correlation is a critical requirement for any metric.

- Predictive models require local data to have meaning for the organization.
- Actual data must look like the model's, or the prediction is not valid for the project.

Lesson 14.4   Metrics will change over time: Initial measurements will give an idea of what measurements we should make in the future.
This will bother some who want absolute continuity, but we are virtually guaranteed that our initial metrics will need tuning.

Lesson 14.5   Measurement requires sensitivity.

- Don't read too much into numbers.
- Don't overanalyze or overnormalize data.
- Manage variation by changing the process.

Lesson 14.6   Employ expert statistical help for all but the simplest analysis.

References

[Booch94] Booch, G. *Object-Oriented Analysis and Design with Applications.* 2nd ed. Redwood City, California: Benjamin/Cummings, 1994.

[DeGrace93] DeGrace, Peter, and Leslie Hulet Stahl. *The Olduvai Imperative: Case and the State of Software Engineering Practice.* Englewood Cliffs, New Jersey: Prentice Hall, 1993.

[DeMarco82] DeMarco, Tom. *Controlling Software Projects.* Englewood Cliffs, New Jersey: Prentice Hall, 1982.

[Deming86] Deming, W. Edwards. *Out of the Crisis.* Cambridge, Massachusetts: MIT CAES, 1986.

[Humphrey95] Humphrey, Watts. *A Discipline of Software Engineering.* Reading, Massachusetts: Addison-Wesley, 1995.

[Jacobson92] Jacobson, I. *Object-Oriented Software Engineering: A Use Case Driven Approach.* Reading, Massachusetts: Addison-Wesley, 1992.

[McConnell96] McConnell, Steve. *Rapid Development.* Redmond, Washington: Microsoft Press, 1996.

[Muller97] Muller, R. J. *Productive Objects: An Applied Software Project Management Framework.* San Francisco, California: Morgan Kaufman, 1997.

[Zuse97] Zuse, H. "Lectures in Software Measurement." [World Wide Web site] Berlin, Germany: 1997 [cited March 23, 1998]. Available from http://irb.cs.tu-berlin.de/~zuse/.

chapter fifteen

Inspecting Object-Oriented Software Products

15.1   Why Do Inspections?

Although data continues to mount in favor of using inspections to
improve quality and reduce overall development and maintenance cost,
the effort involved in performing inspection is significant. Some software
teams feel that they cannot afford inspections. We feel that inspections
are the most cost-effective technique of ensuring software quality.
Removing defects at their point of insertion significantly reduces the cost
of their repair. This is the difference between engineering reliable software rather than trying to test reliability in. Efficient inspections are
always a wise investment, but since as much as 20 percent of the development effort may be devoted to inspections, they can come under
scrutiny as potential inhibitors to rapid development. Experience shows
that the increased time spent doing inspections at early stages of development dramatically reduces the amount of rework needed at later
stages. Moreover, inspections serve a secondary purpose as a team building tool, as shown in Figure 15.1.

What about the Cost?

Testing consumes as much as 40 percent of development time. If historical
information is kept on a project, it is likely to show that much time in testing phases is really spent doing rework rather than verifying functionality.
Rework due to design and requirements defects is much more expensive
when found by testing code than by inspecting earlier. If much of the time

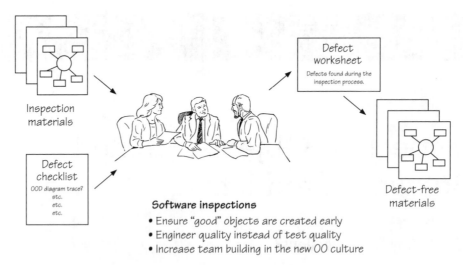

Figure 15.1   The critical role of inspections.

spent in what is normally called testing is really rework, and if inspections dramatically reduce rework, it makes sense to budget extra time in for inspections throughout the development cycle so that the overall project duration can be reduced. Moreover, by their very nature, inspections also find defects that testing cannot, and do it more efficiently than most testing. Testing will not create quality objects, and test engineers should be able to spend their time more productively in necessary activities, such as unit, integration, and acceptance testing, as shown in Figure 15.2.

It's difficult, however, to contemplate an increase in development time given an already demanding schedule. And it is even more difficult in an unstructured project, where any time spent outside of coding and testing may lengthen the project. But the premise of this book is that developers are moving away from unstructured development because it produces poor results in all but the smallest projects, and we assume the reader agrees with the premise.

Experience indicates that inspections use about 15 percent of a project's resources, the majority of which is at the front end. However, the project's net resources are reduced by 10 to 40 percent, and usually the schedule is shortened. It is unlikely that inspections will lengthen the schedule in all but the most pathological projects.

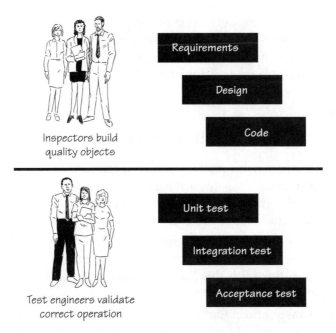

Figure 15.2 Testing will not create quality objects.

We recommend, therefore, that the cost of defects be estimated and tracked. If the organization has historical records of similar development projects, they can be used to help gauge the effectiveness of current development. By estimating the cost of defects at various stages, a reasonable feeling can be developed for the value of inspection. In addition, keeping track of defects at each stage and part of a project—from requirements to maintenance and from standards to coding to documentation—provides a good high-level metric on the quality of the product as a whole.

15.2 What Are Inspections?

An inspection is a structured, formal reading of a text with the aim of finding defects. The method originally described by Fagan [Fagan86] was intended for code, but now is performed throughout the development process on requirements, designs, code, documentation, and test plans.

The method for doing inspections is essentially the same regardless of what is being inspected. We do not explain the inspection process in detail here, but give an overview of the process and provide references to some of the excellent books on the subject.

Inspection Phases

The typical phases of an inspection are as follows:

Planning. After a work package is completed, it is scheduled for inspection. Specific roles are assigned for the inspection team, and the materials, such as listings, requirements specifications, and design documents, are distributed to the team members.

Overview. A presentation is made to the team members to familiarize them with the work package to be inspected. If the team is already familiar with the package, then no overview meeting is necessary.

Individual inspection. Each inspector reads the material looking for and noting errors. As mentioned below, different inspectors may concentrate on different aspects of the same work package to speed the process.

Inspection meeting. This is a moderated meeting in which the reader presents the work package, and individual inspectors look for and note errors. The meeting is limited to two hours at the most, and defects are noted without proposing resolutions.

Rework. The author of the work package fixes the listed defects.

Follow-up. The corrections are checked and, if necessary, a reinspection is scheduled.

Inspection Roles

The roles of an inspection team include the following:

Moderator. The person who ensures the readiness of the product for inspection (clean compiles, conforms to style standards, and so forth) distributes the inspection materials, schedules, and runs the inspection meeting. In the inspection meeting, the moderator makes sure that team members remain focused on finding and recording defects.

Reader. During the inspection meeting, the reader presents the work and in some cases paraphrases the text.

Inspectors. The people who read the text of the work package both before and during the meeting, looking for defects. The number of inspectors should be minimized so that the whole inspection meeting has no more than five to nine people.

Author. The person who has created the work package. The author may not be the reader or the moderator.

Recorder. The person who records the defects as they are found and categorizes them according to various criteria, such as severity and error type.

The result of an inspection meeting is an inspection report containing a list of defects and various metrics captured during the process.

15.3 Use a Process When Inspecting

Evidence shows that software inspections substantially improve product quality and help to keep new object-oriented (OO) development on track by reducing and improving defects and reducing cost (see Figure 15.3) [Fagan86]. As with anything new, however, the application of specific concepts may not be fully understood. Even concepts that are well understood may allow several implementations, all equally correct. Inspections and reviews, then, must have a process that preserves their positive characteristics. Documentation is a good example. Those who have attempted to integrate several developers' writing into a coherent document are well aware of the difficulties. Without formal interim reviews, the product will resemble a United Nations meeting—several seemingly unrelated individual elements trying to work together.

Approach software inspections as a rigorous form of peer review. As such, inspections should formally compare developed software with established standards. Standards, of course, vary with the project, but inspections will ensure that the development team follows the appropriate standard. In this way, inspections become the primary means of ensuring software quality. And, of course, processes that do not measure their own effectiveness will degenerate. Therefore, metrics must be kept and analyzed to assure that inspections are properly done and are removing defects. Although the developer is the first recipient of inspection

Software inspections guarantee successful completion of each OO software development phase:

- Requirements inspection of software object
- Preliminary and detailed design of the object
- Implementation and unit test procedures
- Documentation of OO requirements, design, and code

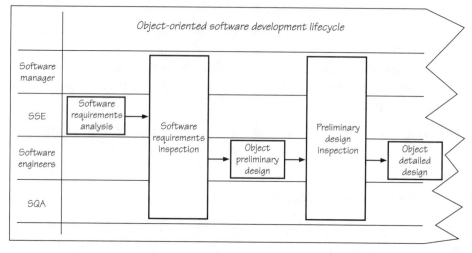

Figure 15.3   Inspection process applies to all phases of OO software development (OOSD).

data, it provides a wealth of metric data. Portions of the project with high defect rates indicate problem areas. Tying the completion of work packages to passing inspection provides a rigorous method of measuring development progress.

Please see Appendix A for more information on inspection processes and the process notation shown above.

15.4   Inspections Yield Metrics and Improve Process

Inspection is not a cheap process. It adds as much as 20 percent to the earlier stages of development and takes up large portions of not only the developers' time, but clerical time as well. Considerable resistance to such an added burden can be expected, and without some data to show the usefulness of inspections, the process may well be canceled. Fortunately, keeping defect data is integral to the inspection process and can provide the sort of information that proves its usefulness. Among the metrics to consider to assure that inspections are being properly executed are defect removal efficiency, faults detected per thousand lines of code (or text), inspection and preparation rates, and reinspection percentage [Barnard94].

The analysis of defects is also an excellent way to identify potential process improvements. For example, defect analysis at the preliminary design level generally shows that a high proportion of the requirements lack sufficient detail and clarity. This might suggest a need for greater rigor in the requirements inspection process and might even indicate doing more analyses before proceeding further. On the other hand, a significantly higher defect rate should be expected in the analysis stage because the problem is just becoming understood. The greatest value comes from finding not only defects, but also the root causes of defects.

While performing more analysis and holding up the design might be seen as a drawback, there is no doubt that the cost of finding and fixing the problems later in the development cycle would be far more costly. It is important to remember, however, that quality cannot be inspected in. At every stage of the development process, there will be inconsistencies and defects, and inspection is shown effective at finding such problems. But inspection cannot compensate for wrong analysis, poor design, or bad implementation. The role of inspection in building quality objects is to find problems with the consistency and traceability of requirements and design, to find problems with the conformance to the method, and to find defects in the code. However, starting with ambiguous requirements or a poor design and iteratively inspecting out defects is an extremely expensive development method.

15.5   Efficient Inspections

Thoroughly reviewing all software on a large project is time consuming. Because of this, inspection processes should be optimized by defining specific, complementary roles for individual reviewers. For example, one reviewer may ensure all requirements are sufficiently allocated in the design, while another may verify a unit's testability. The number and specific responsibilities of the reviewers must be formally documented for each type of material reviewed. We have found that inspection checklists are a good way to ensure that several independent reviewers cover all the bases. In addition, be sure that the preparation stages for reviews are enforced.

It is important not to mix purposes when doing inspections. The inspection process is designed to find and record defects, nothing else. Adding more functions, more participants, or more time to the inspection process will substantially reduce its efficiency. In particular, determining how to deal with defects should be done separately from the inspection (although it may be done immediately following the inspection while the issues are still fresh in the minds of the participants). Commit instead to holding other formal reviews for progress assessment and development on the project.

Before a product is inspected, it should have had as many defects removed by automated processes as possible. For text-based documents, this means at least that typographic errors and spelling errors have been removed beforehand. Conformance to layout standards should also have been done. For code products, clean compiles, text formatting, and coding standard checks should have been applied before inspection begins. This allows the inspection team to focus on finding defects that automated methods would miss.

15.6   Implementing Inspections

It is important to make the first use of inspections a success. How to be successful depends on the organization. Some groups have started by completely reworking the whole development process and have included inspections for all projects at all phases. For others, the risks of failure would be prohibitively high. If the organization has little experience with formal development processes, the learning curve for going to total inspection, along with the other process changes OO development requires, might just be too high. While it is true that inspecting requirements and design yield higher returns in defect removal and rework reduction, code inspection is better understood.

Inspection appears to be useful in team building and product understanding. While it is not clear that having the meeting results in finding higher numbers of defects than the premeeting reading activities, it does appear that the process as a whole adds to the team's ability to understand the project and develop better development skills. For example, involving the developer in test plan inspections helps the developer understand the expected use of the product. Naturally, the inspection process must have been properly implemented to have a beneficial effect, and the most effective way to assure proper implementation is to have formal training in inspections.

As stated earlier, it might be better to start with a moderate project that is important enough to be valuable but not absolutely critical to the company's survival. By choosing people who are committed to the project's success and who are capable of achieving it, you can make use of the start-up effect. The start-up effect uses the extra enthusiasm, attentions, and skills of the specially chosen staff to make greater than usual gains on an initiative. Although the start-up effect is often used to describe why new methods and processes fail to work after initial success, you can exploit the effect to give a worthwhile method the extra boost it needs to offset resistance to its use.

Even so, expect the early inspections to be less productive. The inspection materials themselves will have defects that must be recognized and corrected. People will not completely understand their roles. Initial materials will have an initially higher level of errors because producers may not be attuned to the process. Expect the process to change often, at least in minor ways, when starting up. The goals of the inspection must be explicitly stated and clarified. Start with checklists; develop a consensus of quality, major/minor defects; checklists help remind the team of expectations and standards. Definitions of major, minor, and trivial defects must be solidified and categorizing defect types must be learned. If moving from a pilot project to general use, expect a drop again in effectiveness until the process has been assimilated.

15.7   Suggestions for Inspections

The following are some suggestions about inspections in OO-based development.

General Suggestions

Review products for specific qualities of object orientation. These qualities range from consistent abstraction levels for generic objects and methods, to appropriate use of inheritance. Additionally, potential for reuse may be scored and documented. These types of reviews will help reinforce OO concepts by revealing several applications in the project domain. Applying these theories is the best continuous education available.

Develop quantifiable metrics to ensure adherence to a specific technique. These measurements should concentrate on the specifics of the application of the technique itself. They may include definition of an object, correct use of graphics, and other documentation.

Inspect the quality of documentation, including graphics. Standards should be developed to define documentation quality. These standards are often overlooked in software development, especially when CASE tools are introduced as documentation aids. We've found that while good graphics increase maintainability, poor graphics detract. Remember that the customer's main perception of system development quality is through the documentation.

Do inspections for more than code. While it's obvious that code will benefit from inspection, the benefits of inspecting requirements, design, and test plans are greater still.

Get formal training on inspections. Implementing inspections badly can be worse than having no inspections at all. A good training course not only explains the roles and processes of inspection but will also illustrate the difference between proper and poor inspection processes, provide template checklists, and generally assure that first inspection efforts have a chance for success. Inspection training can be done in just a few days. If the organization is unused to working with formal processes, a short follow-up course may also be useful.

Recommendations for the Initial Implementation

Don't eliminate pieces of the process or roles within the process. To make sure the process has value, it must be formal and repeatable. While modifications can and should be made after inspections have been adopted, certain phases such as rework or reinspection appear to be necessary for the process to work. Likewise, keep the roles well defined.

Don't skip measurement. The value of the process and its efficacy must be measured. If you decide to make changes to the process, the only way to know if they work or not is to measure. To see if inspections are working at all, you must measure the defect rate. High levels of downstream errors indicate problems with the inspection process. In one study [Shirey92], it was found that inspections did not appear to have benefits. Analysis of the data found major problems with the inspection process which were then corrected. This would not have been possible without measurement. Until you start estimating and tracking defects, you cannot analyze them for process improvements.

Management must be committed to the process. Although this is obvious to the point of triteness, it is nonetheless essential for success. In particular, this means that time must be allocated to inspection preparation, meetings, and follow-up. Time for analysts doing the inspection reading must be allocated; it is not an optional or spare-time activity. It also means that inspections cannot be abandoned to alleviate schedule pressures.

Work for timely beginnings and ends to meetings. The inspection process is already time-consuming. Meeting delays make it more time-consuming still.

Do not bunch up or speed up inspections. Studies have found that careful reading finds the optimum number of defects and reduces the number of reinspections. Attempting to speed the process up by inspecting more pages per hour, or lengthening the meeting time is counterproductive. The same reasoning that limits inspections to two hours at a time indicates that having multiple inspections in a day using the same people will also diminish their effectiveness.

Don't start inspecting every phase at once. Work on a few pieces and add pieces as you've settled in. However, make sure that within a phase, especially requirements analysis, you perform thorough inspections for all components.

Don't bother to do inspections if you don't apply them properly. This sounds harsh, but inspections are costly to implement and are worse than useless if improperly done. Among the common failures in inspections are found defects not being addressed, no reinspection of corrected work, no metrics collection, and no process improvement. These are all errors that make the inspection process fail.

15.8   Automating Inspections

What we have described so far is a fairly orthodox view of inspections and the inspection process. When Fagan initiated inspections [Fagan76], a paper-based, face-to-face meeting model was the only practical way to perform inspections. Even in his 1986 article [Fagan86], paper-based inspection was still the state of the art. Until recently, the cost of using more automation and distributed services for inspections outweighed the benefits. This cost relationship has changed, and some of the limitations of inspections can now be addressed with new technology. E-mail, conferencing, and even virtual meeting software have almost reached the commonplace in even small high-tech companies, and distributed development is now a well-known practice. Inspection processes in the future should make use of the new technology. Philip Johnson has written an insightful description of the way inspection processes can use technology to improve [Johnson98].

No More Face-to-Face?

We feel that in-person meetings are important when introducing inspection technology to the team. They help teams develop through social interaction. Procedural details and meeting etiquette are easier to convey in person. It gives participants a common basis for understanding the group's goals and dynamics. And formal training is easier to conduct when all participants are physically present. These factors suggest that in-person inspections will continue to be valuable regardless of technology advances. However, physical meetings impose limitations.

The more people who have to attend a meeting the more difficult it is to coordinate. Thus, inspections are traditionally limited to nine or fewer participants. For large inspection artifacts, especially certain forms of technical documentation, this can be too small a review group. If a remote conferencing system is available, then more people can be involved without being physically present. Because much of the reviewing happens outside the review meeting, people could either send their review issues to the person playing the role of reader, or they could remotely participate in the meeting when the parts they had read were being discussed. Such a system could reduce the physical coordination problems while linking in more participants to review larger artifacts.

Outsourcing Inspection

Just as distributed development is now possible, so is distributed inspection not just possible, but practical. There is no reason why two teams halfway around the world from each other could not review each other's work. For some specialized functionality, it would be possible to use outside experts, especially if they were not required to be present at a meeting, to lend their skills to a particular project area. Johnson [Johnson98] mentions a company that provides such a review service for developers using the Microsoft graphical user interface (GUI).

Object-oriented frameworks might be an area that would significantly benefit from outsourcing inspections. The framework's creators could be expected to have the greatest understanding of its use, but having people present at inspection meetings would be impossible to accomplish. An asynchronous review service, however, would be cost-effective for all involved, and not only would the group using the framework benefit, but the framework creators would also get a clear view of the way their product was being used. They would get a clearer technical view of usage, product ambiguities, and shortcomings, and they would be able to produce enhancements that did not break their customers' products.

Seven Recommendations for Future Reviews

Johnson gives seven recommendations for the future of formal technical reviews (FTRs) that are based on the changes in widely available technology [Johnson98]. We summarize them here.

> **Provide tighter integration between FTR and the development method.** Inspections are a general technique that can be applied in any environment. In the future, however, linking the inspection process to the development model may provide even greater returns. Johnson suggests that in the spiral model the number of

---

Tips and Practical Advice

Lesson 15.1   Quality must be designed in; quality cannot be inspected in.
Make use of software inspection process for all software products (requirements specification, Design, code, test plans test), but remember, quality cannot be tested into software. Furthermore, inspection alone is ineffective. Quality results from commitment to quality objectives, well-defined processes, continuous measurement supported by formal software inspection, and process improvement.

Lesson 15.2   Modern inspection techniques improve product quality.

- Inspections provide a source of metrics.
- Checklists ensure coverage of all issues.
- Efficient inspections are a wise investment.

---

turns around the spiral may affect the emphasis and roles in the inspection meetings.

Minimize meetings and maximize asynchronicity. As stated above, meetings are hard to coordinate and necessarily contain inefficiencies that waste valuable time. Using distributed development methods, meetings can be reduced, and as much work as possible can be done asynchronously.

Shift the focus from defect removal to improved developer quality. He points out that increasing developer quality to produce fewer defects is a more important goal than just finding defects. He also suggests using inspections on known high-quality documents as a method of improving skills.

Build organizational knowledge bases on review. Johnson suggests the development of knowledge bases that can go beyond finding defects and provide information to multiple groups. Guideline development is also possible.

Outsource review and insource review knowledge. Outside expertise may be used for inspections, especially in areas where the development staff is not expert. In addition, using outside resources can help develop in-house skills.

Investigate computer-mediated review technology. Johnson suggests rethinking inspections and technical reviews to make the best use of commonly available technology.

Break the boundaries on review group size. As stated earlier, physical meetings are necessarily limited in size. Using remote meeting technology and asynchronous reviews, larger groups can work effectively to inspect larger artifacts.

References

[Barnard94] Barnard, J., and A. Price. "Managing Code Inspection Information." *IEEE Software* 11, no. 2 (March 1994).

[Fagan76] Fagan, Michael E. "Design and Code Inspections to Reduce Errors in Program Development." *IBM Systems Journal* 15, no. 3 (1976). pp. 182–211.

[Fagan86] Fagan, Michael E. "Advances In Software Inspections." *IEEE Transactions on Software Engineering* 12, no. 7 (July 1986): 744–751.

[Johnson98] Johnson, Philip M. "Reengineering Inspection." *Communications of the ACM* 41, no. 2 (February 98). pp. 49–52.

[Shirey92] Shirey, G. C. "How Inspections Fail." *Proceedings of the 9th International Conference on Testing Computer Software* (1992).

chapter sixteen

Integrating Software Documentation

16.1   Rethinking Documentation

Organizations underestimate the value of documentation. Good documentation describes the system's purpose, the developers' understanding of the problem domain, and the solution addressing the problem through analysis of the system. It exposes the design of the system and its construction, as well as the logic behind physical connections. Documentation is more accessible to humans at a variety of levels than is the source code that implements the system. While software encapsulates an organization's acquired experience in both the development of programs and in application domains, trying to glean this experience from the source code is often difficult for programmers and virtually impossible for nonprogrammers. The only way to make accessible the accumulated experience and knowledge realized in the software is to record it in documentation.

Good documentation records the system's history: it delineates the evolution of understanding of the system throughout its lifetime, and it records the adaptation of the system to new usage environments. It is usually the only link that maintenance personnel have to the original designers and the evolution of the system. An historical view gives a sense of the magnitude of effort required to bring the system to its present state and gives a guide to the efforts required for future changes.

Documentation is the most visible sign of software quality: the source code and support environment of the system are seldom viewed by anyone other than the development staff. In these senses, documentation is the most valuable software asset of the organization. It is imperative then that the link between documentation and the system is strong, and the documentation must reflect the actual requirements and design of the system. To assure such a connection, we may want to revise the way we think of documentation.

The first revision is to discard the idea that documents should be written once and then filed away. Iterative development is necessary in object-oriented (OO) projects, and as requirements and designs are refined, so should their documentation be refined. The documents should accurately account for the state of development, adding completeness as the work progresses. This can be done only by documenting iteratively as an integral part of the development.

The second revision in our thinking is to start regarding hard-copy documentation as a snapshot of a continually evolving entity, just as we think of code listings as snapshots of the source, rather than as the source code itself. By thinking of snapshots, we focus on the idea of an evolving documentation base closely tied to other development artifacts. It makes the requirements for computer-aided software engineering (CASE) tool compatibility clearer, because it is likely that graphical material and detailed information about requirements and design must be acquired from the CASE system. This view also makes the need for configuration management more obvious: changes in analysis, for example, are reflected in the CASE system, and thus are integrated into the documentation stream.

The third way in which we must change our thinking is to start regarding documentation as an asset. Documentation poses software development risks for the reasons that everybody knows: it is difficult and expensive to write documentation. It is harder still to keep documentation synchronized with software. Effective user documentation, especially tutorial information, is much more of an art than a science, and it often takes much longer than planned. Errors in printed documentation tend to be exceptionally irritating to the customer and very costly to correct. In environments where production software changes rapidly, all the costs of creating and updating documentation are magnified. For some reason, documentation is chronically underestimated in software development planning. Developers who come to regard the documentation as unreliable or out-of-date will ignore it. And finally, documentation is still thought of as an expense that must be borne to get the software done. It is no wonder that organizations tend to regard documentation as a virtue observed more in its breach than in its practice; organizations avoid doing it, even though they know they should. Poor documentation is worse than none at all. A few examples will illustrate this risk.

If software changes and updates do not consistently result in corresponding document changes, the documentation is (correctly) perceived to be unreliable and is not used.

- If the development documentation does not use the same modeling terminology and preferably the same modeling diagrams as the analysis and design, the mismatch will make developers and maintainers avoid documentation.
- A writer in a traditional environment will work on his or her own sections. In those cases where the same information is required in different sections, different writers will have different and probably conflicting descriptions.

We think that documentation should be viewed as the basis for protecting the software investment. Although much is written about reverse and reengineering software, the reality is that large systems are very difficult to understand. A system that has been in place for any length of time will have many fixes and enhancements that complicate the code. In a shockingly large number of existing systems, there is no configuration control that spans the lifetime of the system. Given these difficulties, the cost of analyzing software to maintain or enhance it is prohibitively high. Moreover, the original designers and implementers of the system may no longer be in the organization or may be needed in other areas. Even if they are available, they most likely will not remember details of the system at a level to make it easy to maintain. The bottom line is that analyzing code is difficult, and it is a poor way to handle an asset such as software. Good documentation, however, provides information about the software that makes it accessible even to those unfamiliar with the system. It doesn't eliminate the need to analyze and reverse engineer the source code; it just makes the effort manageable. Further, good documentation will provide useful information about the magnitude of effort involved to make major changes to the software or to replace it with newer technology. The difficulty in our view of software and documentation to this point has been that we view them as independent entities. It is as if we thought of automobiles and automobile engines as separate and usable without each other. Software and documentation similarly need each other.

16.2 Development Documentation

Development documentation must provide a clear indication of how the design corresponds to the system's requirements and how it realizes the OO methodology chosen for the project. It must be possible to trace in either direction between requirements and implementation. Both consistency and completeness are important here. Documentation saves the essential development details that implement software engineering goals, such as efficiency, correctness, understandability, and modifiability. It must also conform to documentation standards. Documentation saves development details that implement software engineering goals, as shown in Figure 16.1.

Mapping an OO technique to documentation standards can be difficult. The problem is compounded with extensive use of graphics. This difficulty is usually traced to the term *standard,* implying "applicable for all developments except mine." What is worse, OO development was probably uncommon when the documentation standard originated. Undoubt-

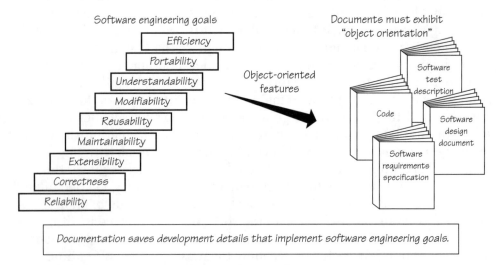

Documentation saves development details that implement software engineering goals.

Figure 16.1   Importance of OO software documentation.

edly, the documentation standard will need to be revised for compatibility with an OO development technique.

We have found that the best approach is to tailor the documentation standard to the specific technique before the development begins. This includes translating all the terms given to the development phases, concepts, and deliverable pieces. It is important to define and maintain focus on the real purpose of the documentation: to record and direct the development and deployment of the system. If the documentation is not trusted by the developers it becomes useless. Technique-specific graphics (possibly generated by CASE tools) should be integrated into specific documentation sections. Diagrams are indispensable to complex designs, just as visual aids are indispensable to building architecture. Diagram integration may prove to be surprisingly difficult to achieve. The mapping is likely to require several revisions; however, the results are well worth the efforts. In addition to the graphics, if detailed documentation of interfaces is part of the standard, it is worthwhile to let the CASE tool generate that as well, and to develop a way to include the information automatically.

Object orientation lends itself to the formulation of requirements and decomposition from the problem domain down to details. Requirements documentation can be organized in the same way: describe first the principal objects that map the domain. Then continue describing objects, interactions, flows, and other analysis artifacts as they relate to each other according to the OO method you have chosen. Avoid making just an alphabetical catalog of objects and methods: These are cumbersome and provide less useful information about the architecture of the system.

The minimum requirements for documentation are the following:

- Unfailing consistency between the documentation and the analysis, design, and implementation of the software. This is a metarequirement without which the other requirements are meaningless.
- Documentation must include analysis, requirements, design, code, and test documents (both plans and results). User manuals must also be done.
- Description of the purpose of the system and reference to the software development plan (SDP). The SDP will either contain

or reference domain information, environment, and hardware/ software constraints.

- List of the object classes arranged by model level, along with the expected links and associations between them.
- For each object, a description of its interface.

This minimum is difficult enough in itself, but there are many more types of documentation and many more issues to be considered. The SDP is the primary document that provides links and descriptions of other documents.

DOD-STD-2167a and MIL-STD-498

Although not commonly used in commercial industry, the U.S. Department of Defense software development standards, DOD-STD-2167a and MIL-STD-498, provide a useful framework for identifying development documentation. They list the following documentation items:

- System/subsystem specification
- System/subsystem design description
- Software design description
- Interface design description
- Computer operation manual
- Computer programming manual
- Software user manual
- Software transition plan
- Software version description

Not all of these documents will exist in all development projects. In addition, documentation for items listed in the SDP (as we describe in Chapter 3) such as risk management, subcontractor management, corrective actions, test plans, and security are required. The standards may not be formatted to everyone's liking, but they contain valuable information that should find its way into the documentation stream of any significant development.

16.3 User Documents

User-oriented documentation has a different purpose from development documentation. Development documents provide people intimately involved with the system a clear and detailed path between the requirements and the implementation, while user documents guide people, who may have no interest in the structure of the system, in its effective use. For user-oriented documentation, mapping to documentation standards is only the first requirement. For example, the IEEE standard for user manuals provides only the form that the document should take: intended audience, table of contents, index, references, and so on. This form, while necessary, provides no guidance on methods for making readers understand the purpose or the expected usage of the program.

User manuals, because they are completed after analysis and design, tend to be more stable than development and maintenance documents. To users, they are more than just snapshots of the system at a particular state. For that reason, user documents are also more likely to exist primarily in hard copy. Frequent changes and updates to user manuals can be irritating to people trying to use the system and suggest that the product is incomplete.

What are some ways in which we can make user-oriented documentation useful? One way is to use scenarios or use cases as the basis for documentation. If the use cases cover the expected system usage, then describing use cases should give a user an accurate and relevant guide to operation. Likewise, if the use cases bear little resemblance to the usage, or if the use cases leave too much of the system's operation undocumented, then the analysis was probably wrong or incomplete. Other suggestions include:

♦ Avoid hierarchical catalogs of the system's commands and procedures. This is not the way people learn to use software, nor is it an effective way to familiarize a user with a system.

♦ Avoid tutorial exercises that don't impart useful skills. The purpose of the tutorial is usually not to make users wholly familiar with every feature but to give them initial mastery of enough of the system so they can acquire by themselves the added skills they need.

- Keep some of the paper-based forms in on-line user documentation. For example, tables of contents, indexes, and references that look like the paper-based forms aid in navigating on-line material. Keyword searches, annotations, and links, of course, should be added.

- Consider providing both hard-copy and on-line documentation. While on-line documentation is both trendy and useful, it is often awkward or impossible to switch between documentation and program screens. In addition, on-line documentation cannot be studied off-line.

16.4   Other Documentation Issues

Customers

If customer approval is required for documentation decisions, include the customer in the early discussions. Customers will often be the ultimate system maintenance agent and may have strong feelings on specific documentation issues. Simple agreements early in a program may avert many later headaches.

Documentation in Software Engineering

Effective software engineering (like other engineering disciplines) guarantees neither success nor perfection, but for all significant projects, the lack of software engineering virtually guarantees failure. While consultants continue to thrive on projects that have no documentation, such projects become increasingly intractable as they age. Major upgrades benefit little from previous work or scheduling. The implication, of course, is that most projects have a life span that will see maintenance and enhancement, and these phases will cost as much as or more than the original development. Without documentation of the design, development plans, and maintenance history, a system must be analyzed anew each time.

Configuration Management

Software configuration management is essential for all but the smallest documentation suites. Without configuration management, documentation integrity is impossible. The internal form for documentation in most word-processing and document-processing systems is a binary file rather than text. Besides the text and graphic information, document-processing systems keep information about the style and format of the documentation, none of which is plain text. In this way document source is different from source code, and, therefore, it imposes an additional burden for configuration management. You must develop a document control mechanism that deals with binary information. The expertise to develop such a system will almost certainly have to come from outside the technical documentation groups and should be done before development begins.

Inspections

Inspections should be done for all documentation. For user documentation especially, beware of the political issues involved. Good user manuals and tutorials are still more art than science, and many technical writers, even more than programmers, dislike having their work publicly scrutinized. This reluctance is exacerbated by the fact that members of the inspection team have poor writing skills. To avoid trouble, follow some of the basic inspection rules.

- Documents must be spell checked, proofread, and formatted before distribution to the inspectors.
- Make the inspection focus on finding defects, such as incorrect descriptions, unclear passages, omissions of information important to the user, and deviations from documentation standards.
- Avoid issues of writing style.
- Remember that the intended user will probably have far less interest in the internal workings of the program than the developers, so when thinking about a documentation omission, be sure that it affects the user's ability to work with the system.

Minimality

Documentation is expensive. Use the minimum needed to accurately capture the principal features of the development. Automate as much documentation as possible, tying it to CASE information, and avoiding redundancy. Low-level details are best kept in CASE tools and extracted automatically to other documentation. Documenting for reusability, however, requires a greater level of documentation.

Organizational Issues

An object-oriented approach to documentation forces a change in the way documentation is organized and will probably force a change in the organization of the technical writing staff. As Bist points out, writing about a top-down-structured program meant that the technical writing tended to be divided into sections handled by different writers. In the object-oriented model, "all writers must design the information as a group—several times in an iterative way. Since writers share many files, they must agree on a common format and style for each object" [Bist96]. Even if it hadn't been required before, the larger number of smaller files necessitates a configuration management and change control mechanism.

Just as the development group's efforts will shift so that more time is spent in analysis and design, so too will the writing staff's time change. More time and effort will be spent designing the program and its documentation, and the writing implementation will consist of many more units of information, each in its own small file. Emphasis will change from writing in isolation to writing in groups, and each writer will have to develop a greater knowledge of coworkers' efforts to eliminate redundant descriptions.

The impact of these changes should not be underestimated. Writers, like programmers, have not traditionally worked as close-knit teams. They have been able to pick larger chunks of information to document as logical units. The new mode compels a tighter cooperation not only with other writers, but also with software developers and software development CASE tools. The higher commitment at analysis and design and lower commitment during the testing cycle will change staffing loads. Training must include configuration management and OO concepts as well as problem-specific issues.

16.5   Summary

We have made a case in this chapter for rethinking our views of documentation. Documentation is often slighted because it is high risk and

Tips and Practical Advice

The following practical tips have been mentioned throughout the chapter and are summarized in Figure 16.2 for convenience.

Lesson 16.1   Organize requirements, design, and testing documents hierarchically by objects and include the links between them.

Lesson 16.2   Integrate graphics with text. Use CASE and modern illustration/word-processing tools.

Lesson 16.3   Adopt an object-oriented approach to the documentation.
This means that writers will use the same analysis, design, and implementation data that the software developers use. Instead of writing monolithic documents, writers will include links to other writers' work so as to eliminate redundancy and conflict [Bist96].

Lesson 16.4   Configuration management of graphics and text is critical.
Remember that document-processing systems are not necessarily text based, and change control will require extra effort.

Lesson 16.5   Standards provide a more flexible framework for documenting object-oriented software.

Lesson 16.6   Time and money saved by delaying documentation wastes more time and money later in the development.

Lesson 16.7   Documentation requires experience to determine a proper balance between too much and too little.
Too little requirements specification documentation and too little design documentation can cause a maintenance nightmare. Forty-five percent of the total effort for documentation requirements for military software developments as compared with 22 percent of the effort spent on the same activities for commercial applications. Documentation is a high risk in cost and schedule.

1. Organize requirements, designing, and testing documents by object

2. Integrate graphics (notation) with text

3. Configuration management of graphics and text is critical

4. DOD-STD-2167A and MIL-STD-498 (SDD) provide a more flexible framework for documenting object-oriented software

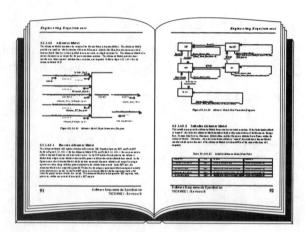

Figure 16.2   Generating OO software documentation.

seems peripheral to the development effort. We feel this is wrong. It must be viewed as an asset integral to the software itself. It must change as the software changes, and it must be under the same requirements for completion and control as the software product it accompanies.

Development documentation must exhibit the same properties of object orientation that the software embodies. To do this, it must be modular, linked, and based on the same evolving information base as the software itself. This means it must cease to be a paper-based artifact. The paper copy should be thought of as merely a snapshot of the current state of the document. User documentation likewise must evolve. User documents have often suffered from the syndrome of *total comprehension before first use.* This is simply impractical for most systems. User documents should evolve to a form that allows early mastery of essential components and gradual acquisition of more advanced skills.

References

[Bist96] Bist, Gary. "Applying the Object-Oriented Model to Technical Information." *IEEE Transactions on Software Engineering* 39, no. 1 (March 1996).

Sample Process for Software Inspection

Process Documentation Template:

Item	Description
Process Title	Defines process name, such as Software Inspection Process
Process #	CSP-ddd
Date	January 20, 1998
Created/Modified By	Software process group (SPG)
Definitions	Defines all the special concepts and roles in the process
Rationale	A software inspection is a method to identify and document defects and problems found during the inspection process.
Definitions	A) Defects: A *defect* is an error in a software product including documentation, requirements models, designs, code, test plans/procedures/result, user documentation, and so forth. A defect prevents the software from meeting its requirements or meeting standards. Defects are classified according to severity, type, mode, phase generated, and phase found.
	B) Severity:
	Critical. A major defect has no known work around and will cause the system to fail in meeting a requirement.

Major. Causes a malfunction or unexpected result and would lead to an incorrect response or misinterpretation of the information by the user.

Minor. It is undesirable but would not cause a malfunction or unexpected result and is undesirable but would not be detected by the user.

C) Type:

Requirements Defects:

Requirement Wrong (RW): An error exists in the requirements that are included.

Requirements Missing (RM): The requirements are incomplete.

More Detail (MD): The requirements are ambiguous as written. Need enough detail so that there's only one correct interpretation of the information present.

Interface (IN): An error exists in an interface defined between objects.

Standards (ST): The specification does not meet the standards.

Design:

Logic (LO): An error exists in the logic.

More Detail (MD): The design is ambiguous as written. Need enough detail so that there's only one correct interpretation of the information present.

Standards (ST): The code and ADL, including headers, does not perform to required specifications.

Performance (PE): If the object is time-critical, alternate designs may be discussed to optimize performance.

Higher Level Design (HL): The preliminary design does not correctly implement the requirements.

Requirements (RQ): A requirements error was detected at the detailed design inspection.

Interface (IN): An error exists in an interface defined between objects.

Precision (PR): The precision of a data entity is incorrect.

Test Code (TC): An error was found in an object test case.

Code:

Logic (LO): An error exists in the logic.

More Detail (MD): The design is ambiguous as written. Need enough detail so that there's only one correct interpretation of the information present.

Standards (ST): The code and ADL, including headers, does not perform to required standards.

Performance (PR): If the object is time-critical, alternate designs may be discussed to optimize performance.

Higher Level Design (HL): The preliminary design does not correctly implement the requirements.

Requirements (RQ): A requirements error was detected at the code inspection.

Interface (IN): An error exists in an interface defined between objects.

Precision (PR): The precision of a data entity is incorrect.

Test Case (TC): An error was found in a unit test case.

D) Mode:

Missing.   Information that is specified in the requirements or standards, but is not present.

Extra.   Information that is not specified in the requirements or standards but is present.

Wrong.   Information that is specified in the requirements or standards and is present but incorrect.

E) Phase Generated: Phase in which the defect was introduced. For defects found in inspections, this is the current phase.

F) Phase Found: Phase in which the defect was found. For defects found in specifications, this is the current phase.

G) Additional Information Needed per Defect:

Source SDR (if any): (Not applicable for defects found in inspections)

Date Defect Found

Date Defect Corrected

Document or Code in which defect found

Mhrs to Correct Defect

H) Inspected Items:

Software inspection process is suitable for all software products such as:

User manuals

Software development plan

Software requirements specification

Software design document

Code

Test procedures

Test plans

Software Inspection Process

The typical phases of an inspection are as follows:

Planning.   After a work package is completed, it is scheduled for inspection. Specific roles are assigned for the inspection team, and the materials, such as listings, requirements specifications, and design documents, are distributed to the team members.

Overview.   A presentation is made to the team members to familiarize them with the work package to be inspected. If the team is already familiar with the package, then no overview meeting is necessary.

Individual inspection.   Each inspector reads the material looking for and noting errors. As mentioned in the following, different inspectors may concentrate on different aspects of the same work package to speed the process.

Inspection meeting.   This is a moderated meeting in which the reader presents the work package and individual inspectors look for and note errors. The meeting is limited to two hours at the most, and defects are noted without proposing resolutions.

Rework. The author of the work package fixes the listed defects.

Follow-up. The corrections are checked and, if necessary, another inspection is scheduled.

Roles and How	The participants on a software inspection and a general description of their responsibilities are as follows:

Moderator. The person who ensures the readiness of the product for inspection (clean compiles, conforms to style standards, and so forth), distributes the inspection materials, schedules, and runs the inspection meeting. In the inspection meeting, the moderator makes sure that team members remain focused on finding and recording defects.

Reader. During the inspection meeting, the reader presents the work and in some cases paraphrases the text. This should not be the author/developer but should be a key inspector.

Inspectors. The people who read the text of the work package both before and during the meeting, looking for defects. The number of inspectors should be minimized so that the whole inspection meeting has no more than six to nine people.

Author. The person who has created the work package. The author may not be the reader or the moderator. Answers questions during inspection. Fixes the problems found.

When	Whenever needed and scheduled.
Regulations	Inspections should not be combined.
	Inspections should not exceed the recommended number of attendees.
	Inspections should not exceed two hours meeting time.
	Any exceptions must be documented in the Project Development Plan (PDP) for that software project.
	(. . . other regulations).
Checklists	Note: Must be prepared by the author.
Forms	A sample form is included in Software Requirement Specifications Inspection Sheet.
Notes	Lists problems encountered and participants' suggestions.

Software Requirements Inspection Defects List

Project:
System:
Class:

Name

Author:
Moderator:
Reader:
Tester:
Requirements:
# of Inspectors

Prep. Time

Inspection:

Reinspection:

Total:

Group Insp. Date:
Start Time:
End Time:
Group Insp. Date:
Start Time:
End Time:
Group Insp. Date:
Total Overview Time:
Total Preparation Time:
Total Time Used:

H:MM
H:MM
H:MM

Est. Rework Time:
Actual Rework Time:
Reinspection Required?
Est. Rework Date
Actual Rework Date
Passed (Moderator Signoff)?
Pages Inspected:
Rqmts Inspected:

DEFECT SUMMARY:

Defect Severity
Critical   CR   O
Major   MA   O
Minor   MI   O
    TOTAL: O

Defect Class
Missing   M   O
Wrong   W
Extra   E   O
    TOTAL: O

Defect Type
Reqmts Wrong   RW   O
More Detail   MD   O
Standards   ST   O
Reqmts Missing   RM   O
Interface   IN   O
    TOTAL: O

Page	Section/Line No.	Defect Type	Defect Severity	Defect Class	Rework Complete	Defect Description

Note: You have to create a similar sheet for other inspected items.

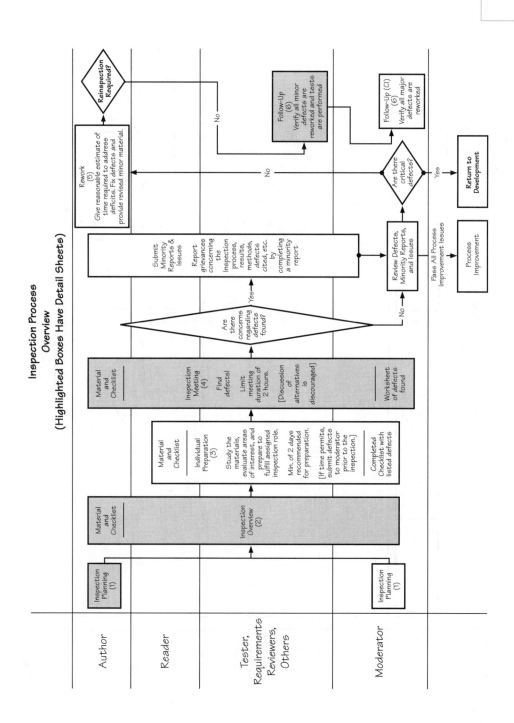

Inspection Process
Overview
(Highlighted Boxes Have Detail Sheets)

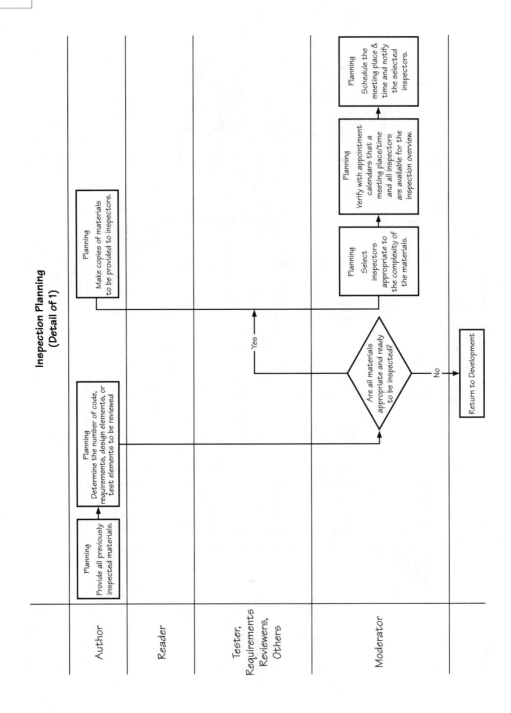

Inspection Planning
(Detail of 1)

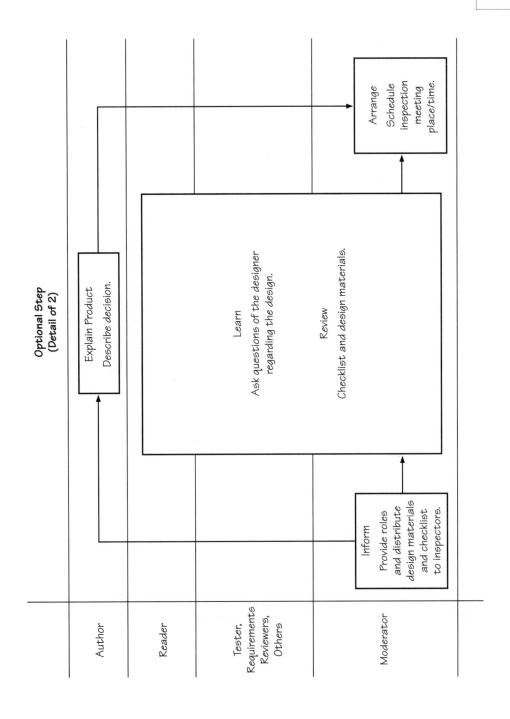

Optional Step
(Detail of 2)

Author

Explain Product
Describe decision.

Reader

Tester,
Requirements
Reviewers,
Others

Learn
Ask questions of the designer regarding the design.

Review
Checklist and design materials.

Moderator

Inform
Provide roles and distribute design materials and checklist to inspectors.

Arrange
Schedule inspection meeting place/time.

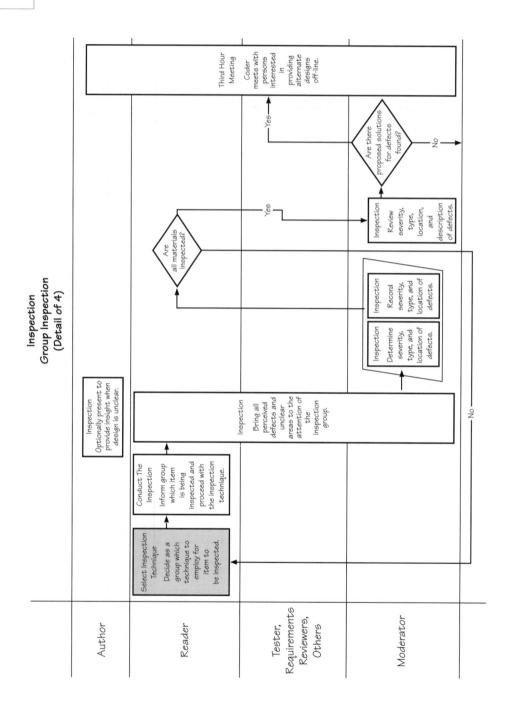

Inspection
Group Inspection
(Detail of 4)

> ### Group Inspection
> ### Select Inspection Technique
> (Notes for Detail of 4)
>
> ◆ Determine by group agreement and organization policies the inspection technique to be used for current item to be inspected.
> ◆ Inspect the product covering a line at a time. Reader tells group which line is being analyzed for defects.
> ◆ Ask inspectors whether any defects were discovered in entire section being inspected. Reader tells group which section is being looked at and asks which defects were found.
> ◆ Cite defects by referring to worksheet. Reader refers to defects previously specified by inspectors.
> ◆ Record all defects.

Mapping the Graphical Inspection Process to Roles

This document describes the activities of each person with a role in the inspection process for each inspection phase.

Author

Planning step
  ◆ Review document and ensure it is ready to be inspected.
  ◆ Provide moderator with the document to be inspected.
Overview step
  ◆ Present document at overview meeting explaining the inspection's purpose and background.

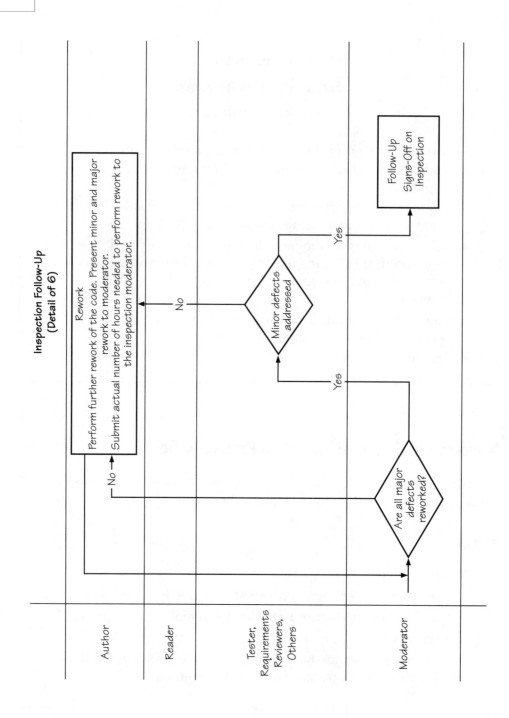

Inspection Follow-Up
(Detail of 6)

Author

Reader

Tester,
Requirements
Reviewers,
Others

Moderator

Rework

Perform further rework of the code. Present minor and major rework to moderator. Submit actual number of hours needed to perform rework to the inspection moderator.

Minor defects addressed

Are all major defects reworked?

Follow-Up
Signs-Off on
Inspection

No

No

Yes

Yes

Preparation step

- Prepare for inspection meeting by studying document, recording defects, and making notes on the document.

Inspection step

- Participate as an inspector in the inspection meeting.
- Listen to the interpretations of readers/inspectors and verify that the document's intent is understood and accurately communicated.
- Report on identified defects.
- Give estimate for rework time.

Rework step

- Correct the defects documented on the defect list.

Follow-up step

- Present corrected document to moderator for sign-off.

Moderator

Planning step

- Ensure that document is ready for inspection, meets entry criteria.
- Collect inspection document, standards, requirements, and other supporting material.
- Select inspection roles and inspection team.
- Decide if document needs to be chunked into several inspection meetings.
- Make copies of inspection document and supporting materials.
- Arrange and schedule overview meeting and send out meeting notices.

Overview step

- Chair the overview meeting.
- Assign roles to the inspection team.
- Provide guidance on inspectors' roles and responsibilities.

- Distribute inspection material at end of overview meeting.
- Record overview time.
- Ensure that inspection meeting has been arranged and meeting notices have been sent out.

Preparation step

- Prepare for inspection meeting by studying document, recording defects, and making notes on the document.

Inspection step

- Chair the inspection meeting.
- Collect preparation times from the team.
- Determine if adequate preparation was made by attendees.
- Keep team focused on finding defects not solutions.
- Participate as an inspector.
- Ensure that all defects are categorized and recorded on defect list.
- Record issues.
- Determine if reinspection is necessary.
- Record inspection meeting time.
- Record rework estimate time.

Follow-up step

- Ensure that author has corrected all defects.
- Sign-off reworked document.
- Generate inspection summary report.

Reader

Overview step

- Understand author's presentation of document's intent.
- Understand inspection team role.

Presentation step

- Prepare for inspection meeting by studying document, recording defects, and making notes on identified defects.

Inspection step
  - ◆ Read document aloud and interpret meaning at inspection meeting.
  - ◆ Report on identified defects.

Rework step
  - ◆ If requested, assist author in correcting defects.

Tester/Other Inspector

Overview step
  - ◆ Understand author's presentation of document's intent.
  - ◆ Understand designated inspection team role.

Preparation step
  - ◆ Prepare for inspection meeting by studying document, recording defects, and making notes on the document.

Inspection step
  - ◆ Report on identified defects.

Rework step
  - ◆ If requested, assist author in correcting defects.

Summary of Tips
and Practical Advice

Chapter 2   Transition Planning

2.1   The transition to object-oriented software engineering (OOSE) is a mission with problems.

2.2   There is little guidance for object-oriented software development (OOSD) project managers on how to transition to OOSE.

2.3   Careful selection of the first object-oriented project is very important.

2.4   On average, the transition of a single software development team to OOSE takes at least a year.

Chapter 3   Effective Development Planning

3.1   A software development plan (SDP) must be the first document produced.

3.2   An SDP policy should be in place.

3.3   The existence of a complete and responsive SDP is not a guarantee of project success.

Chapter 4   Dealing with Culture Change

4.1   Transition planning is critical.

4.2   Thinking in terms of objects is essential.

4.3   Upper management must fully support the transition and provide the support and resources needed to change.

4.4   Management must change as much as the team.

4.5   Resistance must be actively managed.

4.6   The customer must understand the transition of project processes and tools.

4.7   The culture must be prepared.

4.8   The change must be sold to the team, to the customer, and to management.

4.9   Personality conflicts usually aren't.

Chapter 5   Selecting the Right Object-Oriented Technique

5.1   Avoid use of the functional decomposition front-end to an object-oriented method.

5.2   Stick to the method.

5.3   Selecting the appropriate technique is critical to project success.

5.4   Technique selection will impact virtually every activity in the new software development process.

5.5   Most verification and validation (V&V) activities remain ad hoc.

5.6   Software engineers must adapt.

5.7   There are some hidden risks that are associated with each object-oriented technique.

Chapter 6   Selecting the Right Computer-Aided Software Engineering Tool

6.1   Computer-aided software engineering (CASE) tool support is important for object-oriented development projects.

6.2   The selected tool must be true to the technique.

6.3   Object diagram complexity dictates the need for CASE tools.

6.4   Selecting a CASE tool follows technique selection.

6.5   CASE tools can have negative impact if improperly applied.

6.6   CASE selection must be based on a need-driven process.

Chapter 7   Staffing and Organizing the Project

7.1   Staffing the first object-oriented project requires special consideration.

7.2   Development teams' or developers' attitudes and attributes are one of the major keys to success or failure of adapting the object-oriented technology on the project.

7.3   Development of a large system may require an object orientation guru to ensure that the methods and tools are rigorously followed, as well as to provide follow-up training to the development team when needed.

7.4   Specialized software disciplines (e.g., OORA, OOD, Ada, C++, Java, and testing) help the development process.

Chapter 8   Training

8.1   Involve the entire team at early requirements analysis sessions.

8.2   Training is essential for new object-oriented development teams.

8.3   Train for the whole life cycle.

8.4   The method of training must be carefully selected.

8.5   Training should be spread over a number of weeks.

8.6   Training examples are much easier than real problems.

8.7   Laboratory participation is mandatory.

8.8   Object orientation learning curve is relatively steep.

8.9   Organize the training so that participants are not distracted.

8.10 Do not substitute on-line or self-directed training for the major pieces.

Chapter 9   Dealing with the Legacy Systems

9.1   Legacy systems must be recognized and dealt with effectively.

Chapter 10   Budgeting for Reuse

10.1   To support change, the system needs to have it built into the system.

10.2   The whole notion of changeability must be a fundamental business decision.

10.3   Do not expect huge gains from the first reuse effort.

10.4   Designing for reuse requires extra effort.

10.5   Reuse is not free.

Chapter 11   Analyzing, Modeling, and Prototyping

11.1   OO analysis and design dramatically enhance requirements' traceability.

11.2   Reduce risks by using prototypes early in the development phase.

11.3   Prototyping provides better and more accurate feedback for user interaction.

Chapter 12   Effective Tracking and Controlling

12.1   Avoid wishful thinking for project estimates.

12.2   Estimates must come after analysis.

12.3   Pay attention to interfaces.

12.4   Conduct a postmortem.

Chapter 13   Defining and Documenting the Development Process

13.1   The development process must be documented.

13.2   Use a project process team.

13.3   Measure processes rather than people.

13.4   Software development processes map the abstract theories of the object-oriented technique into concrete and repeatable actions.

13.5   Processes cannot be acquired off the shelf but must be developed over time.

13.6   Warning: Poor process use is crippling.

13.7   Process-oriented development lets team members contribute effectively.

Chapter 14   Applying Software Metrics

14.1   Metrics provide the ruler that measures success or failure.

14.2   Metrics provide a means of measuring process quality and identifying potential bottlenecks.

14.3   Correlation is a critical requirement for any metric.

14.4   Metrics will change over time: Initial measurements will give an idea of what measurements we should make in the future.

14.5   Measurement requires sensitivity.

14.6   Employ expert statistical help for all but the simplest analysis.

Chapter 15   Inspecting Object-Oriented Software Products

15.1   Quality must be designed in; quality cannot be inspected in.

15.2   Modern inspection techniques improve product quality.

Chapter 16   Integrating Software Documentation

16.1   Organize requirements, design, and testing documents hierarchically by objects and include the links between them.

16.2   Integrate graphics with text. Use CASE and modern illustration/word processing tools.

16.3   Adopt an object-oriented approach to the documentation.

16.4   Configuration management of graphics and text is critical.

16.5   Standards provide a more flexible framework for documenting object-oriented software.

16.6   Time and money saved by delaying documentation wastes more time and money later in the development.

16.7   Documentation requires experience to determine a proper balance between too much and too little.

appendix c

Annotated References

We list here selected references and give short descriptions of each reference's particular contribution. This list is not intended to be exhaustive but is rather intended to provide pointers to important literature that gives background and extension to the subjects covered in our text.

Magazine/Journal Articles

[Bach95] Bach, J. "Enough About Process: What We Need Are Heroes." *IEEE Software,* 12, no. 2 (February 1995).

This article provides an antidote to the claims that put processes before people in software development. While we don't agree with all of Bach's conclusions, it's refreshing to have somebody remind us that people, and not processes, create software.

[Bist96] Bist, Gary. "Applying the Object-Oriented Model to Technical Information." *IEEE Transactions on Software Engineering,* 39, no. 1 (March 1996).

This article is one of the few discussions about matching technical documentation to object-oriented development methods. Bist describes important features of OO technical documentation and suggests organizational principles for documentation as a whole.

[Brooks87] Brooks, Fredrick P. "No Silver Bullet: Essence and Accidents of Software Engineering." *IEEE Computer,* 20, no. 4 (April 1987).

This article expresses what experienced practitioners understand: Developing software is inherently hard, and there are no magical ways to make software simple to produce. He predicted that there was no technology coming up in the coming decade that would give an order-of-magnitude improvement in software development. Although written over a decade ago, Brooks's thesis is as hotly discussed and debated today as it was when it was published. The article and a retrospective commentary on it are included in the 20th anniversary reissue of his classic book, *The Mythical Man-Month.* His conclusion is that he was right about his prediction. This is one of the foundational articles of software engineering.

[Fayad96a] Fayad, M. E., W. T. Tsai, and M. L. Fulghum. "Transition to Object-Oriented Software Development." *The Communications of the ACM,* 39, no. 2, pp. 108–121 (February 1996).

This article provides the foundation for this book. It advances the proposition that while object-oriented (OO) approaches to software development are becoming increasingly prevalent, the transition is a mission with problems. Although research on the technical aspects of object technology is plentiful, many divergent opinions exist. There is also little guidance for development project managers on how to effect the transition to object-oriented software engineering. The article identifies the three major stages of the transition: (1) planning and preproject stage; (2) technology insertion stage; and (3) project management stage. Important issues are identified for each stage, and proven approaches based on real project experience are suggested.

[Schein96] Schein, E. "Three Cultures of Management: The Key to Organizational Learning." *Sloan Management Review* (Fall 1996).

Schein is a pioneer in the study of organizational culture. In this article, he identifies different corporate subcultures and their particular interests along with the way they interface to others outside their group. This article provides clues to understand conflicts within corporate culture. A "must read" for any manager working on culture change.

Columns

[Fayad97a] Fayad, M. E. "Software Development Processes: The Necessary Evil." *Communications of the ACM,* 40, no. 9 (September 1997).

Each of these columns is part of the "Thinking Objectively" series, in which various topics in object-oriented software development are explored. This particular column discusses the necessity of introducing repeatable processes into the software development life cycle. Issues covered include the value of documented processes, resistance to and problems with process documentation, and how to start organizing processes.

[Fayad97b] Fayad, M. E. and M. D. Laitinen. "Process Assessment: Considered Wasteful." *Communications of the ACM,* 40, no. 11 (November 1997).

This column questions the generally accepted first step of process improvement: the assessment phase. It cites the lack of data supporting software process improvement (specifically the CMM) in smaller companies and the lack of good tailoring of the CMM to those companies.

[Fayad98] Fayad, M. E. "The Art of Managing Multiple Processes." *Communications of the ACM,* 41, no. 5 (May 1998).

This column discusses the issues of managing multiple processes in multiple projects. It discusses the concepts of prototyping processes and when to combine processes done by different groups into common processes.

[Laitinen98] Laitinen, M. D. and M. E. Fayad. "Surviving a Process Performance Crash." *Communications of the ACM,* 41, no. 2 (February 1998), pp. 83–86.

The proposition of this column is that there is a learning curve associated with adopting a process orientation, and there can be a temporary reduction in productivity until people become comfortable with processes. Suggestions are given to deal with the learning curve.

Theme Issues

[Fayad95] Fayad, M. E. and W. T. Tsai. "Object-Oriented Experiences and Future Trends." *Communications of the ACM,* 38, no. 10 (October 1995).

This theme issue assembles a group of authors who share their experiences in transitioning to object-oriented technology in their work environments. Two articles describe managerial issues in the transition of a development group of 150 people to object-oriented development on IBM's AS/400 project. Technical issues include the use of design patterns for distributed systems in communications companies, testing and maintenance, and scientific parallel processing.

[Fayad96] Fayad, M. E. and M. Cline. "Managing Object-Oriented Software Development." *IEEE Computer,* 29, no. 9 (September 1996).

This theme issue describes the lessons learned in managing over 100 object-oriented projects. Among the issues covered in the articles are strategy, dealing with development iteration, productivity, reuse through frameworks, project traceability, and practical experiences. Managerial concerns in OO such as planning, staffing, training, scheduling, cost estimation, documentation, development, legacy systems, and metrics are specifically covered.

[Fayad97] Fayad, M. E. and D. Schmidt. "Object-Oriented Application Frameworks." *Communications of the ACM,* 40, no. 10 (October 1997).

This theme issue describes the design and use of application frameworks and their value as a high-level means of reuse as well as a way to capture the essence of successful software patterns, architectures, components, and programming mechanisms. Areas covered in the articles include the design and evolution of frameworks, domain partitioning, framework use in large systems, framework tailoring guidelines, evolving from applications to frameworks, frameworks for educational purposes, and practical experiences in framework construction. Case studies in multimedia, broadcasting, banking, and computer-integrated manufacturing augment the theoretical discussions.

[Schmidt96] Schmidt, D., M. E. Fayad, and R. Johnson. "Software Patterns." *Communications of the ACM,* 39, no. 10 (October 1996).

This theme issue covers various topics in software patterns, including social-architectural interaction, software adaptability, real-world pattern pros and cons, and practical examples of pattern use. The practical examples of pattern use include training, fault-tolerant distributed state sharing, patterns for parallel locking, and concurrent and distributed control systems. Articles also describe how patterns can aid reuse and simplify modeling and design, and how they make a step toward the creation of the software equivalent of engineering handbooks.

Books

[Bennatan92] Bennatan, E. M. *On Time, Within Budget: Software Project Management Practices and Techniques.* New York: John Wiley & Sons, 1995.

The book concentrates on modern software management practices and techniques that have been developed and refined over the past decade. Project management is presented as an acquired skill and not an innate talent. This is a practical text and not a theoretical work. Many methods and techniques are described without their theoretical basis. However, extensive references are provided throughout the book for those interested in the theoretical background. A comprehensive list of references and recommended reading appears at the end of the book.

[Boehm81] Boehm, B. W. *Software Engineering Economics.* Englewood Cliffs, New Jersey: Prentice-Hall, 1981.

This classic of software economics introduces the COCOMO estimation model and provides encyclopedic discussions on the cost and benefit issues in software development. Included in the book are case studies, evaluations of life-cycle models, cost analysis, performance models, economies of scale, decision analysis, value analysis, risk analysis, maintenance cost considerations, and productivity improvement.

[Booch94] Booch, G. *Object-Oriented Analysis and Design with Applications.* Redwood City: Benjamin/Cummings, 1994.

This is another classic book on object-oriented analysis and design. Like the Rumbaugh and Jacobson books, it lays out the concepts of objects and object-oriented modeling using Booch's own notation. From the models, the book proceeds to implementation concepts using C++ and touches on various practical programming issues. Included are a series of sample applications which are described in phases from analysis through maintenance. This is a useful book for learning object-oriented concepts.

[Brooks95] Brooks, F. P. *The Mythical Man-Month,* Anniversary Edition, Reading, Massachusetts: Addison-Wesley, 1995.

Although it describes the development of a long obsolete IBM mainframe operating system, OS/360, this 20th anniversary edition of Brooks's 1975 book is as worthwhile to read today as it was when it was first published. The software industry's short history and its relentless advancement make the added retrospective essays a real boon to understanding software management. Most of the original information has worn well, but the added commentaries illuminate how the best understanding of that time has yielded to new understanding. An extra bonus in the book is the inclusion of his classic essay, "No Silver Bullet," and a ten-year retrospective commentary on that as well.

[Demarco87] DeMarco, T. and T. Lister. *Peopleware: Productive Projects and Teams.* New York: Dorset House, 1987.

Tom DeMarco has written many worthwhile books on software management and human issues in software. Many software developers avoid working for managers who have not read this book.

[DeMarco95] DeMarco, T. *Why Does Software Cost So Much?: And Other Puzzles of the Information Age,* New York: Dorset House, 1995.

This 1995 book of essays on software provides, among its many delights, an interesting view of the software crisis: It doesn't exist. This is useful reading for software developers who have trouble explaining why software takes so much time and effort to build.

[Deming86] Deming, W. Edwards. *Out of the Crisis.* Cambridge, Massachusetts: MIT CAES, 1986.

Although not directed at software development, Deming still has more to say about quality and metrics than any other author. His analysis of problems is compelling and his recommendations for restructuring organizations are still radical even though a dozen years have past since he made them. This book is essential reading for anyone developing a metrics or quality assurance program or anyone involved in changing corporate culture.

[Gamma95] Gamma, E., R. Helm, R. Johnson, and J. Vlissides. *Design Patterns: Elements of Reusable Object-Oriented Software,* Reading, Massachusetts: Addison-Wesley, 1995.

This book has quickly become the classic description of software design patterns. It describes the ideas behind software patterns, relates them to object-oriented programming, and describes the contexts in which patterns should be used. The largest portion of the book is devoted to describing in detail 23 of the most commonly used and useful software design patterns. This book is essential reading for object-oriented designers and programmers and for those dealing with application frameworks.

[Glass92] Glass, R. L. *Building Quality Software.* Englewood Cliffs, New Jersey: Prentice-Hall, 1992.

Robert Glass is a prolific author who has written many books on the human issues involved in software development. Unlike so many books that treat software development as purely a technical issue, Glass uses both research and experience to illustrate how technical issues and human issues must be considered together when looking at software organizations. He describes practices that work and those that do not. This book discusses in detail a variety of techniques and issues in the area of software quality, including design approaches, formal methods, programming languages, inspections, testing, V&V, and metrics. He provides case studies in software quality.

[Glass98] Glass, R. L. *Software Runaways.* Upper Saddle River, New Jersey: Prentice-Hall, 1998.

Anyone who has experience with large software projects knows that they are notoriously hard to keep under control and is undoubtedly aware of software projects that failed. In his typical fashion, Glass combines useful studies with war stories about large projects that failed and comes up with a useful synthesis of information that can be applied to new projects to gauge their susceptibility to failure.

[Humphrey89] Humphrey, W. S. *Managing the Software Process.* Reading, Massachusetts: Addison-Wesley, 1989.

This is the classic description of software development using the Software Engineering Institute's Capability Maturity Model (CMM). Any discussion of software process begins with this book which has exerted a strong influence in the development community. The book's orientation is toward large defense software contractors with traditional management hierarchies. Some of the recommendations and procedures will not map well to small organizations outside this environment.

[Humphrey95] Humphrey, Watts. *A Discipline of Software Engineering.* Reading, Massachusetts: Addison-Wesley, 1995.

In this book, Humphrey introduces the idea of a Personal Software Process (PSP) which is designed for individual programmers to measure their own effectiveness, and by doing so, to improve their skills. Only a few studies have been done to assess the value of the process, which is heavily oriented toward statistical measurement. The principal difficulty with this approach is the time and effort required to make it work. In this respect it resembles a diet or exercise regimen. Such activities work only if they are followed over long periods. In addition, for the PSP to work, companies must give employees significant amounts of time to engage in non-work-related activities. This area bears watching.

[Jacobson92] Jacobson, I. M. Christerson, P. Jonsson, and G. Övergaard. *Object-Oriented Software Engineering: A Use Case Driven Approach,* Reading, Massachusetts: Addison-Wesley, 1992.

This book provides a useful approach to object-oriented development, based on use cases. A *use case* is a description of a single complete user interaction with a system. By identifying all the major use cases for a system, the analysis can be completed. A technique is given for moving from use cases to object definition and continuing through implementation. While use cases have drawbacks that are not described in this book, the book provides a useful view of OO development.

[McConnell96] McConnell, Steve. *Rapid Development.* Redmond, Washington: Microsoft Press, 1996.

McConnell's book has already become a classic in software management. It is probably the most comprehensive collection of practical software management advice available today. It covers a variety of development methodologies, although its treatment of object-oriented issues is sparse. It stands in contrast to books like Humphrey's *Managing the Software Process* in that it does not assume its readers are part of a large defense contracting organization. This is essential reading for software developers and managers.

[Paulk95] Paulk, M. C., C. V. Weber, W. Curtis, and M. B. Chrissis. *The Capability Maturity Model.* Reading, Massachusetts: Addison-Wesley, 1995.

This book is a companion piece to Humphrey's *Managing the Software Process.* It describes the five-level Capability Maturity Model (CMM) in detail and identifies key practices appropriate for each level. Again, the CMM was designed for large defense systems, so the book's recommendations for tailoring practices to smaller organizations in other business areas are vague and problematic.

[Rumbaugh91] Rumbaugh J., M. Blaha, W. Premerlani, F. Eddy, and W. Lorensen. *Object-Oriented Modeling and Design.* Englewood Cliffs, New Jersey: Prentice-Hall, 1991.

Rumbaugh's book is a classic in object modeling and design. It introduces the widely used OMT modeling notation. It includes detailed sections on static, dynamic, and functional object models. It pays attention to the areas of analysis, system design, and special considerations for object design. It also covers various aspects of implementation, including interfaces with non-object-oriented languages and databases.

[Senge90] Senge, Peter M. *The Fifth Discipline.* New York: Doubleday Currency, 1990.

This important book describes systems thinking for organizations. Even more than the diagrammatic views of systems, its description of how feedback and balancing processes in organizations cause recurring organizational problems makes some apparently irrational events understandable. Perhaps its most important contribution, however, is its presentation of dynamic processes that take place over months or years and are normally not noticed by people who are affected by them.

[Shaw95] Shaw, M. and D. Garlan. *Software Architecture: Perspectives on an Emerging Discipline.* Englewood Cliffs, New Jersey: Prentice-Hall, 1995.

This book is an introduction to the field of software architecture. The book focuses on informal descriptions, and touches lightly on formal notations and specifications and on tools to support them. This book will appeal both to software developers who are looking for new ideas about system organization and to students looking for useful perspectives in software architecture.

[Weinberg91] Weinberg, G. *Quality Software Management: Systems Thinking.* New York: Dorset House, 1991.

This is the first of four volumes on software management by Weinberg, a well-known long-time writer of software issues. This book augments Senge's *Fifth Discipline,* giving an alternate view of systems thinking, but tailoring it to the particular issues of software development.

index

Software Development Planning Guideline for Object-Oriented Projects

When someone wants to start a business with funds from a financial institution, one item that is always required is a business plan. This plan tells what the business will do, what resources are needed, what competition exists, what events will take place in getting the business started, who is involved in the business, and what their qualifications are. Without such a plan, one has little chance of getting funds. However, in the software industry many companies are investing huge amounts of resources in software development projects without requiring even the most basic plan to tell them exactly what the software will do, what resources will be used, what competing products exist, what and when events will take place, who is going to work on the project, and what their qualifications are. Our hope is that this document will help the software development community become more aware of the care that can be taken to avoid taking the huge risks described above.

This document, "Software Development Planning Guideline for Object-Oriented Projects," can be specialized based on DoD-STD-2167A and MIL-STD-498 for military and government projects or based on the ISO 9000 Series and IEEE Standards for commercial projects. It must be stressed that this is intended as a guideline, and project-specific tailoring is required. The major purposes of this document are: (1) to provide guidelines for those involved in writing a software development plan (SDP) with a special emphasis on object-oriented projects; (2) to provide quality and reusable SDP; and (3) to reduce development time and cost of preparing the SDP.

We have been privately selling the printed version of this document for $400. The companies that have purchased this document with either focus have been happy with the quality and the results of using this material. To order either version of this document, please contact Dr. Mohamed Fayad at m.fayad@computer.org and fayadm@acm.org.